Extremes of Fortune

FROM
GREAT WAR
TO
GREAT ESCAPE
THE STORY
OF
HERBERT
MARTIN
MASSEY
CBE DSO MC

EXTREMES OF FORTUNE

ANDREW
WHITE

Published in 2020 by Fighting High Ltd,
www.fightinghigh.com

British Library Cataloguing-in-Publication data.
A CIP record for this title is available from the
British Library.

ISBN – 13: 978-1-9998128-8-1

Designed and typeset in Adobe Minion 11/14pt
by Michael Lindley. www.truthstudio.co.uk.

Printed and bound by Gomer Press.
Front cover design by www.truthstudio.co.uk.

For Eleanor, Camilla and family,
and for the real Group Captain Ramsey.

Contents

Acknowledgements

Biographical books are, by definition, largely works of research, the more so if the subject is deceased and the author cannot rely on first-hand accounts. Many hours have been spent by me in various archives in compiling the story of Herbert Martin Massey's life, but that research alone cannot tell the whole tale – any author seeking to discover the detail, especially the personal elements, relies on the assistance of others to complete the picture.

My deepest thanks must first go to Camilla Skinner (Martin's grand-daughter), her brothers Edward, Simon and Ben, and their mother Eleanor (Martin's daughter-in-law) for their wonderful support, contributions and trust, without which this book would never have got off the ground. Camilla has been on hand throughout to fill in gaps, find documents and photographs, and dig out family anecdotes to add to the mix. Eleanor has very kindly welcomed me into her home and allowed me to go through the veritable treasure trove of artefacts and ephemera that she holds about her father-in-law, without which much of this book would not have been possible.

I would not have been able to trace Camilla and her family without the kind assistance of Colin Clark, then proprietor of Hilton House Hotel, who passed my details on to them. Especial thanks also go to Helena Coney, secretary of the Hilton and Marston History Group and keeper of the group's archive, who has given so much enthusiastic and valuable information, and photographs, about Hilton House and the history of the Hilton community.

Two experts on the Great Escape have been extremely helpful to me through sharing letters, documents and photographs, and I am very grateful to Steve Martin and Ben van Drogenbroek for their contributions and interest.

I am indebted to Air Marshal Andrew Turner for making the time in his busy schedule to kindly write the foreword for this book. Air Marshal Turner is a friend of the Massey family, and has a wealth of operational experience as a support helicopter pilot in the RAF, a role in which he has amassed over 5,000 flying hours in a variety of theatres. At the time of writing (September 2019), he is Deputy Commander Capability at Headquarters Air Command, and is responsible for the strategic planning and delivery of all aspects of Royal Air Force capability, including people, equipment, infrastructure and training. Air Marshal Turner also sits on the Air Force Board as the Air Member for Personnel and Capability.

The following people, in alphabetical order, have provided me with considerable and generous support through their time, advice, material and permissions: Peter Aitkenhead, Assistant Librarian at the Museum of Freemasonry; Malcolm Barrass; Chris Buswell; Rob Davis; Henry Eagan; Julie Green; Judith Herring, Oundle School Archive Assistant; Ruth Hooper, Archivist, Spondon Historical Society; Steve Johnson of the No. 6 Squadron Association; Elspeth Langdale, Oundle School Archivist; Pino Lombardi; Suzanne Make; Phillip Millward of the No. 6 Squadron Association; Patrick Minns; Colin Moore; Dr Christopher Morris, Honorary Secretary, Archivist and Editor of the RAF Habbaniya Association; Dr Robert Owen; Steve Russell; Charles Sale; Mark Sutherland; Squadron Leader Colin Thomas, No. 6 Squadron History Officer; and David Wiggins, Assistant Curator at the Museum of Military Medicine.

My thanks also go to Matthew Boddington and Jean-Michel Munn, both pilots of replica BE2s, for their insights into flying the aeroplane. Especial thanks to Clare, as ever, for her support and encouragement during the writing of this book, and I once again offer my sincere apologies for all the times she has tried to talk to me while I was writing and received a vague, distracted response.

contact via the publisher, and all reasonable endeavours will be made to correct the error. As for any factual inaccuracies, they are entirely mine.

Preface

My first book, *Fire-step to Fokker Fodder*, told the experiences of an infantry officer and airman named Jack Lidsey through the diary writings that Lidsey had made during his time in the trenches and in the skies over the Western Front in the First World War. Jack had been a pupil at my school, and had worked in my home town, so I felt a strong personal connection with him which, coupled with my love of military history, compelled me to tell his story.

The final chapter of that book was a conclusion, in which I followed up the 'What happened to ...' stories of other men about whom Lidsey had written – the people he had shared the horrors of the First World War with. Some had been killed during the war, but many others survived and went on to have long and interesting lives. One of them was Herbert Martin Massey, a 19-year-old member of Lidsey's unit, No. 16 Squadron of the Royal Flying Corps, based in France in 1916 and 1917. A Google search and a leaf through certain books on my study shelves elicited some scant information about Massey, but not much more than that he had stayed on in the (by then) Royal Air Force after the war despite terrible injuries, had been wounded again in the 1930s, had been made a prisoner of war in the Second World War and had somehow been involved with the Great Escape. These seeds of information began to grow in my mind. Who was this man, and how had he survived such adventures?

My initial research showed that much of the available information about him was wrong, such as that which said that he had been an amputee and therefore one of the first limbless pilots to return to flying (long before Douglas Bader). Or the many references to him as 'a veteran escaper who had already been in trouble with the Gestapo' – a quote about someone else entirely, that has been misread in a book, incorrectly applied to Massey, and repeated mistakenly many times over. Most allusions to him, whether online or in print, seem to not know how to use his name – many hyphenate his middle and surname to get Martin-Massey, and the majority call him Herbert rather than Martin, the name by which he was known to all. No website that lists him, including his Wikipedia page, seems to know exactly when he had died other than some time in 1976. Those that do give a date appear to refuse to believe that he could have died on 29 February, and so quote March instead.

Tracking down Jack Lidsey's family had proved difficult, and, once I had decided that Massey's story was one that deserved further investigation, I steeled myself for another protracted search for his relatives to see what they knew about him. I saw online that Massey had had a blue plaque placed on his childhood home in Derbyshire, now a hotel, back in 2016, so the hotel manager seemed a good person to start with. Fortunately, he still had the email address for Massey's granddaughter, Camilla, and I sent my details to her. And that was that – contact established almost straight away. More details came from Camilla and her brothers, convincing me that Herbert Martin Massey should be the subject of my next book. I could scarcely believe that his story had not already been told. The more I discovered about him in the National Archives and other repositories, the more my admiration for him grew. Here was a truly remarkable man who was, in my mind at least, the personification of the Royal Air Force's motto *Per Ardua Ad Astra* – 'Through adversity to the stars'.

Last year saw the seventy-fifth anniversary of the Great Escape, and the passing of the last of the escapees. Now is the time to remember and recognise the man who bore the weight of that momentous event, and its aftermath, on his shoulders. His story prior to that, though, is no less extraordinary – in fact the more so.

Readers of *Fire-step to Fokker Fodder* will recognise some of the descriptions and quotations in the chapter about Massey's First World War, particularly those about the design and history of the BE2. These are common to the stories of both him and Jack Lidsey since they flew the same aeroplane, at the same time and place, and on the same squadron. Spellings of place names in Palestine and Poland, such as Ramleh and Sagan, have been kept as they were at the time rather than modernised.

Air Marshal Andrew Turner

CB, CBE, MA, MSC, BA, FRAeS, CCMI, RAF

Last century our great nation twice went to war in Europe and both times this triggered an array of eye-watering acts of gallantry from an enormous cast of men and women who, in their own eyes, were just doing their bit. Individually, the citations are awe-inspiring and barely able to perceive, but only some have been serialised, characterised or venerated in post-war populist reflections in book, film or art. The story of Air Commodore Martin Massey, CBE, DSO, MC, RAF, has thus far not been captured in this way and this biography puts that right. As the reader will immediately detect, Martin's story is one of selfless commitment, courage, derring-do, never-say-die and gallantry and it is hard to equal, then or since. It is an important work of a notable character in a period of unparalleled bravery and it is a compelling read.

Martin's story starts unremarkably and in humble beginnings as the century turns. He was commissioned at Sandhurst, joined the Royal Flying Corps at the time of the Somme and strapped into a hopelessly outclassed BE2 observation aircraft in France. He quickly demonstrated aptitude, guile and three-dimensional instinct in reconnaissance, artillery-spotting and bombing roles, in perhaps the most congested and contested airspace ever known to man. Rapidly recognised for his flying, fighting and leadership skills, at the age of eighteen he was appointed as a flight commander on No. 16 Squadron. In the first of several personal disasters, he was shot down, burned, very seriously injured, shipped home and torpedoed before convalescing in England; he was awarded the Military Cross. What followed was equally spellbinding as recovery led to a tour in Iraq, a skating accident with repatriation to the UK, staff time, flying instruction, private secretary in the Air Ministry, piloting flying boats and then, rather sedately, staff college. He took command of No. 6 Squadron flying Fairey Gordons in Egypt, and then, after re-equipping to Hawker Harts, deployed the squadron for the Palestine Emergency in 1936 and was at the genesis of air–land battle doctrine and its developing tactics, some of which remain in place today. Shot again, almost comedically saved by his cigarette case, he is awarded the Distinguished Service Order and a Mention in Despatches. Promoted to Group Captain and posted to bombers, he took command of RAF Abingdon flying Whitleys and won two more Mentions in Despatches for his outstanding work in training bomber aircrews. Prior to an auspicious posting in the United States, Massey manoeuvred himself on to two of the 1,000 bomber raids and, out of luck, was shot down again, this time being captured and sent to Stalag Luft III at Sagan.

As the senior British officer, Massey was an enormous character in the camp, recognised for his leadership, stature and unrelenting demeanour and recognisable for the stick he carried as a consequence of injuries in France 1917, Iraq 1923, Palestine 1936 and Germany 1942. Highly respected by his men and equally by his captors, he controlled the camp in the manner one would expect. Yes, times were difficult, but he held the line, complied where the Geneva Convention compelled him to do so, but no more than its protocols demanded. His natural style in command and timing put him at the helm of the Great Escape. Although its design, construct, the digging enterprise, the deception plans, and onward escape preparations were the labours of others, ultimately it was Massey who authorised the breakout. Perhaps one of the century's greatest moments of defiance and pluck, regrettably he was also the first to be informed of the recapture and execution of the fifty escapees, and it was he that, upon repatriation, brought home the news of the murders, which led to the prosecution of the perpetrators. He was as gallant in attack as he was compassionate and humble in taking responsibility for his men's actions. Invested as Commander of the Most Excellent Order of the British Empire for his service, post-war retirement was notably quiet, given his extraordinary first fifty years. He died peacefully in 1976.

Andrew White has perfectly captured the man in this fantastic and breathless biography. He gallops us through this scintillating story of gallantry, commitment and selfless duty with cursive style and pen-perfect pictures. Such is the framing of the aviation moments, that one can almost taste that characteristic blend of cockpit sweat, leather and kerosene that pervades aircraft of the era. He brings to life this remarkable character from this dramatic era of conflict, who was blooded by both wars and twice between, and was decorated six times by three different kings. He has brought back to life Martin Massey's innate leadership style, deep sense of personal ethics and engaging charisma that made this person so great. Above all, one is left shamed by the sheer achievements of this man before he was nineteen, twenty-five, forty and fifty years of age.

This biography of Air Commodore Martin Massey, CBE, DSO, MC, RAF, is instructive in proving what is truly possible if one sets aside personal interests, holds high ethics and takes life on with head, heart, hands and feet. The story is as compelling as it is consuming, aptly complements the canon of its era and is highly recommended for student and sofa-surfer alike.

Headquarters Air Command
RAF High Wycombe
October 2019

A Family Perspective

I cannot express how grateful I am to have crossed paths with Andrew White via the blue plaque in my grandfather's honour at what was his family home in Derbyshire. I was unaware of its existence and it was at my father's funeral that someone mentioned it, so I had to enquire! It was only a few weeks later that Andrew also contacted the hotel and that is how the connection between he and my family got off the ground.

Our beloved deceased Dad, John Massey, was extremely proud of his father and all that he achieved in his lifetime and career. As I have said to Andrew many times, it is just so unfortunate that Dad is not around to appreciate all the most amazing information that he has unearthed.

My parents John and Eleanor had cleverly and carefully stored an enormous amount of memorabilia from Martin's life, of which Andrew has been able to read and photograph and use in this book. It was wonderful seeing Andrew's face light up as he worked his way through so many photographs, school reports and piles and piles of RAF-related paperwork stemming from so many years ago.

My grandfather was known to his four grandchildren as Goppy, and my memories of him are a little vague as I was only seven years old when he died. But I can picture him, impeccably dressed, walking with a stick, maybe a little strict at times with his young, lively grandchildren, but he was a kind man and most certainly had an air of authority surrounding him. My eldest brother Edward and I would spend as much as three weeks during the long school summer holidays with Goppy and Grannie at The Red House in Pilton, days of Enid Blyton books, trips to the beach at Croyde and gardening as a penance for bad behaviour! What my brothers and I remember extremely clearly are the many Christmases we spent watching *The Great Escape* film, and I think we can safely say that we know this version of such an incredible story very well.

As a family we are indebted to Andrew for writing this book and uncovering and releasing such an incredible account of Goppy's extraordinary life and career. We hope that those who choose to read this book will find it equally as interesting and enlightening as to what one particular gentleman achieved within his life.

Camilla Skinner
October 2019

Introduction

There have been many books written (and of course a Hollywood film produced) about the Great Escape over the seventy-five years since it happened. Most of them claim to be either the 'full', 'real' or 'true' story of that famous Second World War event, an attempt to facilitate the escape of 200 Allied prisoners of war from the German Stalag Luft III prisoner of war camp at Sagan, now in Poland. Some of the books were written by former prisoners after the war and are therefore first-hand accounts, but, as with any record of personal experience, such works can be clouded by memory, the passage of time, and by the writer's perceptions and bias of events that he may have figuratively been viewing from a distance. Similarly, the German commandant of Sagan wrote his own memoirs long after the incident but, as we shall see, he probably had ulterior motives for what, and how, he wrote. Other works are an amalgam of documentary evidence and novel, in which the author has introduced imagined dialogue within historical fact to make more of a story. Finally, some of the books are purely documentary, a record and analysis of official papers and personal statements. There are also published biographies of some of the main personalities in the Great Escape, most notably Roger Bushell, the man credited with hatching the ambitious plan and who oversaw its implementation, and Harry 'Wings' Day, a rumbustious senior officer at the camp and habitual escaper. All of these books have their part to play, and each adds something to an overall appreciation of what happened on that night of 24/25 March 1944.

One man, though, warrants barely a mention in most of these books, featuring only in passing as a peripheral, somewhat avuncular figure, and one who is overshadowed by the likes of Bushell and Day who cut the more colourful and heroic characters. Yet heroism comes in many forms, and his contribution to the Great Escape and the aftermath of it demands far greater recognition. Herbert Martin Massey was the senior British officer at Stalag Luft III, the man to whom fate handed the responsibility for the welfare and discipline of the captured British airmen, a role he neither asked for nor expected to find himself in, but one in which he ultimately excelled. As head of the prisoner population of the camp, it was Massey alone who sanctioned the mass breakout. He could at any time between the plan's genesis and execution have vetoed it had he felt that the risks were too great. It may well have been Bushell's scheme, but Massey was the authority behind it. It was to him that the Germans broke the news of the shooting of fifty of the recaptured escapees, the deaths of whom (as will be explained later) he could not have foreseen and for which he therefore cannot be blamed, and which perhaps, to a greater or lesser degree, remained on his conscience thereafter, although we can never know that for certain. And it was Massey who brought the news of the murders home to Britain shortly afterwards, and upon whose subsequent testimony the British government demanded 'exemplary justice' for the perpetrators.

This book is not intended to be yet another attempt to re-tell the story of the Great Escape; in terms of facts about the escape itself, there is little left to say. Rather, it seeks to give long overdue credit to the man who bore the majority of the responsibility for the scheme, and whose role in it (and, moreover, in the day-to-day running of the camp) has been largely glossed over in previous accounts. That said, the question of what warnings were given about the consequences of escaping and how they may have influenced Massey's decisions are given due consideration. But there is far more to Martin Massey's story than the two years he spent in captivity.

The Second World War was Massey's third experience of conflict. As an 18-year-old, he flew with the Royal Flying Corps during the First World War, where his skill as a pilot and a leader of men was very quickly recognised with rapid promotion and decoration. He was shot down in flames in February 1917 by one of Germany's great flying aces, Werner Voss. In that dogfight, Massey's observer was killed and he himself suffered horrific burns, which his doctors did not expect him to survive. But against the odds he did live, and through immense courage and determination he returned to military flying after the war. He was wounded and decorated again during the Palestine Emergency of 1936, where Massey led his light bomber squadron with great tenacity and initiative. During that operation, he helped to introduce, develop and refine many of the RAF's cooperative tactics with the Army that would prove decisive not only in Palestine but on into the Second World War, as well as the more recent conflicts in Iraq and Afghanistan. In 1942, by now at a rank and role in the Royal Air Force in which he was not expected to be directly involved with the fighting, he nevertheless chose to fly and attack the enemy once more, wanting to gain first-hand experience of strategic bombing, which he expected to bring to a new command in the United States of America. On that mission, Massey was shot down and badly injured again, and it was this incident that led to his incarceration at Stalag Luft III.

Martin Massey (as he was always known) was without doubt a highly successful leader, as testament from his fellow prisoners as Sagan, as well as other RAF colleagues throughout his career, bears out. Whether it was as a teenager during the First World War, as a squadron commander in the Middle East, or as a senior officer in the Second World War, he earned respect, praise and indeed affection from those who followed him (and his enemies alike, while at Sagan), as well as recognition from those above him. He was a remarkable person – a man who refused to let injury and disability get the better of him, who consistently displayed tremendous moral and physical courage, and one who steadfastly served Crown and country through thick and thin for more than three decades. His story deserves to be told. To quote one of his former commanding officers, Martin Massey's life was one of 'extremes of fortune'.

Chapter One

Early Years:
1898 – 1915

Ernest Martin Massey was, by his own admission, a somewhat reluctant businessman. He had inherited Mrs Massey's Agency – a company specialising in the supply of domestic staff to the upper echelons of society – upon the death of his mother, Sarah, in 1892 when he was twenty-nine years old. The agency had been established in 1845 by Ernest's grandmother in King Street, Derby, but under his mother's acumen the company had become so renowned that 'throughout the country Mrs Massey's became a household word and she became an authority on matters pertaining to Domestic Service'.[1] But Ernest's first love was painting, and he regarded himself as an artist by profession. Although his occupation on the 1901 census return was listed as 'agent for the supply of domestic servants',[2] by 1911 it had been changed to 'artist',[3] and was also recorded as such in the *Kelly's Directories* from 1891 to 1912. Ernest painted landscapes, and he first exhibited in 1880 at the Royal Society of British Artists, with four of his works shown between then and 1940 (long after his death). He was more prolific at his local museum, the Nottingham Museum Art Gallery, showing thirteen pieces there, but his highest honour came in 1895 when a painting entitled 'Morne Farms' was exhibited at the Royal Academy of Arts in London. Despite his disinclination towards business, Ernest was nonetheless successful in running Mrs Massey's Agency, and under his supervision the agency introduced 'certificates of character' (now better known as references) for potential domestic staff. Of greater significance was the opening in 1920 of the London branch of the business in Baker Street, under the management of his daughter, Ruth.[4] Family lore holds that the London office supplied staff to the Royal Household and to 10 Downing Street.

The prosperity of the agency allowed Ernest and his family to live in comfort. He and his wife, Florence, owned Hilton House in the village of Hilton in Derbyshire, around nine miles to the south-west of Derby itself. Inherited from his mother along with the business (his father had predeceased her), and the home to several generations of Masseys, Hilton House was a large, three-storey, six-bedroomed property that also boasted servants' quarters; Ernest's studio; a schoolroom; stabling; a harness room; a coach house; coal house; laundry; and a greenhouse. The main entrance to Hilton House certainly made a statement, featuring heavy, seven-foot-high oak doors with mouldings and ornate iron hinges. In the large garden was an ancient mulberry tree and a great weeping ash, and there was also an orchard. Ernest employed four domestic servants, namely a nurse, a cook, a housemaid and an under-nurse, who all lived-in at Hilton House.[5] The Masseys also owned the first motor car to be seen in the village, no doubt quite a sight and talking point in rural Edwardian Derbyshire. Hilton itself was a reasonably prosperous, mainly farming, community. The major landowner and lord of the manor was the Duke of Devonshire and most of the farmers were his tenants but there were a few freehold farms, including one on Hilton Common owned by the Masseys. In addition to Hilton House there was another significant house in the village called Hilton Lodge, at one time a property of politician Sir Oswald Mosley. Evidently also a philanthropist, Ernest was secretary of the Hilton reading rooms.

Ernest had married Florence Lilian Warwick on 17 July 1895. She was almost nine years his junior, and was, like Ernest, Derbyshire born and bred. The couple's first child, their daughter Margaret, was born the next April. A son followed on 19 January 1898, Herbert Martin Massey, so named after his father's brother who had died at the age of twelve in 1876.[6] Six more children arrived in fairly short succession thereafter, two boys and four more girls. Young Herbert was baptised in the local parish church, St Mary's, by the Reverend H.W. Lamb on 20 February 1898, but for the rest of his life he was to be known by his middle name of Martin.

Ernest's means were such that he could afford to have Martin educated privately. For his early years of learning, Martin was probably home-tutored in the schoolroom at Hilton House, along with his siblings, under the instruction of a governess. When he came of school age, he was sent first to nearby Derby School Preparatory in 1907, aged nine. He was only to spend two terms at the school, though, and by Christmas that year, Ernest decided to move his eldest son to Spondon House School, just outside Derby. His two reports[7] while at Derby Preparatory were average; both recorded his overall conduct as 'good', a word repeated singly throughout most of the subjects, occasionally prefixed with 'very'. Even in Latin, where he came top in his class, his master simply recorded that he 'has worked very well'. Only his science master goes into any detail or shows any enthusiasm for his pupil; in that year's Midsummer term, he wrote of Martin that he 'works well and attends to what is going on'. The following term, Michaelmas, the same master enthused that Massey 'has done very well indeed; always seems interested and works excellently'. Perhaps this apparent general lack of passion on behalf of the teaching staff is what prompted his father to move him to Spondon House, where, since the school was some sixteen miles from Hilton, Martin became a boarder.[8]

Spondon House School was housed in a Georgian mansion, apparently built around 1785 as a dower house, a secondary seat of the Drury-Lowes family on their Derbyshire estate, Locko Park. In 1854 a preparatory school was opened in the house as a 'school for the sons of gentlemen'.[9] The founder and first headmaster, the Reverend Thomas Gascoigne, set the tone by forbidding the boys from mixing with the humbler children of the village. Gascoigne was succeeded by the Reverend Edward Priestland in 1874, who was somewhat better disposed towards the hoi polloi and opened the school's cricket pitch to anyone who wished to play, and he even managed to organise a match for the school team against the Australian touring side of 1898.[10] Under Priestland, the school flourished and gained a reputation as one of the best in the area. By the time Martin arrived at the school, the headmaster was Mr C.H.T. Hayman, himself a first-class cricketer, and Spondon's involvement in the game is probably what inspired Massey's prowess at cricket. Academically, Martin's time at Spondon House could best be described as 'mixed'. His first school report there placed him at the bottom of his class, but he was at least showing potential: 'He worked well for the latter half of the term but his exams were disappointing. I hope next term that he will realise that he must work all the time in school. He does not yet understand the art of mental application and so fails at work to be learnt by heart. He has the makings of an excellent boy'.

Poor showings in examinations were to be a common theme throughout most of Martin's subsequent schooling. Overall, his form master said that 'If he put as much energy into his work in school as he puts into his games and boxing, he would do well.' By the end of that school year, the feeling was that 'I think he has tried his best, but he must nail back his head in exams.'

He began the following academic year little better. That first half-term, 'he seemed to have forgotten everything after the long holidays, but he is now getting on well and showing more enthusiasm in his work'. His application began to pay dividends, but his attention was obviously still held more by the school's sporting activities since, by the end of term, 'he had decidedly improved this term and is taking his work more seriously. If only he were as good in school as he is at games, he would take quite a high place in his form.' The rest of that year continued in the same vein – some improvement in classroom attainment where he was showing 'far more energy', but limited by his passion for sport: 'he is splendidly keen out of doors'. He finished that year, 1909, creditably well, coming second in his form out of seven pupils, having shown a respectable improvement in all subjects bar French ('his work is half-hearted'). His English master recommended that he do as much reading in the summer holidays as possible 'in order to enlarge his ideas … any interesting boy's book will do'.

In addition to sport, young Martin's love of the outdoors was further demonstrated by his membership of the Spondon School Boy Scout troop. He 'has shown exceptional keenness and worked very well both on parade and in field work. Pays attention to what is said. Has passed all the tests for a 2nd Class Scouts' badge, except the "signalling". Turnout and equipment very good. Is to be promoted corporal.' Much of what was reported here was to stand him in good stead for his later military career.

The next year saw a dramatic improvement in Massey's schoolwork. Early on, he studied 'excellently' and 'really put his back into it'. The recommendation that he read more evidently paid dividends since his English teacher recorded that 'he has quite surprised me and possibly himself with the way he has improved in this subject. It only shows what a little real hard work will do.' French was still a struggle, though, 'to be sternly tackled next term'. There was a cryptic comment by his form master regarding his disappointing showing in the mid-year exams, however, speculating that 'I rather fancy that his little outing somewhat unsettled him.' What that 'outing' was we can only speculate, but was surely an unauthorised activity that caused a scare or got him into trouble somehow. His mysterious excursion notwithstanding, he finished the year strongly, coming top of his class. His master noted 'I have nothing but praise for his work', and that 'I am pleased to see him taking non-athletic prizes.' At last, he was matching his sporting performances with intellectual effort.

Massey's final year at Spondon, 1911, saw him slip back a little in terms of placing within his form, but since there were only five boys in it to begin with (and only three by the end of the academic year), it was hardly a major concern. All of his reports that year credit him with 'excellent work', and although 'languages will never be his strong point' he was described as 'an excellent boy both in and out of school'. His valedictory summary from his form master prior to leaving the school once again contained a puzzling comment – that 'he has done an excellent term's work and deserved a happier ending'. Considering the apparent quality of his efforts in class, we can only venture that some misfortune had befallen him – perhaps it was his performance in exams again.

For Martin's secondary education, his parents chose to send him as a boarder to Oundle School in Northamptonshire, Ernest's own alma mater. The school is an ancient one, with its history dating back to 1556 when Sir William Laxton, Lord Mayor of London and Master of the Worshipful Company of Grocers, endowed a 'Free Grammar School' in Oundle, where he had been educated at the original Gild School founded in 1506.[11] Martin Massey entered Oundle on New Year's Day 1912, when he was a couple of weeks short of his fourteenth birthday. He went into Laxton House where, despite his small stature, he soon reaffirmed his earlier sporting talents. *The Laxtonian*, the Oundle School chronicle, noted that 'Massey has plenty of cricket in him and ought to be useful next year as both a bat and in the field.'[12] And so it was to prove since Martin played for his House XI in 1912, featuring prominently. He was a successful bowler – in a match against Grafton House that season, he took seven wickets, and a further six against Dryden House in the next match; he took another eight against Dryden the following year. He was an upper-order batsman, too, and occasionally opened the innings, contributing valuable runs. In a letter home to his parents dated 12 July 1914,[13] Martin's enthusiasm for the game shone through:

Dear Daddy and Mother,

Speech day went off very well and we are now settled down to work again. Rain prevented our House match beginning until Friday when a half was given.
Scores:
1st   School House 201
1st   Laxton 121   Myself 61 not out, I carried my bat
2nd   School House 190 for 1 wicket
This is how it stands now.

On account of my score I played for the First Eleven against Lord Lilford's Eleven yesterday at Lilford. The match ended in a draw in their favour, I made 25. His place[14] is huge and very beautiful, he has large aviaries where he keeps birds from all countries, he has also other wild beasts. Everything is keep [sic] straight and neat, lilyponds with fountains springing up everywhere. Great was our joy last night for Laxton has won the shooting cup, with 1 House colour and the other three just ordinary shots, really they did wonderfully well, and at last we possess a cup in the 'Dining Hall'.

Our school certificate exams begin tomorrow and the only school matches left are the Old Oundelians match and a 2nd Eleven against the masters. Our final is I am afraid gone too far, we cannot pull ourselves together now, some fellows did bat so atrociously first innings.[15]

The swimming House races we have a good chance for, also the House drill competition.

I do not think I shall go to camp this year.

Could I draw 10/- out of my banking account, I want a little for one or two things.

Mr Squire has given me a ripping pair of pads for my 61.

Love from your loving son,
Martin

He played Fives for Laxton House, too, and in 1913, *The Laxtonian* noted that 'very good games have been seen [especially] in the Juniors between Safuentes and Massey'.[16] Similarly in rugby, in which he was noted to 'make very good openings and is a good attacking three-quarter. He gives and takes his passes well.'[17] He represented the school in the sport, and in a game against Trinity Hall on 11 November 1913, he 'did wonderfully well, considering his size and experience', culminating in Massey (at fly-half) making the final pass for Oundle to score the winning try. Against R.A. Little's team in December 1914, 'an attack by Massey, Clifford and West put Owen over the line', but this time Oundle lost the match. Sport was to feature throughout Martin's subsequent military career, with rugby (he represented the RAF in the 1919–20 season), football, tennis, cricket, golf, polo and hunting all appearing on his service record.

The improvement that Martin had been showing in the classroom during his latter terms at Spondon continued, in the main, at Oundle, although his lack of prowess in exams continued to cause him difficulties.

He was evidently clever enough, but the majority of the time just could not do himself justice under the pressure of exam conditions. His first year's reports concluded that, although his work was 'excellent' (apart from in Singing, where 'he does his best' – obviously not a candidate for the school choir), it was 'a little disappointing in examinations'. However, his work throughout this time was always at least satisfactory, if not good, with each year's report being signed off by the headmaster, Mr Sanderson (known as 'Beans' to the boys due to the enthusiasm and energy – 'full of beans' – with which he administered corporal punishment), as 'good' and on one occasion, 'A good term – I am pleased to see this.'

Oundle School was, and still is, noted for its engineering and design courses. Boys would usually go into the 'classical side' of the school on entry and remain there throughout their schooling if their future lay towards Oxbridge; but if their vocation was to be in either science, medicine or engineering, then they would transfer to the 'engineering side' at around fifteen years old, where technical and scientific subjects would replace classical languages.[18] Likewise, boys who either showed little aptitude for the classics or whose destinies were planned for the commercial world were also placed on the engineering side. Martin found himself on that side of the school, probably because he was his father's eldest son and therefore the heir to Mrs Massey's Agency, and so was expected to inherit the family business. He did well in the engineering arena, and was presented with a workshop prize. Oundle's excellently equipped workshops formed a large part of the school's life and, when the First World War came, boys were actively engaged in making munitions and component parts for other military hardware.

While at the school, Massey was also a member of the Oundle School Officer Training Corps (OTC), evidently showing early potential for command since he was promoted to lance-corporal, continuing where he had left off with the Spondon Scout Troop. The public school and university OTCs had been established in 1908 as part of Richard Haldane's (then Secretary of State for War) reformation of the British Army, and by 1912, the year that Martin began at Oundle, some 27,700 boys and young men had enlisted in them up and down the country.[19] The OTCs were to play an important part in supplying junior officers and soldiers during the coming First World War, highlighted by Oundle's own contribution to the cause – around 90 per cent of its former OTC cadets from 1909 to 1913 were serving in some capacity in 1915, and 'a heavy toll of killed and wounded has been exacted from both officers and cadets'.[20] By the end of the war, 256 Old Oundelians had lost their lives during the conflict.[21]

Martin Massey left Oundle School on 1 April 1915, aged seventeen. By that time, Great Britain had been at war with Germany for almost eight months, and like most other young men of the day he obviously felt it his patriotic duty to serve King and Country. Indeed, he had spent the latter part of his time at Oundle in a class known as the 'Army Boys', a special form that focused on preparing pupils for entry into the military.[22] Any thoughts he may have had towards university and then business apprenticeship under his father were shelved for the time being. His family background and education marked him out as potential officer material, since public school-educated boys were expected to be leaders of men, but, academically at least, Massey seemingly had a good deal more work to do before he would be able to enter the Royal Military College at Sandhurst. To gain the extra knowledge that he needed, he next went to Storrington College in Sussex, not far from Worthing. Storrington had been established in 1871 as a 'cramming school' to 'prepare pupils for Woolwich, Sandhurst and the Universities' under the tutelage of Mr W.A. Fuller, MA, 'aided by Experienced University Staff',[23] and Martin arrived there on 12 April 1915, just eleven days after leaving Oundle. He spent the next two and a half months at Storrington, frantically learning what he needed to know to pass the Army's entrance exam. In the meantime, he completed and submitted his application form for entry to the Royal Military College on 21 May 1915.[24] The form asked who would be responsible for the payment of £35 'towards the expenses of uniform, books etc.' upon admission to the college; Massey's father (described on the form as a 'man of business') appended his name to the declaration, and endorsed his son's application since Martin was under the age of twenty-one.

Martin underwent a medical examination in London on 5 June 1915 to assess his physical suitability for the Army. His height was recorded as 66½in (5ft 6½in), and his chest measured 37½in fully expanded, 35in deflated; he weighed in at 147lb, or 10½ stone. His hearing, teeth, and vision were all judged to be 'good', and he declared himself free from any previous injuries, fits, mental or bodily infirmity, and physical imperfections.[25] Following this seemingly somewhat cursory examination, the president of the medical board, a Lieutenant Colonel Reid of the Royal Army Medical Corps (RAMC), passed Massey as 'fit'. The final obstacle to be overcome successfully was the Sandhurst entry examination, which must have been a concern for him given his lack of prowess in exams up to that point. But Martin passed the test in June, and was ranked 132nd in the order of merit of those examined at the same time. Unfortunately, we do not know how many candidates there were in total, but his 'cramming' session at Storrington had at least paid off. With all the hurdles now cleared, Martin Massey was nominated to a cadetship at the Royal Military College, and his order to join Sandhurst was sent to him on 21 August 1915,[26] just over one year after the First World War had begun.

Chapter Two

From Sandhurst to the Skies:
24 August 1915 – 17 April 1917

Seventeen-year-old Gentleman Cadet Martin Massey joined his fellow prospective officers in H Company at the Royal Military College Sandhurst for the Officers' Course of Instruction on 24 August 1915. Most of his comrades were, like him, the product of public schools and the associated OTCs. Due to the urgent wartime need to increase the throughput of regular officers into the rapidly expanding field army, the course had been shortened in 1914 from its usual length of eighteen months to just three, but inevitably the quality of the training, and by definition that of the graduates, suffered. Consequently, the course was extended to six months by the end of 1915 when Martin was already a cadet (a decision that was applied retrospectively, thereby affecting his intake of recruits), and continued to grow longer still until, by the end of the war, it stood at one year's duration.[27] In terms of content, some elements of the course syllabus had advanced little since the turn of the century, and in certain respects not since Napoleonic times. One cadet of Martin's age who was at the college at the same time as him, Douglas Lockhart, described his experience at Sandhurst:

> Everything was of course telescoped, as the War Office wanted all the young officers it could get. I had come straight from Wellington [College] aged just over 17, and the policy for people of my age was to put us through in five months. Obviously it was impossible to fit into so abbreviated a course all that we needed to know. But it was more than doubtful whether the authorities knew what a young officer needed to know in World War I. One had a strong impression that, on a basic scheme of training designed to fit us for the Boer War, all

sorts of extras were tacked on as the World War showed itself to be following a disquietingly different line of development. I have a vivid recollection of my Company receiving careful instruction on forming a square, fixing bayonets and preparing to receive a cavalry charge (we were formed up shoulder to shoulder, rear rank standing, front rank kneeling on one knee, so that I rather fancy this particular item dated back to pre-Boer War times). On the other hand, we spent a number of evenings defending trenches against another Company, lighting flares and throwing imitation bombs [grenades] at the attackers.[28]

The college regime was punishing and exhausting, with the working day starting, with drill, long before dawn and going on into the evenings. On nights when there were no manoeuvres, the cadets were to be found in their rooms poring over their books, revising for the following day's instruction. There was no free time during the day, with constant, rapid changes of uniform required between lessons, from barrack dress to PT kit to fatigues, back to barrack dress before outdoor games kit, and then black tie for dinner. Any brief spare moment was spent resting before the next ordeal.

Shortly before gaining their commission at the end of the course, the successful gentleman cadets were directed to submit their application for posting to a regiment of their choosing. The 'First Appointments' form asked the new officer for three choices of regiment, with the proviso that 'candidates are warned to consult their parents or guardians before stating their wishes, as changes cannot be made when once an officer has been gazetted [his commission confirmed in the London Gazette]'. How strange this seems nowadays – the young officer was about to be placed in command of men in the field in wartime, yet he still had to ask his parents' advice about where he should be sent. Massey's choices, and his reasons for them, were submitted on 6 March 1916:[29]

1. The Notts and Derby Regiment (Sherwood Foresters) – My family has resided and owned property in Derbyshire for many generations past.
2. The Northamptonshire Regiment – Was at school (Oundle) in Northants for four years.
3. The South Staffordshire Regiment – None [he gave no reasons for this third choice].

Massey was awarded his first choice, and was gazetted, along with two other graduates[30] destined for the Sherwood Foresters, on 6 April 1916 in the rank of second lieutenant.[31] Given that he spent a little over seven months at the college, rather than six, it seems that he had some sort of misfortune during the course – perhaps it was a recurrence of his difficulties with exams, or some physical injury sustained while training, that held him back temporarily. One of the problems with the increased numbers of cadets at Sandhurst during wartime was overcrowding in the barracks, which brought with it a heightened likelihood of communicable diseases such as mumps,[32] so it is also possible that he became ill at some point.

Leaving Sandhurst the day after being gazetted, 7 April, Massey was posted notionally to the Sherwood Foresters' 3rd (Reserve) Battalion, but he never served with his chosen regiment. Instead, he volunteered for fly-ing duties, a decision that he appears to have taken while at Sandhurst since his 'particulars' form,[33] completed just prior to entering the college, asked him whether he was 'desirous of entering Cavalry or Infantry', to which he responded 'Infantry'.[34] How and exactly when he was bitten by the flying bug we will sadly never know, but in all likelihood his interest was aroused during a lecture about the Royal Flying Corps (RFC) during the Officers' Course. Had Martin harboured an ambition to fly from the out-set, he would probably not have gone to the Royal Military College at all, but rather proceeded as a direct entrant to the RFC's 1st Officer Cadet Battalion at Denham in Buckinghamshire (which had been established earlier in 1915), where he would have undergone a two-month basic military training course (similar to that at Sandhurst) before commencing flying training. Having then successfully passed out as a pilot, he would have been commissioned as an officer in the RFC. As it was, Martin was sent straight from the Royal Military College to the RFC's No. 3 Reserve Squadron, based at Shoreham-by-Sea in West Sussex, for a 'course in aviation', arriving there on 11 April. No. 3 Reserve Squadron's remit was to provide basic flying training for potential pilots, with instruction being given on the Maurice Farman Shorthorn aircraft. The Shorthorn was a heavy and cumbersome French design that had been in service with the Royal Flying Corps prior to the war as a light bomber and reconnaissance aircraft, but was now obsolete and had been relegated to training duties, a role for which it was particularly unsuitable.

Learning to fly at that point in the war was, at best, a somewhat hap-hazard and risky process, and at worst, downright dangerous – lethal, even. A much-needed overhaul of the RFC's flying training procedure (what would become known as the Gosport System, designed by Major Robert Smith-Barry) was more than six months in the future when Martin began his time with No. 3 Reserve Squadron, so he was subjected to the older, more perilous, methods of teaching. The flying lessons at Shoreham were ridiculously short, lasting between five and fifteen minutes, with the aircraft not going above 1,000 feet in altitude, and only then in benign, flat calm, weather conditions (training flights were not permitted when the wind speed exceeded five knots), and always within sight of the airfield. Such conditions were generally only available early in the morning or in the later afternoon, and so a typical day for a Shoreham trainee would have been:[35]

7–8.30 a.m. Early morning flying available if required.

8.30 a.m. Breakfast.

9.00 a.m.–12 noon. Lectures. Flying if required.

1.00 p.m. Lunch.

2–4.00 p.m. Lectures. Flying if required.

4.15 p.m. Tea.

7.00 p.m. Dinner.

Of course, 'flying if required' should also be taken to mean 'if weather permits'. The emphasis of the instruction was on taking-off and landing – aerobatics were practically unknown, and were limited to simple loops and stall turns, which even then were tried by only the boldest, or most reckless, of students. Spins were never attempted because they were known to be courting certain death. There was an almost total lack of communication between pupil and tutor while airborne since, in the days before intercoms or even voice pipes, there was no method of conveying instructions other than by gesturing frantically, passing scribbled notes (assuming the slipstream did not whisk them away first), or even by hitting terrified students. On the ground, scholars and instructors were strictly segregated because of the Army's societal hierarchy, and any interaction was actively discouraged – they were even kept apart in the mess hall – which meant that a bond could not be formed between them. When it came to taking to the air for a lesson, the learner pilots were expected to rest their hands and feet lightly on the controls while the instructor flew the aeroplane, and to somehow absorb what was happening by 'feel'. One student, Paul Maltby (who was later to be Martin's commanding officer in France), recalled that:

reliance had to be placed mainly on sight, hearing and the seat of our
pants to tell us what was happening to our machines … it still left
vast areas unexplained to the pupil, who had perforce to find out
about them by himself. We were in fact, largely self-taught … it could
be most unbalancing to get into a mess and afterwards be unable
to understand how it came about or how one had succeeded in
recovering control, which could well leave one wondering if it could
happen again; the only way to learn was to try once more and find
out. We shook ourselves up in inverse ratio to our natural aptitude.
The overall result was that the flying life of an individual, apart from
war or accident, was in those days short … this process of finding
out for oneself took time, even for the best pilots. But time was what,
in a rapidly expanding service, could not be given to the new entry
in 1916–17.[36]

The quality of the instructors themselves also left a lot to be desired. Maltby
wrote that 'some taught tolerably well, some not so well'.[37] Most of them
were woefully inexperienced, having just graduated from the training
programme themselves, and so were scarcely better qualified aviators than
those they were teaching to fly. One such new (or 'green' instructor, as they
were known) summed up the situation thus: 'I was fully aware that, except
for having acquired a knack for landing properly, my flying abilities were
limited to the unreliable performance of gentle turns, and the thought
that in the near future aircraft in which I flew would be controlled by one
whose ignorance of the art of flying was only slightly more intense than
my own depressed me considerably.'[38]

   Overall, the Shoreham syllabus was pitifully brief, necessitated by the
increasing demand for pilots at the front. Some students received only
ninety minutes of training with an instructor before going solo, and in at
least one case, just thirty minutes. Cecil Lewis, who had been at Oundle
at the same time as Martin, described his introduction to solo flying in the
Maurice Farman Longhorn (similar to the Shorthorn):

One and a half hours' dual stood to my credit. I had trundled around
the aerodrome with Sergeant Yates, my instructor, doing left-hand
circuits, and made a few indifferent landings.
   'You'd better go solo this afternoon, if the wind drops.'
   'Yes, sir.'
   'Remember to take plenty of room to get off.'

'Yes, sir.'

Last week George had neglected that important point, caught the upper lip of the concrete, and gone arsy-tarsy down into the meadow on the other side.[39]

One student at Shoreham, Duncan Grinnell-Milne, witnessed the terror of a fellow trainee who was told that he was to go solo: 'He had been warned the night before, after half an hour in the air with the senior instructor. "You'll go solo at dawn tomorrow," he'd been told briefly. And if for "go solo" the words "be shot" had been substituted he could not have been more upset.'[40] When Grinnell-Milne's own turn came, he was no less apprehensive:

'How much dual control have you done?' he [his instructor] asked.

'Three hours and twenty minutes,' I answered, hopeful that so small an amount would induce him to give me more at once.

'Do you think you could go solo?'

The question staggered me. All my past lies flashed before me, whirled in my head and merged into one thumping fib.

'Yes,' I answered, and at once regretted it.[41]

Most trainees were given only around three hours' dual instruction, and a similar number of solo hours, before moving on to another school for advanced training, and even these hopelessly inadequate requirements were often not met. The combination of a lack of purpose-built training aircraft, the hurried courses, poor training methods, and the generally low quality of instructors, meant that the accident rate at the flying schools rose alarmingly. Throughout the First World War, more pilots died while undergoing training than were killed on the front line at the hands of the enemy – some 8,000 out of a total of just over 14,000.[42] Aviation at the flying schools was often not possible because of a lack of serviceable aeroplanes, with many having been damaged or written off by the hapless beginners. Sometimes at Shoreham, as few as three serviceable machines were available from a total complement of twelve. Several pupils gave up waiting and returned to their infantry regiments to take their chances in the trenches instead.

Mercifully and miraculously, Martin survived the Shoreham course and on 21 May 1916 was sent to another training squadron, No. 13 Reserve Squadron based at Norwich, for advanced instruction. Here, the training consisted of longer, cross-country solo flights, with altitudes of over 8,000 feet often being achieved. As well as navigation, students were taught methods of observation, aerial photography, how to read ground-based signals, aerial gunnery and occasionally even bombing techniques. At Norwich, Massey was introduced to the Royal Aircraft Factory Blériot Experimental 2 aircraft, otherwise known simply as the BE2, the aeroplane in which he was to go to war. The BE2 was a single-engined, two-seat tandem biplane, designed by Geoffrey de Havilland, that enjoyed an unenviable reputation within the RFC and was reviled by its crews. Entering service in 1912 in the light bomber and reconnaissance roles, the BE2 had performed well at the start of the First World War but was soon left behind by the pace of technological advance that the conflict brought with it. By 1915, it was an outdated aircraft, having been designed before air-to-air combat had been imagined, and was easy prey for the new German types that were coming into service, especially the Fokker Eindecker. The Eindecker was the first purpose-built fighter aeroplane and featured a belt-fed machine gun synchronised to fire through the propeller, allowing for a far better aim at the target – wherever the aeroplane was pointing, the bullets would go in the same direction. This was a game-changer in the air war, as the RFC had no such technology at the time. The best the British had to offer was armoured deflector plates on the propeller that were supposed to protect the blades against being struck by the host aircraft's bullets, an innovation that did little to inspire confidence and could just as likely ricochet the pilot's own rounds back at him. British and French aircraft losses began to mount, leading to the so-called 'Fokker Scourge' during the latter part of 1915, and with the attrition came a surrender of air superiority over the Western Front to the Germans.

Because the term 'Fokker Scourge' was a creation of the British press, it was slightly misleading and sensationalist. Compared with the intense levels of air fighting that took place in 1917 and 1918, the number of Allied casualties during the 'Scourge' period was relatively small, partly due to the way that the Germans used Eindeckers, issuing them only in small numbers to existing reconnaissance squadrons – it was to be nearly another year before the Germans were to follow the British example of establishing specialist fighter squadrons. Also, there were fewer aeroplanes in use at the time, so the attrition rate was logically smaller. Lastly, despite its advanced armament, the Eindecker was by no means an outstanding aircraft. Nevertheless, the impact on Allied morale of the fact that the Germans were in control of the air created a major scandal in the British media. There is no doubt, though, about the psychological effect that the Eindecker's reputation had on British aircrews. In his classic book *Sagittarius Rising*, RFC pilot Cecil Lewis commented that: 'The Fokker was the menace of the RFC. Hearsay and a few lucky encounters had made the machine respected, not to say dreaded, by the slow, unwieldy machines then used by us for Artillery Observation and Offensive Patrols. Rumour credited it with the most fantastic performance! It could outclimb, outpace, and outmanoeuvre anything in the RFC. You were as good as dead if you as much as saw one, and so on. In short, our morale wanted bucking up.'[43]

Lewis flew a BE2c, along with examples of other Allied aircraft, against a captured Eindecker for comparison, and found that 'all of them gave quite a good account of themselves except the [BE]2c, which in performance, was nowhere'.[44] Paul Maltby agreed, stating that the Eindecker 'outclassed the BE2c in speed, firepower and manoeuvrability'.[45]

The BE2's vulnerability to enemy fighters earned it the Allied nickname of 'Fokker Fodder'. To the Germans it was known, tellingly, as *'kaltes Fleisch'* – cold meat. The C version of the BE2 had a seventy-horsepower engine that gave it a cruising speed of just 60mph, and a maximum of 70mph; even in 1916, in its latest, improved E and F versions, the BE2 could only achieve around 90mph. By then the Germans were replacing the Eindecker with newer, even more advanced aircraft such as the Albatros, which sported two synchronised machine guns and was capable of speeds of up to 110mph, against which the BE2 was virtually helpless. Such was the BE's dreadful performance that no less a person than the legendary British fighter ace Captain Albert Ball, VC, called it 'a bloody awful aeroplane'. The strength of feeling about the BE2, and the state of British aircraft manufacturing in general, was so great that the subject was raised in a heated debate in the House of Commons in March 1916 when the independent MP and former Royal Naval aviator Noel Pemberton Billing sought to reform the leadership of the RFC and to end the monopoly of the Royal Aircraft Factory's supply of aircraft to the military. In an inflammatory speech to Parliament on 22 March, he opined that British pilots were being 'rather murdered than killed' in France because of the BE2's poor performance and called it a 'travesty of a weapon of war'. The Conservative Member for Brentford, William Joynson-Hicks, supported Pemberton Billing's cause, telling the House that:

I myself have been out to the front and seen the organisation of our Air Service there. I saw any number of new machines, all of the same old type of machines that we used when the War began, with the same old engines of eighty-five, ninety, and ninety-five horsepower. What I have been trying to impress, time and time again, is that you cannot meet a German machine of 150 horse-power with an English machine of 90 or 95 horse-power. That is my whole case against the Flying Corps, as I told the right hon. Gentleman in private conference some time ago. What I want is to have someone in charge of the Air Service who will stop the making of these machines. My right hon. Friend knows that a contract was given a little time ago to an English firm for 1,000 90 horsepower engines. They are being pressed for delivery still. Why is not that contract scrapped at once and a new contract entered into, not for 95 horse-power machines, but for 200 horse-power machines? I know that there are other higher horse-power machines being built, but what is the good of turning out 1,000 engines of 95 or 90 horse-power? Up till now our machines have been maids-of-all-work. They have had to carry a pilot, an observer, one or two guns, ammunition, a few bombs here and there, photographic apparatus, and wireless equipment. No wonder they are called Christmas Trees at the front. They are decked all over with all kinds of these things, and they cannot go more than the certain number of miles per hour they went at the beginning of the War. I have no time to describe them. My right hon. Friend knows the types of machines we must have if we are to win the battle in the air.[46]

Warming to his theme, Joynson-Hicks read out part of a letter he had received from 'a captain in the Flying Corps':

He says: 'At the front the tales you are told about our mastery of the air are known by all of us out here to be absolutely incorrect. We have not got the mastery. We have the pluck, we have not got the machines. It may soothe the British public's mind, but we airmen know the truth'. That is not a satisfactory position. That is not really a position in which we ought to put our men, gallant as they are. This man is a gallant man and is a Military Cross officer.[47]

The two MPs made compelling, if controversial (and in the case of Pemberton Billing, self-serving, since he owned an aircraft manufacturing business), arguments, and their speeches led to the formation by the Government of the Bailhache Committee (chaired by Sir Clement

Bailhache, a High Court judge) to investigate the issues raised. However, the long development times involved in designing, building, and testing new aircraft meant that, for now, the BE2 would remain in service and in large numbers.

Aside from its slow speed, there were other reasons why the BE2 was so unloved. Firstly, the pilot sat in the rear seat so that the machine's centre of gravity would not be unduly disturbed if it was being flown solo, thus placing the observer in the front cockpit, which was directly over, and between, the wings. This meant that the wings, struts and bracing wires that surrounded the observer, and the engine directly in front of him, restricted his field of view (the best sight he could get was slightly forwards and straight down, due to the stagger of the lower wing) and hampered the operation of the camera and/or the Lewis gun (for self-defence) – hardly ideal for an 'observer'.

Secondly, since the BE2 had been designed before the war, no consideration had been given to arming it for self-protection and in any case, in its early versions, the aeroplane's engine was not powerful enough to cope with the additional weight of a gun, ammunition and mounts. As the war progressed and improved engines were introduced, front-line squadrons began to experiment with 'home-made' solutions for mounting a Lewis gun. These ad-hoc designs were later adopted officially but, even in modified form, were still far from ideal. The observer's Lewis gun was able to be mounted in only one of three positions at a time: one on each of the forward centre section struts to either side of his cockpit, and one behind him, between his and the pilot's cockpits (known as the Strange Mount after its inventor, Captain L. Strange). If the arc of fire needed changing, the observer had to stand up, lift the 28lb weapon off its swivel mount and heave it from one position to the next – not easy in flight while under attack and when the BE2 was manoeuvring. As Paul Maltby put it, 'It takes little imagination to picture his difficulties in a bucking aeroplane in a dogfight.'[48] If the marauding fighter was coming in from behind, which was usually the case following the introduction of the Eindecker, it meant firing rearwards over the pilot's head (using the Strange Mount) while kneeling on the front seat. Maltby noted that: 'Fire from his [the observer's] cramped cockpit was very limited – the engine and propeller masked everything ahead; the top plane [wing], umbrella-like, masked almost all the upwards field of fire while the bottom plane in the centre of which he sat, did the same downwards. The fuselage and tail plane, with the pilot's head sticking out of the former, obscured most of the rearwards field.'[49]

Another Lewis gun could be mounted either in a fixed position along-side the pilot's cockpit on the fuselage (angled outwards at forty degrees to prevent it shooting off the propeller), or to swivel mounts on the rear centre section struts in front of the pilot. Aiming and operating this second weapon, especially changing the 97-round magazine,[50] meant that the pilot's attention was distracted from actually flying the aeroplane, so it was usually only carried when the pilot flew alone. In short, the BE2 was 'very ill-provided for the air fighting which lay in store for it, but it was the best that could be improvised'.[51]

Thirdly, the aerodynamic design of the BE2 led to problems. Competing theories on aeroplane design in 1912 held that either an aircraft should be built as inherently *unstable*, meaning that the airframe will naturally devi-ate from straight and level flight and must be brought back to steadiness by corrections from the pilot, or inherently *stable* so that any movement away from straight and level must be initiated, rather than corrected, by the pilot. The unstable aeroplane will therefore be more manoeuvrable, but will be trickier to fly, than the more forgiving (but less agile), stable design. The BE2 was built to be stable, hardly surprising given the inexpe-rience of pilots and the paucity of flying training in those early years of manned flight. It was so steady that it could be flown for long periods (in good weather) without the pilot touching the control column and would right itself if upset by a sudden gust of wind. Such gentle manners were so unusual in early aeroplanes that pilots called the BE2 'Stability Jane', or 'The Quirk'. Stability also made the BE2 a very good platform for obser-vation and photography, which is what it had been designed for, but of course this did not help it under dogfight conditions when agility is the key to survival.

His flying training at Norwich completed successfully, and moreover safe-ly, Massey was awarded his Graduation Certificate (number 1625), which stated that he was 'qualified for service in the Royal Flying Corps',[52] and on 7 July 1916 he was posted – proudly sporting his brand-new RFC pilot's 'wings' on the left breast of his tunic – to No. 16 Squadron in France. The amount and quality of training he had been given was, by any standards, paltry – from beginning to end, the entire course of learning how to fly had lasted exactly three months, and he was now expected to face the enemy in the air. For those who managed to survive the perils of flying instruction, many (in the years up to 1917) were sent to operational squad-rons in France and Belgium with as little as fifteen to twenty hours of solo flying in their log books, and were often completely unfamiliar with the aircraft type they were expected to fly and, moreover, fight in. Their hard-pressed new units did what they could to give the novice pilots 'some further flying, gunnery and air fighting instruction, but precious little was possible'[53]

Embarking on 12 July 1916, Massey arrived at the squadron's airfield at La Gorgue in northern France four days later. La Gorgue was some seventeen miles south-west of Ypres, in what Paul Maltby described as a 'nursery … a quiet sector in which battle-worn formations were rested and in which new ones were introduced to trench warfare'.[54] The bulk of the squadron's work was to help train the 1st Australian Corps in working with aircraft, something they were unused to since they had previously been in Gallipoli where air cooperation had been minimal. There were still regular offensive operations to be undertaken, though, as Martin was to discover. The airfield at La Gorgue was 'a bad one – small, dusty or a mire according to the weather, with a "star-fish" of concrete tracks in the centre for taking off and landing in bad weather';[55] the concrete was renowned for bending, or even tearing off, the BE2's tail skid during a hard landing. As for accommodation, the squadron personnel were billeted in farms and scattered hamlets around the local area, and barns and other large buildings were commandeered to provide workshops and offices.

No. 16 Squadron had been formed in February 1915 at the large RFC HQ aerodrome at St Omer to carry out a mixture of offensive patrolling and reconnaissance duties, operating a combination of British and French aircraft types but now using solely the BE2. The squadron was known as a 'corps squadron', reflecting its close cooperation duties with the ground Army, and one of its main tasks was to 'spot' for the artillery, watching to see where shots were falling and then to transmit aiming corrections by wireless back to the gun battery. One of the squadron's early commanding officers was Major Hugh Dowding, who later masterminded RAF Fighter Command's victory in the Battle of Britain during the summer of 1940,[56] but the CO when Massey arrived was Major David Powell. Powell had, just a few months earlier, expressed his grave concerns about the quality of new arrivals to his squadron in a letter to the general officer commanding the RFC's 5th Brigade, in which he wrote: 'It is not understood how an officer who is reported to be fit for [duty] overseas should, on arrival in France, be found to be so completely unsuited for the duties of a pilot, unless the officers who were responsible for his training and graduation made a very grave error in judgement.'[57] Arguably, the most serious deficiency in flying training was in the realm of aerial combat, in which 'a great mistake was to send them out [to France] knowing so little about air gunnery … many hardly knew how their guns worked, much less how to use them or how to manoeuvre if attacked. Hence the numerous casualties amongst the last joined.'[58]

The best advice that could be given to a new, operational, BE2 pilot on what to do if attacked by a German fighter was summed up by No. 16 Squadron pilot and 'A' Flight commander Captain Eric Routh, who wrote that: 'When a new pilot reported to me my advice was 1: Ceaselessly search the sky, however much you may trust your observer. 2: If a Hun gets behind you, never dive away from him; feint, sideslip, anything you can think of, but don't dive. 3: Look over your shoulder to see if he is getting a lead on you; if he is, it is time to do something.'[59]

Instead of being pitched straight into operational sorties, Martin, like any new pilot, needed to learn the layout of the local area and get to know landmarks from the air, and would also have had to prove his competency as a pilot to the CO, especially so considering Powell's misgivings. His first flight with his new squadron was on 18 July 1916 in a BE2c, serial number 2688 (a machine in which he was to have a sobering experience a short time later), doing 'circuits and bumps' at La Gorgue for almost an hour that evening. The weather that day had been 'clouds, mist and rain; unfavourable weather for any successful flying,'[60] but presumably it had cleared sufficiently later on to allow for a few laps of the airfield. No doubt watched critically from the ground by Major Powell and the other squadron pilots, Massey managed to complete two landings, which were recorded simply as 'OK'.[61] The following day he flew three times; two sorties were 'engine tests', the first of which was curtailed after only twenty minutes, the engine having a 'burst cylinder'. Then, in the late afternoon, he was sent aloft with Lieutenant Westcott, one of the squadron's experienced observers, to take a look around the district, learn the landmarks, and get his bearings. Most probably, Westcott guided Massey out towards the Western Front so that Martin could take his first look at the trenches and perhaps experience some anti-aircraft (AA) fire.

Now deemed ready for the front line, Massey's first operational sortie of the First World War came on 20 July 1916. Flying again with Westcott, he took off at 11.20 a.m. on a counter-battery patrol[62] and spent over two hours in the air, but to no avail – no muzzle flashes were seen, and no movement by enemy road traffic was noted. Martin was probably disappointed that his first experience of the war was a routine one, but he surely knew that he had been fortunate first time out. Having been initiated, he then got stuck into the squadron routine of spotting for the British artillery and carrying out reconnaissance sorties, all part and parcel of life on a corps squadron.

Less than two weeks after his introduction to operational flying, though, he was involved in a major attack against the Germans. On 1 August, some sixteen aircraft of the RFC's 2nd Brigade, of which No. 16 Squadron was a part, along with an escort of eleven fighters, attacked the railway station, sidings, and supply dumps at Ledeghem, around ten miles due east of Ypres. Massey was one of five No. 16 Squadron pilots sent on the raid, and he flew solo to compensate for the weight of the two 112lb bombs carried by his BE2. Leaving La Gorgue at 1.50 that afternoon, Martin 'dropped bombs on the south of the sidings between there and houses'.[63] Overall, the attack was deemed a success, apparently having caused 'much damage and started 3 fires'.[64] Massey landed just over two hours later, having taken the war to the enemy for the first time. He had been lucky, however, since 'during the raid on Ledeghem Station … enemy machines came up in force'[65] and there were several furious dogfights that he had, either by luck or judgement, managed to avoid.

The next day was to prove somewhat less successful. Flying once more with Westcott, Martin took off from La Gorgue at 1.25 p.m., to undertake a reconnaissance mission. He was once again at the controls of 2688, the BE2 he had flown on his first trip with No. 16 Squadron back in July. The aircraft was a 'presentation' machine, paid for by the people of Nigeria and it carried proudly that country's name on its fuselage. No. 2688 had been built under licence by Ruston, Proctor and Company, a Lincoln-based industrial equipment firm best known as a manufacturer of narrow – and standard-gauge diesel locomotives and steam shovels, but who also built cars, steam locomotives and a range of internal combustion engines as well as aeroplanes. While flying over Maugré, about five miles south-west of Lille, Massey and Westcott saw what appeared to be an emplacement for four small guns facing west-south-west.[66] They were not able to photograph the structure because German AA guns opened up on them, causing severe damage to 2688. Massey nursed the ailing aircraft back to La Gorgue, managing skilfully to land despite the harm suffered by his machine. Fortunately neither he nor Westcott were injured, but the luckless 2688 was so badly damaged that it could not be repaired by the squadron riggers and had to be sent away to the RFC's No. 2 Air Depot at Candas whose engineering facilities were better equipped. Even there, though, the aeroplane was deemed beyond repair and it was written off on 13 August.

A new commanding officer arrived at La Gorgue to take the helm of No. 16 Squadron on 5 August 1916. Major Paul Maltby, arriving on promotion from No. 15 Squadron, replaced Major Powell that day, which just happened to be Maltby's twenty-fourth birthday.

Massey dropped bombs again on 7 August. This time, his target was an enemy kite balloon (such tethered dirigibles were used by both sides to spot targets for their respective artillery), a particularly hazardous undertaking since there was a risk of being caught in the explosion if and when the balloon's inflation gas ignited. Along with two other pilots, Martin (again solo) first flew to the RFC airfield at Abeele to refuel before heading towards Armentières to search for his prey. The first machine, piloted by Lieutenant Thompson, failed to locate either a balloon or its shed and so returned with a full bomb load. Massey, however, saw an enemy inflatable and attacked it, dropping fifteen 2lb bombs, but without success. The balloon was hauled down hastily by its ground crew and, since his remaining bombs had jammed on their racks, Martin then headed for home. Second Lieutenant Augustus Bird in the third BE2 also bombed a balloon that he had spotted on the ground, causing a great deal of thick smoke and provoking a stiff response from the German AA gunners, both of which prevented Bird from seeing any conclusive results.[67] The trio landed some two hours later, doubtlessly frustrated that they had nothing more positive to show for their efforts. The rest of August 1916 played itself out with Massey flying on most days, mainly on artillery observation and reconnaissance sorties, but also with the occasional bombing mission such as that on the 17th when, 'in spite of the weather ... aeroplanes for the most part had to fly low',[68] he and Captain Waller bombed a sugar factory. Their bombs not only missed the target, but also failed to hit a train leaving the factory as they attacked. Many of that month's usual sorties were interspersed with 'hostile aircraft', or HA, patrols. Quite what a lone BE2 was supposed to achieve on an HA patrol is unknown, since attacking a German aircraft in one was an extremely unwise undertaking for all the reasons already described above. Martin was fortunate in that, during all the HA patrols that he flew, he saw no sign of enemy machines.

At the end of the month, No. 16 Squadron relocated to Bruay-la-Buissière, some thirty miles south-west of Lille. The airfield was on the southern side of Bruay, a town built around the coal mining industry. There were four mines in the local area, and the town was dominated by the Bruay Mining

Company, the chief local employer. The move to Bruay heralded the end of the squadron's so-called 'quiet period', since they were allotted to IV Army Corps, which was facing the dominating feature of Vimy Ridge a few miles to the east, and it was immediately apparent that 'serious fighting was in store here'.[69] The accommodation at Bruay was similar to that at La Gorgue (namely beds in local houses), but was more concentrated since Bruay was a town and therefore the billets were less scattered than in the hamlets of the previous rural area. Several months later, though, the squadron managed to obtain four large wooden huts; one they converted into a canteen and mess for the other ranks with a small sergeants' mess at one end; one became the officers' mess with dining and ante-rooms; and the remaining two were divided into small bedsits, one for each aircrew member – 'no unit was better housed in France', according to Maltby. At least one of the squadron observers disagreed with him, however. Second Lieutenant Jack Lidsey had been on leave in England when the huts arrived, and he was horrified to find that, on his return, the aircrew had been turned out of their comfortable billets in the town and moved into the 'wretchedly cold and soakingly damp huts'.[70] Lidsey decided to stay on in his Bruay quarters, paying for it himself until such time someone noticed he was not living in the huts with the others.

Martin's first sortie from the squadron's new base was on 5 September 1916, a flight that proved to be frustrating and probably not a little embarrassing. The weather that day was 'unfavourable'[71] but nevertheless Massey was airborne at 9.15 a.m. to carry out a counter-battery patrol with Lieutenant Diamond as his observer. They were up for two and a quarter hours during which time 'no [muzzle] flashes were seen', because 'observation [was] difficult owning to mist'.[72] Diamond was obviously having difficulty working out where they were, probably due to a combination of the bad weather and unfamiliarity with the new area, since they 'landed at Hubersent owing to losing the way'.[73] This is somewhat of an understatement given that Hubersent is well to the west of Bruay, not far from the English Channel coast – they had overshot their home airfield by around forty miles. One can imagine the banter from their fellow aircrew once they had eventually made their way back, probably accompanied by some sterner words from Major Maltby.

Just after the move to Bruay, Maltby decided to deploy one of the squadron's flights, 'B' Flight, to a former French Army airfield at Savy-Berlette (also known as Savy-B, or just Savy), a short distance away to the south, as a liaison experiment since the airfield was closer to the artillery batteries with which the aircraft were working. Maltby felt that Bruay was 'very far back from the lines for a Corps squadron'.[74] Martin Massey landed at Savy for the first time on 16 September following an artillery shoot with C Battery, 51 Brigade Royal Field Artillery (RFA), which had been curtailed when a German kite balloon had popped up to range counter-battery fire back at the British guns. As part of Maltby's liaison trial, Massey 'arranged targets with D Battery' of the same artillery brigade.[75] With the new targets agreed, Massey and his observer, Captain Waller, took off to conduct the shoot with D Battery, but unfortunately their wireless aerial (unwound from a spool alongside the pilot's cockpit when transmitting) had become free and caught in a patch of thistles as their BE2 took off, snapping the antenna and rendering it useless, and they were back on the ground at Savy fifteen minutes later, the mission aborted. Undaunted, and with repairs made rapidly to the aerial by the groundcrew, they took off again a short while later to try again, this time successfully – German trenches and a supply dump were hit by the British gunners. The enemy were not about to let Massey and Waller work at will, however, and a 'great deal of machine gun and rifle fire was heard and felt'[76] as they transmitted to the artillery battery below. Waller saw where the AA fire was coming from and sent the enemy's coordinates to the British guns, which shot back and silenced the Germans, leaving the BE2 to continue its task unhindered.

Massey was to experience two further flying mishaps during September 1916. The first came on the evening of the 19th when he and Waller were on a transit flight and the engine of their BE2c, serial number 4494, cut out. According to the RFC's daily communiqué, the weather had stopped most flying activity in the mid-afternoon. At the time, around 8.00 p.m., they were twenty-five minutes into the flight and, with no airfield nearby, Massey had no other option than to force-land, wrecking the aircraft in the process. Both men were fortunate to walk away unhurt. The second incident was on the 26th, when Martin was again flying a solo bombing sortie, this time at night. The targets were enemy positions in the village of Harnes, just north-east of Lens, but Massey could barely make them out due to the effectiveness of the German blackout precautions. Nevertheless, he dropped his eight 20lb bombs but saw no resulting fires,[77] so he headed for home. For some unrecorded reason, Martin crashed on landing at Bruay at 4.35 a.m., destroying his BE2c, serial number 4378, in the process. He had now written off three aeroplanes in a little over two months. Perhaps, in the dark, he had misjudged his approach, but whatever the cause, he had once again escaped serious injury; it seemed that Second

Lieutenant Martin Massey bore a charmed life.

The first day of October bought a frustrating mission. No. 16 Squadron was tasked to join in a bombing raid on the railway station at Orchies, some thirty miles due east of Bruay. They were to be escorted there and back by British FE2b and FE8 fighters, which were to rendezvous with the bombers above Bruay before the entire formation headed off to the target. Massey and several other pilots took off (solo as usual for bombing) at 10.00 a.m. and climbed to 7,000 feet to meet the fighters, which had apparently not arrived. The BE2s then circled the airfield for almost two hours, catching fleeting glimpses of the FEs in the distance that were 'too far away and too high to catch',[78] until finally one of the BE pilots, Captain Barker, took the initiative and led the bombers, unescorted, off towards the front line. They had flown over enemy territory for 'some distance', according to Massey, when they were turned around, landing back at Bruay over two and a half hours after they had taken off, with all their bombs still on the racks and having achieved nothing. Nonetheless, the RFC daily communiqué reported that Orchies station 'was bombed by the 1st Brigade, many bombs falling on the permanent way and rolling stock'.[79] Whoever had carried out the raid, it certainly was not No. 16 Squadron.

Martin was to have greater success the following day, though, earning him an entry in a diary kept by Major Maltby called the 'Honours Book' (in which he recorded noteworthy events), when he and Waller 'descended to 2,000 feet and scattered a party of men with MG [machine-gun] fire, near Vimy'.[80] His attacking spirit was mentioned for a second time in the Honours Book on 6 October. This time he was paired once again with Waller on a counter-battery patrol in low cloud and rain, which made observation 'impossible'[81] – the weather had been 'continually unfavourable for aerial operations' for several days, with heavy rain and strong westerly or south-westerly winds prevailing.[82] As they made their way back across the lines they spotted a German lorry, which they proceeded to strafe with Waller's Lewis gun, and then drop a couple of bombs on. One bomb was seen to explode on a dugout beside the vehicle, but the other went astray.[83]

On 10 October Massey had his first brush with an enemy aircraft, albeit from a distance and without success. He was flying with Second Lieutenant Duffield as his observer on a counter-battery and photography task in the morning when, at 9.50 a.m., he saw a German aircraft cross the front and continue on over the British lines for 'some miles'. Fifteen minutes later, the hostile aircraft came back, being pursued hard by two RFC fighters, an FE8 and an FE2b. Martin stated: 'We joined in the chase, but were unable to do any good. The enemy machine had its nose well down for earth all the way. We gave up the chase 4 miles east of Givenchy and returned.'[84] No hostile aeroplane was claimed as shot down by the RFC in the area that day, so the enemy pilot evidently shook off his hunters. As they flew back over the German trenches, however, Massey and Duffield's BE2 was 'severely shelled by enemy AA and had the right top plane and main spar shot through'.[85] Another lucky escape.

The date of 16 October 1916 saw another major bombing raid undertaken by the squadron. Nine aircraft took off from Bruay at 8.40 a.m. (although one turned back because the machine would not climb) and headed for Bois-Bernard, halfway between Vimy and Douai, which was 'reported to be full of troops'.[86] For his part in the attack, Massey dropped two 112lb bombs on the target, also spotting a 'very big' supply dump close to a rail siding. Paul Maltby felt that the action was worthy of mention in his Honours Book, although the RFC communiqué of the day seems to damn by faint praise, recording that 'the majority of the bombs fell in the village, destroying a large wooden hut and causing a fire',[87] which does not seem to be much of a return for a significant raid against a target supposedly crammed with the enemy. Far greater excitement was to come a few days later, though, when Martin engaged an enemy aircraft in aerial combat for the first time. Crewed once again with Waller, Massey was undertaking an artillery observation sortie in the late morning of 22 October, at 8,000 feet over Avion on the British side of the lines, when they saw another BE2 below them, but over German territory, with a hostile aircraft on its tail. As he began to descend and cross the front line to help the British machine, Massey saw another German aircraft 'coming quickly in a southerly direction',[88] apparently to join in the attack on the other BE2. Massey and Waller 'cut him off, and fired a drum and a half into him, half with [the] forward gun and one with [the] rear gun (observer's) at 50 yards range'.[89] The German pilot broke sharply and dived 'very steeply' away, and was last seen with a British FE fighter 'right on his tail', at which point Martin had to give up the chase due to once again being outpaced by the fleeing enemy machine and the hotly pursuing FE. A short while later, the FE was seen returning, flying low over the British lines. In their combat report, Massey and Waller reported the hostile aircraft as a 'monoplane', so in all likelihood it was a Fokker EIII Eindecker, which by that time was being replaced by newer and more capable designs. The RFC made no claim against an Eindecker, or indeed any other type of German monoplane, that day, so the FE was probably unsuccessful in its chase and the enemy machine made it back to its home airfield unscathed. Some accounts state that Martin was wounded during his brief fight with the monoplane, but this is not the case. There is no mention of any injury sustained on that date either on his medical records, his casualty card, or the combat report, and a post-war photograph of him in uniform shows only one 'wound stripe' on his sleeve, earned in another aerial battle that will be covered in detail below. Meanwhile, a few miles away near Arras, another No. 16 Squadron BE2, crewed by Captain Roland Mounsey and Captain Richard Saul, joined in a dogfight that had developed between other British FEs and 'eight or nine Rolands [a type of German fighter, but more than likely these were in fact Albatros aircraft – misidentification was a common occurrence]'.[90] Mounsey and Saul, showing enormous valour in their outclassed aeroplane, 'engaged 5 of the enemy machines, and shot down and destroyed 1'[91] – no mean feat in a BE2.

The remainder of October and the month of November were relatively routine for Martin Massey, with his flying consisting of the squadron staples of artillery spotting, counter-battery patrols and reconnaissance, all of which passed without great incident. There were two sorties worthy of note, however, the first of which was on 2 November when, while show-ing Lieutenant Dod, a new observer, around the area, Martin dropped a single 20lb Hales bomb on a rail over road bridge, which probably did wonders for Dod's first-timer's nerves. Then, on the 21st, Massey took part in another night bombing raid, this time against troop billets in Avion, which the daily RFC communiqué noted as 'successful'.[92] During that attack, he dropped six 20lb and two incendiary bombs on the target, land-ing back at Bruay at 6.30 a.m.[93] At the end of November, Major Maltby ordered that 'B' Flight was to return to Bruay to rejoin the rest of No. 16 Squadron since the Savy experiment had 'proved uneconomical'.[94] After dismantling the hangars and huts for transportation by lorry, the observers went by road to Bruay on 29 November, but bad weather meant that the pilots had to wait to fly the BE2s back the next day. Even then, the weather was still marginal, meaning that they made the trip at barely 200 feet.

On 5 December 1916, Martin Massey received the most joyful news that any man serving on the Western Front could have wished for – a leave pass granting him two weeks' furlough. He would have travelled home straight away, by train to the coast and then troopship to Folkestone, from where he would have caught a train home to Hilton, via London. Many a man found this sudden dislocation hard to deal with, for one day he was fighting for his life in the trenches or the air, and the next was at home with his family in Britain, back in a world with which he was unfamiliar and struggling to make himself understood. Having prayed so fervently for leave, many could not wait to return to the front – back to normality.

When he arrived back at Bruay on 19 December, there was surprising news waiting for Massey. He was promoted to temporary captain and was appointed a flight commander on No. 16 Squadron. To be promoted and given the responsibility of leading up to ten other pilots, and a corresponding number of observers, is remarkable enough, but for one so young (he was still a month short of his nineteenth birthday), and with only five months' experience of front-line flying, is nothing short of extraordinary. No doubt there were others more senior to him, both in terms of time served in rank and time on the squadron (and therefore more experienced), but Martin's leadership qualities, which would serve him so well in the future, were obviously coming to the fore already. As soon as he returned from leave, he was back in the air and back in the Honours Book. Major Maltby noted that on 20 December Massey, flying with Duffield in the front seat on a counter-battery patrol, 'saw 12 active [German] batteries and, sending them [their positions] down on wireless, reduced barrage to a great extent. Also brought in a lot of valuable information.'[95] On Christmas Eve, the pair were once again flying together, this time on an artillery observation sortie with 161 Siege Battery when their BE2 developed engine trouble and they force-landed just ten minutes after taking off. This time the machine, and the crew, survived intact. Christmas Day 1916 ushered in bad weather to Bruay making flying impossible, which no doubt came as a great relief to the 'three poor pilots'[96] who had been ordered to carry out a bombing raid early on Christmas morning.

As 1917 arrived, early January brought decent flying weather and so Martin busied himself with the usual No. 16 Squadron tasks. The German Air Service was active too, evidenced on 11 January when they conducted a bombing raid against Bruay, setting fire to 'C' Flight's hangar and destroying five BE2s as well as a good deal of vehicles, spares and equipment. Human casualties were mercifully light, with just three airmen requiring minor treatment.[97] Almost as soon as it began, the attack was over; there had not even been time to man Bruay's anti-aircraft machine guns by the time the bombers had disappeared, although 'several enthusiastic optimists'[98] managed to grab rifles from the aerodrome's armoury and fire off a few rounds at the fleeing raiders. In retaliation, No. 16 Squadron bombed the German airfield at Douai less than an hour later. The winter weather deteriorated during the latter part of the month, though, curtailing flying for several days, but on the last day of January, Massey once again found himself entered into Major Maltby's Honours Book when, paired once more with Duffield, Martin 'carried out a successful counter-battery flight … in addition to carrying out a pre-arranged shoot; weather was very misty'.[99]

The skies above the Western Front around Arras, where Massey often found himself, were the hunting grounds of several of Germany's most prolific fighter pilots of the First World War. Manfred von Richthofen, the famous Red Baron, led his Jasta[100] 11 from the airfield at La Brayelle near Douai, scoring his first victory over No. 16 Squadron on 1 February 1917 when he shot down a BE2 flown by Second Lieutenant Percival Murray, with Lieutenant Duncan McRae as his observer. They were not to be his last victims from Bruay. Von Richthofen's great friend and rival was Werner Voss, a man who came from a humble family in contrast to the aristocratic Red Baron. Voss had served as a private soldier in the cavalry before promotion to NCO status, and was then commissioned as an officer in 1915, albeit in the reserves due to his flat feet and weak knees. Undeterred, Voss volunteered for flying training, and immediately proved to be a natural and gifted pilot. After a period as a flying instructor (he was the youngest instructor in the German Air Service, aged nineteen), Voss was sent to Jasta 2 in November 1916 where he met and befriended von Richthofen (before von Richthofen was promoted to command Jasta 11), often flying as his wingman. So impressed was the Red Baron with Voss's skill that he considered him to be the only pilot capable of challenging him for the position of top scorer. On 1 February, the day that von Richthofen shot down Murray and McRae, Werner Voss brought down an Airco DH2 of No. 29 Squadron, his fourth aerial victory; he was now just one 'kill' away from being classed as an 'ace'.

On Sunday, 4 February 1917, Voss (along with others from his squadron) was on patrol from Jasta 2's base at Pronville, probably in an Albatros D.II since the D.III, a newly introduced variant and his usual mount, was suffering from some teething problems, notably structural failure in the lower wings and was grounded. But, armed with two synchronised 7.92mm machine guns and powered by a Mercedes in-line engine, the D.II was still vastly superior to the BE2. Indeed, Major Maltby later wrote that such was the threat posed by the Albatros that his observers often had to abandon their primary role and simply act as lookouts against a surprise attack[101] (meaning that the pilot had to carry out whatever task the sortie demanded as well as fly the aeroplane), and that 'the Squadron was destined to suffer severely at their hands'.[102] As he flew around the Givenchy-en-Gohelle area (just north of Vimy Ridge) at 2.40 p.m. that day, Werner Voss spotted a BE2d and manoeuvred into position to attack it. The British aircraft's pilot was Martin Massey. His observer in the front cockpit was Second Lieutenant Noel Vernham, a 27-year-old married man from London who had been a 'motor engineer's improver'[103] before the war, and who had served as a private in the Royal Army Service Corps prior to commissioning in the RFC the previous September. Massey and Vernham's task that day was artillery observation, which usually meant not having the security of a fighter escort. Martin's fellow No. 16 Squadron flight commander Eric Routh wrote:[104] 'When on artillery spotting, we had no direct fighter protection. If your observer did not keep awake, your first intimation of trouble would be a warning round from our own AA or the very nasty "rat-a-tat-tat" of the Hun machine gun. I developed a rubber neck whilst on that job. It was essential. Those that did not possess that commodity paid the highest penalty.'

Despite Martin's flying experience and expertise, his machine was no match for Voss's Albatros and there was nothing he could do – bullets from the German's twin Spandau machine guns tore into the unfortunate British aircraft (serial number 5797), setting it on fire. The BE2d sported two fuel tanks, one directly in front of the observer (between him and the engine), and the other behind him, between him and the pilot. Conflagration in either of them was usually lethal, especially so considering the wood and fabric construction of the airframe. Massey fought to keep the blazing machine from smashing into the ground and managed, with immense courage and skill, to crash-land the stricken aeroplane about a mile inside the British lines. Despite side-slipping all the way down in an effort to keep the flames away from himself and his observer, and to prevent the fire from spreading further, Massey suffered terrible burns to his legs and feet, but at least he had survived – although only just. Noel Vernham was not so fortunate, however; as a result of being hit by Voss's bullets he was killed instantly. Finally, after his several flying misfortunes, Martin Massey's luck had run out. Voss, though, had now joined that elite group of fighter pilots, the 'aces'. Vernham was not to be No. 16 Squadron's only fatality that day, sadly. Lieutenant Alfred Steele, another Londoner who was aged twenty-five, and Lieutenant James Boyd (a Canadian, and like Vernham aged twenty-seven) had also been killed, probably in the same melee as Martin had found himself. Steele and Boyd had courageously forced down an enemy aircraft from Jasta 2 but were almost immediately shot down by Leutnant Erich König of the same Jasta, his fourth victory.

There are two surviving eye-witness accounts of Martin's valiant efforts in bringing his burning BE2 down,[105] both compiled the following day by British artillery officers, most probably from the gun batteries with whom he and Vernham were working. The first was written by the commanding officer of 64 Battery RFA, a Major B. Carne, addressed to the adjutant of his higher authority, 57 Brigade RFA:

> Herewith a short account of the gallant manner in which Lieut H. Martin Massey, Sherwood Foresters and RFC, brought down a burning aeroplane under control on 4th Feb 1917. Flames were seen to be coming out of the machine when it was at some height. The pilot, Lieut Massey, at once planed downwards, and steered his machine in such a manner that the flames did not spread. As soon as the machine touched the ground the flames at once enveloped the observer, and it was impossible to rescue him. Lieut Massey jumped as the aeroplane landed and enquired for his observer; his boots were burned off his feet, his breeches were also in flames and he had two cuts on his face – his coolness and pluck were wonderful.

Second Lieutenant Arthur Mann, also of 64 Battery RFA, wrote his version of events to Major Maltby at No. 16 Squadron:

> I have the honour to make the following report, upon the gallant handling by the pilot of one of your planes, set on fire in an air combat near the Battery position on the afternoon of the 4th inst. The plane caught alight when I should estimate about 3,000 feet up in the air. Opinions of witnesses I have spoken to today place the height at probably 5,000 feet. The pilot, I understand, was Lt Massey; the plane I refer to was the wrecked one you yourself saw during your visit here yesterday. Lt Massey's handling of the burning plane can only be described as superbly magnificent. From start to finish there was every sign of the coolest nerve. There was no rush towards earth as might have been expected and forgiven. The machine was brought down in circles, Lt Massey seeming to have in mind the frequent changes of course, so that the flames should not get too strong a hold on any one part. I say this because the flames at each turn of the machine seemed to die down and then appear in fresh parts. The

plane was under absolute and perfect control right up until the moment of landing; in fact, Lt Massey, flying low, seemed to choose a landing place. This was done in spite of the pain Lt Massey must have been suffering from the bad burns received upon feet and legs.

Interestingly, both of these accounts, despite being addressed to different recipients, are written on notepaper headed 'Hilton, Nr Derby' – Martin's home – which has been scored out. The heading would seem to indicate that this was Massey's own stationery, but who gave it to the authors? It was unlikely to have been Martin, since neither writer mentions visiting him on the wards, and in any case he probably did not have a stock of personal writing paper with him in hospital just the day after being shot down (and was in no condition to be writing letters anyway). Most likely, it was Major Maltby who asked for the accounts and gave them the paper after he visited the crash site, but why he gave them Massey's personal notepaper rather than No. 16 Squadron's official stationery, or why the gunners could not have used their own, is a mystery.

Over fifty years later, in 1968, Paul Maltby wrote that Massey had been 'attacked by several Albatrosses' and that:

> after a fighting descent of several thousand feet, their machine caught fire and the enemy withdrew. Massey was then able to side-slip the rest of the way down, thereby deflecting the flames from himself, the fuselage and tail-plane. But he had to straighten up for the touch-down, when the heat became so intense that he threw himself out. The ground was deep in snow and Massey fell into a snowdrift which broke his fall, doused his burning clothing and saved him. He was soon rescued by the Canadians. Massey's burns were so severe that the doctors of the Casualty Clearing Station and Base Hospital told me that he could not possibly live (the treatment of burns was still in its infancy). But Massey held on and many weeks later was fit enough to be sent to England … perhaps his extreme youth helped; he was not yet 19 years old, although already a Captain and a flight commander having, like many other enthusiastic boys of that time, falsified his age when he had joined up. His is a story of extremes of fortune. … He is alive today, 1968, despite the medical forecasts in 1917![106]

This account is probably fogged somewhat by the passing of the years (Maltby himself noted that 'fifty-odd years is a long time for the memory to span'), since both Carne and Mann did not mention Massey falling into a snowdrift, and neither did Maltby himself at the time, as we shall see below in a letter he wrote straight away to Martin's father. Further, Maltby's assertion that the medical staff told him that Martin was unlikely to survive his injuries is also at odds with what both he and his wing commander wrote to Ernest Massey directly after the incident. Moreover, Maltby is incorrect in his statements that Martin was 'not yet 19 years of age' (he had celebrated his nineteenth birthday the previous month), and that Massey had 'falsified his age when he had joined up' – all of Massey's application forms for the Army show his correct date of birth, and there is also a copy of his birth certificate, issued in 1915 specifically as part of his Sandhurst application, in his Army file held in the National Archives at Kew.

Noel Vernham's wife, 22-year-old Violet (whom he had married less than three months earlier, on 17 November 1916), wrote to Paul Maltby on 9 February, as soon as she heard the news of her husband's death:

5 Warrington Crescent
Maida Hill
London W

Dear Sir,
I had a telegram yesterday reporting that my husband, 2nd Lieut Noel M.H. Vernham, was killed in action on the 4th inst.
   I should be so very grateful for any particulars you could let me have. Either the above address or 1 Cranbury Terrace, Southampton will find me.
   We are waiting so anxiously for any news
   Yours faithfully
   V.K. Vernham

Without fail, Major Maltby made it his solemn duty to write to the relatives of his squadron's casualties, and he did so to Violet when he received her letter. She wrote back to him on 16 February, her grief bravely supressed yet still unmistakable in her words:[107]

1 Cranbury Terrace
Southampton

Dear Capt [sic] Maltby

So many thanks for your kind letter – it was a great relief to hear that there was no suffering and that his death was instantaneous. I should be so glad of a photograph of his grave.

   Could you send his things home to me? I think there was a small miniature photograph of myself in his tunic pocket, and a little brown book of Shelley's poems, also a photo of myself at his billet and there may have been one or two little personal things of his – anything so long as it was his, it is all I have left.

   He was so happy in his work

   Yours Truly

   V.K. Vernham

PS Could you possibly let me have two photographs of his grave – one for his mother?

In his will, Noel left his personal effects and estate, valued at £161 8s 8d,[108] to his young widow. Violet later gave Martin a keepsake, her husband's silver vesta case engraved with his initials, which he was to treasure for the rest of his life. Second Lieutenant Noel Mark Hodson Vernham was buried a few days later at Aubigny-en-Artois cemetery, not far from Bruay.

   Martin would undoubtedly have been given first aid at the crash site, but would then have been evacuated immediately to a casualty clearing station (CCS). In addition to his horrendous burns, one of Voss's bullets had creased his left cheek, and he had a head wound most probably caused when he had thrown himself from the burning BE2. Given that Vernham was buried at Aubigny, it seems likely that he and Massey were taken to 42 CCS, based in the village, the closest medical facility to where they came down. Established in February 1916, 42 CCS had seen plenty of patients in its time, although it had not always enjoyed the best of reputations. An inspection on 2 June 1916 by the matron-in-chief of the British Expeditionary Force, Maud McCarthy, stated that the CCS 'is not by any means satisfactory, it is dirty, ill-managed and a lack of interest and management everywhere'.[109] By the following February, however, things were better, due in no small part to McCarthy's tireless and tenacious efforts to improve the general standard of nursing on the Western Front.

   Major Paul Maltby wrote to Martin's parents on 5 February, the day after the shooting-down:[110]

Dear Mr Massey,

As your son's CO, I am taking the liberty of writing to you to give you news about him. I am afraid he may not be able to write himself for a few days as he is feeling rather seedy after his accident [Maltby was evidently a master of understatement]. I expect that you will have heard officially before this letter reaches you, but I thought that you will probably like to have details.

He went out yesterday with 2/Lt Vernham as his observer on an artillery observation flight, the shoot being worked by your son. He turned towards our lines after having a shell burst and was about to send down the observation by wireless when he saw his observer turn around and man the machine gun quickly. He then saw a small German machine diving at him. Vernham managed to fire about 50 rounds at the German before he was himself hit and collapsed. Your son was turning his machine about to attack the hostile machine when apparently the petrol tank was hit and burst into flames.

How your son managed to keep control while his machine was alight is simply miraculous. He managed not only to bring it down, but landed it on our side of the lines. His first thought was to save his observer from the burning wreckage but he collapsed from exhaustion before he could do anything. I'm glad to say that I don't think that Vernham suffered at all as he was hit several times, one shot of which must have been instantly fatal.

I saw your son in hospital this morning. He was looking much better than I had expected. His legs are burnt rather badly but luckily he had on very thick clothing so the burns are not deep [Maltby was either wrong in this or was not wanting to shock Massey's parents further]. His hands and one cheek are also rather blistered and he has a bullet graze in his neck [it was actually his left cheek] which I am glad to say is very slight. He was wonderfully cheerful and is doing very well, but must be suffering rather a lot. However, he sticks it wonderfully. They tell me at the hospital that he should be alright quite soon. I have promised to let you know how he gets on, as he does not feel like writing himself.

He behaved simply splendidly all through and I feel very proud of his having been in my squadron and I only hope he will not be overlooked. He deserves anything.

I am sending his kit to hospital with him and I hope it goes down safely with him. Kit used at one time to be very often lost in hospital, but things are better now.

If you could let us know how he gets on after leaving hospital here,

we should all like to hear. He has been with us for some time now and
had just been made a Flight Commander. I am afraid I shall have a
job to fill his place.

Hoping soon to hear that he is fit and about again.

Yours sincerely

P.C. Maltby

A further letter was sent to Ernest on 6 February, this time from Lieutenant
Colonel Thomas Carthew, the CO of 1st Wing, RFC:[111]

Dear Mr Massey,

Although I know that his sqdn [sic] commander will have written
to you about your son, I feel that I should like to add a line myself.

I saw him in hospital yesterday and again today, and am glad to tell
you that, although the burns on his legs are severe, and his beauty has
been impaired for a time, all the medical authorities seem confident
that there will be no permanent injury. The nursing sisters are full
of praise for the plucky way he bears the pain, and General Game[112]
and I when we visited him yesterday found him fairly cheerful and
very patient.

His work has come under my observation a good deal since I took
over command of the Wing, and he has shown great keenness and
dash all the time. As you probably know, he has already been
recommended for the appointment of Flight Commander and I am
confident that he would have done the work well. His first thought,
despite his own injuries, when the machine landed, was for his
observer, and from first to last he behaved in a cool and gallant way.

I have made him promise to let me know how he gets on when he
gets to England and I hope that as he can't write (his right hand is
burnt somewhat) you will do so for him.

I am very sorry to lose him from my Wing, and shall always be glad
to have him back.

Yours sincerely

Thomas Carthew

In a similar vein, Carthew also responded to a letter from one of Martin's
sisters, reassuring her that 'All the nurses, and the doctor, at the CCS, where
he was taken to out here, assured me that he was going on quite well.'[113]
In his journal, Ernest Massey, waiting anxiously at Hilton House for more

news of his son, confided that 'It [Martin's story] is a tale of pluck and heroism which warms one's heart in the midst of all these sorrows and forebodings. These letters [those above from Maltby and Carthew] will be preserved amongst my most precious documents',[114] as indeed they have been by his descendants for over 100 years.

The CCS would have given Martin sufficient stabilising treatment to allow him to be taken to a base hospital in France, a fully equipped general hospital for the more serious cases, and he was accordingly admitted to No. 10 British Red Cross Hospital at Le Tréport on the English Channel coast on 8 February. The hospital was a small one, with just fifty beds, and was also known as Lady Murray's Hospital after its founder who had established it in June 1916. Located in the former Golf Hotel on a plateau above the seaside town, the hospital was a civilian facility staffed by the Voluntary Aid Detachment, which came under the direction of the RAMC, but the control of the Red Cross.

As soon as he received the news that his son had been hospitalised, Martin's father applied to the War Office in London for permission to travel to France to see him. Such visits were, for obvious reasons, a fairly unusual occurrence during the First World War, but perhaps Ernest had connections through the clients of Mrs Massey's Agency and was able to pull strings. On the night of Saturday 10 February, when it was 'close to bed-time', he received a telegram telling him that his request had been granted. Immediately, he and his wife packed a bag, dressed themselves as warmly as they could against the 'bitter' winter ice and snow, and caught a taxi (obtained 'with great difficulty' from Derby) at midnight for the railway station. They arrived in London at 6.00 a.m. the following morning and made their way to the St Pancras Hotel, from where Ernest telephoned the War Office and was asked to report there at 9.30 a.m. In Whitehall, he and Florence were met 'with great kindness' and were given the necessary travel permits. They left London at 12.40 p.m. and arrived in Folkestone at 3.00 p.m., where they boarded the next available ship for France. The realities of war were brought home to them when, prior to sailing, the passengers were ordered to don 'cork jackets' in case of a U-boat attack. Two Royal Navy destroyers escorted the ship across the English Channel to deter such an occurrence, and they arrived safely in Boulogne at 5.00 that afternoon. A Mr Bannerman of the Red Cross was there to meet them as they disembarked and escort them to the Hotel Crystal, the headquarters of the British Red Cross in France. There, a very welcome and much-needed cup of tea was provided by the matron, Mrs Boycott.

Two hours later, a motor car ('a 35hp Sunbeam with no hood') arrived to take them on the freezing and treacherous eighty-mile journey to Le Tréport. Ernest wrote that 'during the past five years or so I have had a good deal of experience in motoring, but never have I had as trying and adventurous ride as this one'. The car's headlights apparently kept going out, which did nothing to deter their 'most capable and patient chauffeur' who 'kept up a great pace wherever possible'. At one point they left the road completely and almost overturned in the dark, but they nonetheless arrived at No. 10 British Red Cross Hospital at midnight, shaken but in one piece. Despite their travails and the late hour, Ernest and Florence immediately tried to go to Martin's bedside but were refused by the doctors (who doubtlessly did not want his recuperating sleep disturbed), but they at least found that 'our boy still lived, and that there was hope that he would recover. God knows the feeling of thankfulness that stirred his mother's heart and mine.' They slept soundly that night in a small ward of the hospital.

Eventually the next day, 12 February, they were allowed to see their son. Ernest recorded that 'lying in a snow-covered hut in the grounds of the hospital, we found our boy suffering and sadly defaced, but happy for the moment in our coming and surrounded by all the comforts and alleviations that his condition permitted, and by kind and friendly nurses too'. Martin's wounds were shocking for his parents to see:

> One side of his face showed scorching from the fire, across his left
> cheek ran what seemed a deep groove where the bullet had passed,
> and there was a cut over his brow where he had struck something
> when he had leapt from the blazing machine – 30 feet, he says, to
> the ground – both wrists were bandaged and his hands were a little
> burnt. It was however in [his] legs and lower back part of the body
> that the burns were most serious. How serious I know not at this time
> of writing. To write of what we three felt and thought would require a
> more able pen than mine, and maybe in writing for my own kindred
> those feelings were too sacred to dilate upon. The picture however
> stays with me of the lad lying on his back, with his burnt face
> upwards, upon which there was still a look of peace and happiness
> despite the pain.

They made small talk while the medical staff went about their business in the ward, the nurses 'greatly busy, and occasionally a doctor passing to and fro'. They had to leave Martin for a time while he suffered the 'torture' of having his dressings changed, and it was only when they returned that 'we realised better how he suffered – the first flush of our coming had passed, and the added pain of disturbing the poor burnt limbs had told its tale'. The excruciating pain of having his leg burns disturbed left him weak and dazed, so Ernest left Florence to soothe her son while he went into the town to arrange lodgings for the duration of their stay. There was not much accommodation to be had because of the war, so they had to make do with 'a locked-up house, which had apparently been disused since the previous summer'. The walls of the house were streaming with wet and the bed was damp; also there was no fireplace and no gas, so the place was desperately cold. They spent the night on top of the mouldering bed covers, clad in their overcoats, caps and gloves, and 'handkerchiefs over our mouths to warm the air a little'. But despite the misery of their temporary home, they were at least cheered by the prognosis of the doctors that Martin was probably not going to die.

Ernest Massey stayed at Le Tréport for the next couple of weeks, leaving for home before the end of February 1917 by which time Martin's wounds were healing 'as well as possible, only one knee giving some trouble … my lad's endurance is being sorely tested'. Florence, though, stayed behind to be with their son, 'doing what is possible to ease him in his terrible suffering'. Martin's father was naturally finding the anxiety over his son's condition hard to bear, confessing to his journal that 'once more I make my jottings feeling it possible that my days are drawing to a close'. Presciently, Ernest also wrote that 'perhaps one day he [Martin] will read this and think back, and having endured this time may be the stronger for future trials'. What trials they were to be, though, Ernest could not have foreseen. He wrote to Martin shortly after arriving back at Hilton House,[115] his great fondness for his son emphasised by his salutation of 'My dear laddie'. He mentioned that he had had a letter from Florence telling him that Martin was still improving which was 'very comforting', and 'stressing that your great sufferings are abating somewhat', which allowed him to 'begin to look forward to better things with a little hope'. He told his son that he had received many enquiries after his welfare, with people calling at the house and stopping him in the street for news of Martin, and, perhaps a little insensitively given the nature of the wounds, Ernest told him that 'his ears must be always burning'. But his genuine love and affection shone through when he wrote that 'I wish I could see you again, if only for a few minutes. I want to see you and think of you in less suffering than when we parted.

It has haunted me ever since.' A second letter followed in early March, in which Ernest told Martin that:

> I am indeed proud and happy to get your first letter upon coming out from what has truly been 'the shadow of death'. Looking back upon the better times through which we have all been passing we have cause to be happy and hopeful though the times are still dark and very chaotic. It is good to feel, lad, that in this stage of our joint lives that there is real love and confidence between us, and I am not a bit jealous that the Old Lady [Florence] has been able to do and suffer so much for you and with you whilst I have been away from you and could do little to help or hearten you through your terrible trials, now I hope so far past that what has to be done in the future can be cheerfully faced. Think of the day, laddie, when you come back here; the place will look its best that day and we will all be cheery happy if the fates so wish it.
>
> Well! Good night my dear lad. Kiss your mother for me and tell her I am all right and not worrying.
>
> Your loving Daddy[116]

Florence remained at her son's bedside at No. 10 British Red Cross Hospital until the end of March, by which time she felt able to return home, 'leaving the lad out of danger'. Martin's stay at the hospital was to last until the middle of the following month when he was deemed to be a long-term casualty and therefore eligible for transfer for further treatment in England. On 17 April 1917, as an immobile stretcher patient, he was taken by train from Le Tréport to the port of Le Havre and then put aboard a hospital ship, the *Lanfranc*, for passage home. Built in Dundee and launched in 1906, the 418-feet long, 6,287 gross registered tons *Lanfranc* had been a passenger liner for the Booth Steamship Company, running between Liverpool and Manaus in Brazil before the war until she had been requisitioned by the military for medical duties. In addition to her crew of 123, the ship took aboard that day 52 medical personnel, 234 British casualties and 167 German prisoners of war, many of whom were also wounded, bound for incarceration in England. Sailing with the *Lanfranc* that evening was another hospital ship, the SS *Donegal* (which was carrying the more lightly wounded), and assorted Royal Navy escort ships. Unfortunately for Martin Massey and his fellow passengers, though, the voyage back to England was to prove a far from comfortable one.

Chapter Three

Convalescence in England:
April 1917 – October 1921

At 7.30 in the evening of 17 April 1917 when she was forty-two nautical miles north of Le Havre (about halfway across the English Channel), bound for Southampton and making fourteen knots, His Majesty's Hospital Ship *Lanfranc* was struck by a 50cm type-G torpedo, fired from the German coastal submarine *UB-40* which was commanded by Kapitänleutnant[117] Hans Howaldt. There is a degree of confusion as to whether or not the ship was properly marked, as directed by the Geneva Convention, as a hospital ship – in other words painted white, clearly emblazoned with red crosses, and brightly illuminated from stem to stern. The official Admiralty statement about the attack said that: 'Owing to the German practice of sinking hospital ships at sight, and to the fact that distinctive marking and lighting of such vessels render them more conspicuous targets for German submarines, it has become no longer possible to distinguish our hospital ships in the customary manner. One of these two ships, therefore, though carrying wounded, was not in any way outwardly distinguished as a hospital ship.'[118]

The Admiralty declined to say which of the *Lanfranc* and *Donegal* was not 'outwardly distinguished' (period photographs show the *Lanfranc* as marked correctly but she could of course have been repainted by this time), but in the event it was academic since the *Donegal* was also torpedoed and sunk (albeit by a different U-boat, the *UC-21*) on the same night.

The *UB-40*'s torpedo impacted the *Lanfranc* on her port side towards the stern, between the engine room and the No. 3 hold. The ship's master, Mr W.E. Pointer, immediately ordered all engines stopped so that her boats could be lowered safely once the ship had come to a halt. Three of the lifeboats had been destroyed in the explosion, however. As she slowed, the hospital ship began to list to port, the sea gushing into her through the gaping hole torn by the explosion of the weapon's 160kg warhead. Almost immediately the *Lanfranc* began to settle at the stern; clearly, she was not going to make it home. Her escorts, the Royal Navy destroyers HMS *Badger* and HMS *Jackal*, accompanied by two patrol boats, the British HMS *P-37* and the French Navy's *Roitelet*, rushed to her aid, thereby putting themselves at risk of attack from the lurking German submarines. The patients, most of whom, including Martin Massey, were 'cot' (or stretcher) cases and so unable to move by themselves, were helped to the lifeboat stations by the medical staff, the ship's crew, and the few walking wounded. The first boat away foundered in the rough seas and sank, her survivors picked up by HMS *Badger* and nearby French fishing trawlers that had also come to help. Once all eight remaining lifeboats (plus those that had been lowered from the escorts) had successfully made their escape from the danger area, *Badger* and *Jackal* came alongside the rapidly sinking *Lanfranc* to take the remaining passengers, both British and German, aboard directly. Some men took the opportunity to jump from the dying ship to the decks of the other vessels, but not all made it, and a few fell into the sea through the gap between the ships. One of the British officer patients aboard gave a vivid account of the sinking and ensuing rescue:[119]

> The *Lanfranc* was attacked by a submarine about 7.30 on Tuesday evening, just as we had finished dinner. A few of us were strolling to and fro on deck when there was a crash, which shook the liner violently. This was followed by an explosion, and glass and splinters of wood flew in all directions. The moment the torpedo struck, the Prussians [the German prisoners] made a mad rush for the lifeboats. One of their officers came up to a boat close to where I was standing. I shouted at him to go back, whereupon he stood and scowled; 'You must save us', he begged. I told him to wait his turn. Other Prussians showed their cowardice by dropping on their knees and imploring pity. Some of them cried 'Kamerad', as they do on the battlefield. I allowed none of them to pass me.
>
> Meanwhile the crew and the [medical] staff had gone to their posts. The stretcher cases were brought on deck as quickly as possible, and the first boats were lowered without delay. Help had been summoned, and many vessels were hurrying to our assistance. In these moments, while wounded Tommies – many of them as helpless as little children – lay in their cots unaided, the Prussian morale

dropped to zero. Our cowardly prisoners made another crazy effort to get into a lifeboat. They managed to crowd into one, but no sooner had it been lowered than it toppled over. The Prussians were thrown into the water, and they fought with each other in order to reach another boat containing a number of gravely wounded British soldiers.

The behaviour of our own lads I shall never forget. Crippled as many of them were, they tried to stand at attention while the more serious cases were being looked after, and those who could lend a hand scurried below to help in saving friend or enemy. I have never seen so many individual illustrations of genuine chivalry and comradeship. One man I saw had a leg severed and his head was heavily bandaged. He was lifting himself up the staircase by the hands, and was just as keen on summoning help for Fritz as on saving himself. He whistled to a mate to come and aid a Prussian who was unable to move owing to internal injuries. Another Tommy limped painfully along with a Prussian Officer on his arm and helped the latter to a boat. It is impossible to give adequate praise to the crew and staff. They were all heroes. They remained at their posts until the last of the wounded had been taken off and some of them took off articles of their clothing and threw them into the lifeboats for the benefit of those who were in need of warm covering.

The same spirit manifested itself as we moved away from the scene of the outrage. I saw a sergeant take his tunic off and make a pillow of it for a wounded German. There was a private who had his arms round an enemy trying hard to make the best of an uncomfortable resting place. A Cockney lad struck up a ditty, and the boat's company joined in a chorus of 'All Dressed Up and Nowhere to Go'. Then we had 'Take Me Back to Blighty', and as a French vessel came along to our rescue the boys sang 'Pack Up Your Troubles In Your Old Kit Bag'. The French displayed unforgettable hospitality. As soon as they took our wounded on board they improvised beds and stripped themselves almost bare so that English and German alike might be comfortable. Hot refreshments were provided and cigarettes distributed, and … the ship headed for an English port.

A report in the *Daily Mirror* published a few days after the sinking claimed that 'at the sight of the submarine the Prussians danced on deck, pushing everybody out of the way, even the wounded, hoping that the submarine would save them'.[120]

The first that Martin knew of the U-boat's attack was when he heard the 'great explosion' of the torpedo's charge as it hit its target. The apparent panic and fear displayed by the German prisoners depicted above were also seen by Massey. Almost straight away, wrote his father:[121]

> he and his berth-mate, a Major with a smashed thigh, were carried up
> on deck and lay there helpless amidst great confusion, for in addition
> to our own wounded, the *Lanfranc* carried a number of German
> guardsmen prisoners, some of them slightly wounded. These men
> appear to have been at some liberty and although unarmed, had
> practical control of the deck of the sinking hospital ship and seizing
> the boats in a great panic, and showing intense fear and cowardice.
> Our wounded officers had been deprived of their revolvers, lest it
> should be said that we carried armed men on our hospital ships, and
> no-one seemed able to maintain order. Our severely wounded men
> lay on the deck helpless and without help whilst Germans went off
> in the boat, and my lad tells me that his rage was so great that it
> stimulated him to make the effort to save himself, which happily
> proved successful.

Paul Maltby, again writing over fifty years later in 1968, said that Massey spent 'a long time floating in the salt water before he was picked up. Perhaps his fortuitous saline bath, then unknown as a treatment for burns, may have helped him to recover'.[122] But this account is completely at odds with what Ernest Massey wrote shortly after the sinking in his journal, having been told the story at first hand by his son. Ernest recorded that:

> a small destroyer came alongside the *Lanfranc*. Martin, the Major, and
> other helpless men managed, God knows how, to reach the side of the
> sinking vessel and, waiting their opportunity, leapt or fell onto the
> deck of the destroyer. Not all I fear were saved and some fell between
> the two vessels. Martin however, in bandages to his waist, with a pyja-
> ma jacket and no other covering, found himself on the deck of the
> destroyer [either *Badger* or *Jackal*], and someone covered him with
> a 'British Warm'.[123] Presently, with great suffering, he got below,
> descending through a manhole by a vertical ladder to the cabin of
> one of the officers and was put in a bunk.

No mention here, then, of spending a prolonged period in the sea. If he had indeed been overboard for 'a long time', as Maltby wrote, it is extremely unlikely that Massey would have survived a sudden and lengthy immersion in the cold waters of the English Channel – the average April water temperature there is just eight degrees Celsius, and cold water shock sets in rapidly at anything below fifteen degrees Celsius. He was also hardly dressed for survival, clad as he was in his pyjamas, and was already weak from his wounds. Further, since his burned legs were bandaged to the waist as his father mentioned, he would probably not have been able to swim or tread water to keep himself afloat, particularly as the sea was not calm, unless he had gone overboard with a buoyancy aid. In any event, he would have been dead within a very few minutes.

Another of the men aboard the *Lanfranc* recorded his gratitude to the *Badger* and *Jackal*:

It was wonderful to see the two destroyers … they had their boats in the water almost before you could turn around. One of them came close in alongside us, and the other went circling round and round us, like a sheep-dog, but angry. We floated [in the lifeboat] for just over a quarter of an hour, and we were very nearly all clear of her when she gave one hiss, and went down like a plummet. That last few minutes wasn't nice, you know – like waiting to go over the parapet. Some of us jumped to the deck of the destroyer, and some got knocked about a bit. The destroyer came right in under us … to get the last of us, and only drew away as the suction began.[124]

There were thirty-four fatalities from the sinking of the *Lanfranc* that night – eleven British other ranks patients; two British officer patients; one RAMC medical orderly; thirteen German other rank wounded prisoners; two German wounded officer prisoners; and five members of the ship's crew.[125] The *Donegal* went down with the loss of a further forty-one souls.

Martin and the others rescued from the *Lanfranc* were taken to Southampton where they arrived at 5.00 the following morning. With help, he managed 'with terrible agony' to get himself back up the destroyer's ladder and on deck, which 'necessitated to some extent the use of his poor, burnt feet'. A journalist from the *Daily Telegraph* witnessed the survivors' disembarkation: 'Then they began to come ashore, a long, stiffly-moving file of shaky, utterly weary souls, wrapped about as to their heads, or arms, necks or shoulders, with rain and brine-soaked surgical bandages. Few had had any sleep for several nights; all were new-plucked from the midmost jaws of death among the shell holes; and all had faced the Boche again, at his ugliest, since leaving France. The fatigue in their eyes, which no man may hide in such a case, was pathetic, but there was a look in the same eyes that overrode anything like pathos; the look indomitable'.[126]

A young woman volunteer from the local Young Men's Christian Association (YMCA) was on hand to help with the arrival of the bedraggled and bewildered survivors:

> We have had a most stirring and exciting day. We got down to the Hut this morning to find that part of the crew and some of the wounded soldiers rescued from a torpedoed hospital ship had been brought in to the dock. They were sent in to us to wait for the ambulances. The ship, HM Hospital Ship *Lanfranc*, was struck at 8 o'clock [sic] last evening. Some French fishing smacks dashed to the rescue and brought them in about 8 o'clock this morning. Many of the men were only half dressed, and all were cold and hungry. We made a great horseshoe of our tables round the stove, and got them all a hot breakfast.
>
> Three of them were so badly wounded that they had to be laid on tables. It was awful to see men with their bandages torn off their wounded limbs, and the stories they told bring home to one most forcibly what a ship-wreck of wounded soldiers must be like. Some of the crew seemed all right, but after a while I suppose the shock began to tell, and they looked too dreadful for words. They were all so nice and so brave, for some were clearly in a great deal of pain.
>
> Some of the less badly wounded Germans stampeded and jumped into a boat, partly filled with their own wounded. This they swamped, and the only person saved in it was an English boy, brought in to us with a crushed hand and leg. He was caught by a chain down the ship's side, but it held him until he could be removed.
>
> After the dockers had left, and we had got all straight and tidy, some of the wounded went to the piano and began to sing – they are wonderful! It made us feel queer to hear them sing 'Pack Up Your Troubles In Your Old Kit Bag'. After a little while Miss Waldegrave went to them and said that she felt that they ought to give thanks for being safe – would they join in a hymn? Every man came to the piano, except one who was too bad to move (the worse [sic] cases had been taken away). They sang most wonderfully 'O God Our Help in Ages Past'. Then Miss Waldegrave said a short prayer, and before she

could move away one of the men said might they have 'For Those in Peril On the Sea' for their mates, as they did not know where they might be? I have never heard anything like it. Many broke down. In the middle the cars came to take them away. They finished the hymn and said goodbye. They gripped our hands until it was painful. Many of them ran back two or three times and said 'thank you, thank you; we shall never forget this morning'. We shall certainly never forget them, the stories they told. One of those rescued had neither arms nor legs; another, who had lost both hands and both feet, managed to get on deck unaided![127]

Once safely ashore and made as comfortable as possible, Martin and the other severely wounded men were sent to various hospitals, first to be treated for any injuries caused during the sinking, and then for their battlefield wounds, the reason that they had been travelling in the first place. Massey's medical records, detailing all the diagnoses and treatment that he had had thus far, were lost when the *Lanfranc* went down,[128] so the whole process had to start again. In addition to his records, he had also lost all of his possessions, both personal and military, to the depths of the English Channel, save for 'a 5-franc note and a pocket handkerchief which happened to be in the pocket of his pyjama jacket'.

Along with several of the other survivors, he went first to an annex, known as the Welsh Hospital, of the vast Royal Victoria Military Hospital at Netley, near Southampton. Arriving there the morning after the sinking, on 18 April, he was assessed for immediate first aid and allowed to recover from the trauma of the *Lanfranc* incident before he could be moved to a hospital better suited for the care of his burns. The Welsh Hospital was a wooden-hutted addition to the main Netley hospital, paid for with funds raised by the people of Wales when war broke out in August 1914. It was designed to be dismantled easily and transported to France if need be, but was still in situ in 1917, providing much-needed ward space for the Royal Victoria. The first that Massey's parents heard of the latest disaster to befall their son was when they received a telegram from the hospital on the day that he arrived there, asking them to wire some money to him since he had nothing. Scarcely believing that he had undergone another near-death experience so soon after being shot down, Ernest once more immediately set out to visit Martin. He took the train to London the following morning, arriving at the Welsh Hospital the next day, the 20th.[129] At Netley, he found that some of Martin's burn wounds had reopened, and that he was 'evidently suffering somewhat from his further terrible experience, but was not seriously worse'.

Martin Massey stayed at the Welsh Hospital for only nine days. He was transferred to the Queen Alexandra's Military Hospital in London's Millbank on 27 April 1917 where his long road to recovery began in earnest (interestingly, his father wrote that it was he who 'obtained his removal' to Millbank. Again, he perhaps knew the right strings to pull). His parents came down to visit regularly, and they brought Martin's younger brother John with them for three days in mid-May. The RAMC recognised that the healing process would be a slow one, for its training manual stated that 'the convalescence from extensive burns or scalds may be prolonged and tedious, and after the first ten days a generous diet with tonics will be necessary'.[130] The treatment centred on the dressing of the burns to encourage and protect the new skin that would, in time, form on Martin's legs and feet, and to prevent sepsis, which was by now the main danger to his life. Strips of lint covered with aseptic Vaseline and boric acid powder or boric ointment were applied to the wounds as a balm, and which were then wrapped in cotton wool to keep them in place, as well as to make Martin as comfortable as he could be. His doctors were keen to expose the burns to the air as little as possible, so the dressings were changed only when absolutely necessary, and then only a strip at a time to keep the rest of the skin covered. The RAMC manual further stated that 'when parts beneath the skin have been burnt [which was so in Massey's case] the formation of disfiguring and deforming scars is frequent. To prevent and diminish these results the sufferer requires very careful nursing.'[131] Inflammatory illness, such as pneumonia, was also a common occurrence in burns patients, so Martin was by no means out of the woods yet. There was at least some good news to be had, though. On 4 June,[132] Martin was told that he had been awarded the Military Cross in the King's Birthday Honours List for what Major Maltby called 'consistently good work'[133] while with No. 16 Squadron. The recommendation for the medal said that: 'As a pilot in No. 16 Squadron from 2 September 1916 to 4 February 1917, when he was severely wounded, this officer distinguished himself by the skill, gallantry and determination with which he carried out his duties in Artillery Observation and Reconnaissances.'[134] The decoration was not to be his last.

Martin's father arranged for a pair of crutches to be sent to his son at the Queen Alexandra, and Massey did use them at first to try to move around but was soon told by his doctors to stop and lie in his bed, otherwise he risked damaging the new skin forming over the burns to his feet and reopening the wounds. Some three months after arriving back in England, on 18 July, he was assessed as 'progressing favourably but very slowly'.[135] He had his first formal medical board (to evaluate his progress and his condition) on 4 August 1917. Listing his wounds as '1) GSW[136] Face, 2) Extensive Burns, and 3) Cut Head',[137] the board found that: 'While fighting near Vimy Ridge in his aeroplane on Feb 4/17 he was shot, his machine [was] set on fire and driven down. Both legs and feet were burned, his face wounded by [a] bullet, and his forehead by fall. On his way home HS *Lanfranc* was torpedoed and papers lost. Wounds are healing and is recommended for further treatment at an officers' hospital (Harrogate).'[138]

Despite the encouraging report of an improvement to his injuries, the board assessed that Massey was unfit for General Service[139] and Home Service[140] for the next six months, and unfit for Light Duties at Home for three months. The burns were obviously the most serious of his wounds, and were considered to be 'very severe' at the time of his shooting-down and remained so six months later when the board assessed him. His complete recovery was evidently going to be a lengthy and drawn-out process.

The recommendation that Martin be transferred to Harrogate was accepted by the War Office, and he soon found himself at the Furness Auxiliary Hospital in the Yorkshire town, with his father travelling there with him from London. The Furness had been built in 1903 as the Grand Hotel, but had been converted to an officers' hospital by the hotel's owner, Lord Furness, and donated to the war effort for the duration. Overlooking the picturesque Valley Gardens, the Furness was just one of several buildings turned over to the military for use as hospitals in Harrogate, no doubt due to the town's (by now waning) reputation as a health spa. Massey's relocation once again appears to be the result of his father having good contacts, since Ernest said that 'through the interest of the Duchess of Portland I was able to get Martin moved to the Furness Auxiliary Hospital Harrogate'.[141] Winifred, Duchess of Portland resided at the family seat of Welbeck Abbey near Worksop in Nottinghamshire, and was renowned as a philanthropist among her local mining community; she was more than likely a customer of Mrs Massey's Agency. But perhaps Martin had been moved too soon, or had been overdoing his efforts to become mobile again, since he suffered a relapse in early October 1917, not long after he arrived at the Furness. Ernest wrote that 'during all this time Martin was far from well and his feet had not entirely healed; indeed during his mother's visit and for about a fortnight afterwards he was kept in bed and he had a horrible boil on his lips and suffered greatly'.[142]

Earlier, Martin had set about trying to replace his military equipment that had gone down with the *Lanfranc*. As mentioned previously, he had lost everything – every single item of uniform from his cap to his boots (the most valuable item that he claimed for was two pairs of field boots at £10). All his underclothes were gone too, along with his coats and gloves, his field gear (including helmet, mess tins, prismatic compass (£3 10s), canvas bath and bucket), and sundry other items, the most important of which was his service Webley revolver. All had been packed in his suitcase and a holdall, which had been abandoned in the haste to escape the sinking hospital ship. The complete list of kit ran to three pages of the official Army 'Claim for Indemnification – Officers' form.[143] In true military storeman's bureaucratic fashion, though, Captain Radcliffe of the Army Quarter- master General's Department in Aldershot wrote back to Massey on 27 September 1917 asking him to:

> please forward certificate that you are fit for service necessitating re-equipment with the articles claimed for, and that it was necessary for you to be equipped at the time of loss for both warm and cold climates.
>   1 cap, 1 boots ankle, shoes, 3 handkerchiefs, 4 pairs thick socks, 4 towels, should be deleted as they are beyond the scale admissible in Appendix to ACI 482 of 1917.
>   The contents of holdall should be stated.
>   Claim should be submitted in duplicate when the vocabulary price of the articles issued at Sandhurst will be ascertained and the claim returned to you for completion as regards value at time of loss. Only articles comprised in Appendix to ACI 482 of 1917 can be claimed for.[144]

Of course, there was no certificate of Martin's fitness for service, and nor would there be one for the foreseeable future. The Army was obviously not about to re-equip an officer who had little chance of returning to front-line duty, at least in the short term, with valuable kit. Captain Radcliffe was evidently also curious as to how Martin had managed to get hold of equipment for both temperate and cold weather climes. How little has changed over the years.

Massey's doctor at the Furness was Major R.C. Highet of the Royal Army Medical Corps, who chaired his next medical board on 30 October 1917. The burns healing process was not going particularly well: 'The GSW of the face is healed and the cut of head is also soundly healed. The burns, especially those of the feet which are exceedingly extensive, are not healing as rapidly as might be expected. He is also troubled by boils breaking out on various parts of the body. Evidently Harrogate does not agree with this officer and the Board consider that he would derive more benefit by being allowed to proceed to his home.'[145]

Highet considered that Martin was '100 percent total disabled' and recommended him one month's 'special leave' at Hilton House with a further suggestion that he be treated there by the family's general practitioner, and then to report back to the Furness for another assessment towards the end of the leave period. But it seems that the War Office disagreed, and the special leave was not authorised. Massey's father had arrived in Harrogate to help his son travel home as soon as Major Highet and the Furness medical board had made the recommendation, but by 15 November, two weeks later, Martin was still in the hospital. Somewhat irked, Ernest Massey wrote to the War Office from his lodgings in Harrogate:[146]

> Sir;
> 2nd Lieut (temp Captain) Herbert Martin Massey MC RFC & Sherwoods, now in the Furness Auxiliary Hospital, Harrogate and recommended by medical board sitting at that hospital for one month's special sick leave on date Oct 31st last.
>   I have the honour to refer to the above recommendation in respect to this officer – my son – and to ask whether the matter is likely to receive early attention in order that I may decide as to the advisability of remaining here, as I have done for the last 14 days, in order to assist my son on his journey thus easing trouble and expense on the hospital concerned.
>   I have the honour to be, Sir
>   Your obedient servant
>   E. Martin Massey

By 20 November, there was still no word from Whitehall, so this time Martin decided to try his luck in writing to them himself:[147]

> Sir;
> I have the honour to state that I was boarded on Oct 30th last and the board advised that I should go home on a month's special sick leave.
>   This recommendation was I believe based upon the opinion that

my general health would benefit by a change, after so many months in hospital. As yet I am unable to walk and my only means of getting out of doors is to hire carriages etc which is costing me a great deal of money. My home is in the country, and there I could get out and about without expense.

I am receiving no treatment at present as my legs and feet have only just healed from extensive burns and the new skin is too delicate to massage.

Would you be so kind as to let me know if this leave is likely to be approved as naturally my parents and I are anxious upon the point.

I am

Sir

Your obedient servant

H. Martin Massey Capt RFC

A statement by the commanding officer of the Furness Auxiliary Hospital, Colonel E. Holloway, appended to the back of Massey's letter confirmed what he had written, and added that 'Capt Massey is at present too much crippled to move by himself'. The pleas once more seem to have fallen upon deaf ears at the War Office, however, and Martin was told to remain in Harrogate. In the meantime, his father was doing his best to help him become more mobile, continuing the daily carriage rides and gradually encouraging a few steps with the aid of crutches.

Massey was boarded at the Furness once more on 27 November, when Major Highet again observed that: 'He has recovered from GSW [to the] face and also cut head. The burns of the legs and feet are greatly improved but not yet completely healed. The Board consider that this officer would derive more benefit by being allowed to proceed to his home and recommend one month special leave. He has been informed of the conditions.'[148]

By now, though, Highet was evidently not convinced that Martin would be able to return to duty in the near, or even medium, term, and revised down his assessment of Massey's fitness for General Service from six months to 'uncertain'. He also downgraded his suitability for Home Service to the less strenuous 'Sedentary Employment', but even then remarked that Martin was unfit for such service for at least a month, again grading him as 100 per cent disabled. This time, the authorities at White-hall gave in and accepted Highet's recommendation, and Massey was finally allowed to go home to continue his recuperation in the Derbyshire countryside. Frustratingly, the special leave was approved on 7 December, the very day that Martin's father had, in exasperation, given up waiting in Harrogate and gone back to Hilton since he had 'many matters needing my attention'. The next day, Ernest travelled to Leeds where he met his son who had got there 'in the charge of a nurse, and brought him home at last. That was a good day for his mother and myself.'[149] The small schoolroom at Hilton House was converted into a bedroom for Martin, presumably because it was downstairs and was therefore more easily accessible for him.

Martin had applied to the War Office as early as 12 August 1917 (while still at Millbank) for a 'wound gratuity', a lump sum payable to officers who had been wounded in action, but he had received no such payment almost three months later. With his frustrations, as well as his overdraft mounting (which was not helped by Massey's flying pay being suspended from 4 August 1917 since he was still grounded six months after being shot down), he had written to the War Office on 6 November from the Furness:[150]

Sir;
I have had the honour to apply to you for a wound gratuity on the 12th of Aug/17 and on 25th of Sept/17 and upon each occasion I have had a reply that the matter is receiving your attention, but have had no notification of a gratuity being awarded. I am still in hospital and was wounded on Feb 4th/17 being shot down in flames whilst flying in France. I am as yet unable to walk and am compelled to use carriages etc in order to get out of doors at all, which is of course essential to my recovery, and the cost of which is greatly taxing my resources.

I am therefore anxious to learn whether a decision has been arrived at and also, if so, the amount of the gratuity which has been granted to me.

I am
Sir
Your obedient servant
H. Martin Massey Capt RFC

The delay with approving the payment of the gratuity appears to have been a knock-on effect of losing his original medical paperwork during the sinking of the *Lanfranc*. At some point after his repatriation, Massey's War Office records erroneously recorded that he was wounded as a result of a flying accident and not from being shot down in combat, which would have disqualified him from receiving the endowment. Naturally the Ministry of Pensions, who were responsible for granting the lump sum, needed to check the facts since Massey had told them in his application that he had been injured while fighting. This was at odds with what the War Office understood to be the case, despite his application being backed by the medical board paperwork from both the Queen Alexandra's Hospital and the Furness. There followed a protracted exchange of correspondence between the Ministry of Pensions, Cox & Co (Martin's bank in Charing Cross), the War Office and RFC Headquarters in France to clarify the situation. Headquarters 1st Brigade RFC confirmed to the War Office on 17 September 1917 that: 'Captain H.M. Massey MC, Notts and Derby Regiment, late of No. 16 Squadron, was wounded in action during combat with enemy aircraft, and was not injured as a result of an accident.' [151] Evidently still to be convinced, the War Office's Directorate of Air Organisation (the forerunner of the Air Ministry) wrote to HQ RFC for further confirmation on 28 September, asking them to 'kindly verify the statements quoted above [from HQ 1st Brigade RFC]'.[152] HQ RFC duly did so on 3 October, but the wheels of bureaucracy turned ever slowly. By early December, Martin had still not had any news from the Ministry of Pensions, prompting a further, curt, letter from him:[153]

> Sir;
> I have already applied three times to the War Office, and after each of the first two letters I received the reply that the matter was receiving attention; the last letter that I wrote on Nov 6th last has not as yet even been acknowledged. I am still in hospital and am practically unable to walk. My last medical board was on Nov 27th and the president told me that he considered that I was entitled to a wound gratuity. I should be obliged if you would let me have any information regarding my gratuity.
> I am
> Sir
> Your obedient servant
> H. Martin Massey Capt RFC

Finally, the powers-that-be relented, and a wound gratuity of £250 (equivalent to around £17,000 in 2019) was authorised on 28 December 1917 when Martin was at Hilton House. Some ten months later, in October 1918, he was also awarded an annual Wound Pension of £50 per annum,

Ernest Martin Massey, Martin's father. *(Courtesy Massey family)*

Hilton House, Hilton, Derbyshire; Martin's childhood home. *(Courtesy Helena Coney)*

Spondon House School Scout Troop on parade. Martin was an enthusiastic member of the Troop and is probably in the picture. *(Courtesy Ruth Hooper)*

Martin Massey while a cadet at Sandhurst in 1916, aged 18. *(Courtesy Massey family)*

Certificate No. *1625*

ROYAL FLYING CORPS.

(Officers.)

CENTRAL FLYING SCHOOL,

UPAVON, WILTS.,

7th July. 191*6*.

GRADUATION CERTIFICATE.

THIS IS TO CERTIFY that *2nd Lieut H. M. Massey*

3rd Bn Sherwood Foresters

has completed a *~~*long~~* in the military Wing course ~~at the Central Flying School~~, and is qualified
short

for service in the Royal Flying Corps.

a—. maclean.

Lieut. Col.
Commandant.

* Strike out word not applicable.

W 8197—3244   500   8/15   H W V(P 1163/2)   H. 16/829
1916—7221   1000   5/16

**Above: Massey's flying course
graduation certificate.**
(Courtesy Massey family)

**Right: A Maurice Farman
Shorthorn, the aircraft type in
which Massey learned to fly
at Shoreham.**
(Author's collection)

Above: An airworthy replica Royal Aircraft Factory BE2 at Stow Maries Great War Aerodrome, Essex. *(Courtesy Mark Sutherland)*

Right: Major Paul Copeland Maltby, Commanding Officer of No. 16 Squadron RFC 1916-7. *(Author's collection)*

Far right: Werner Voss, who shot Massey and Vernham down on 4 February 1917 thereby becoming an 'ace'. *(Author's collection)*

An Albatros D.Va, similar to the D.II flown by Voss. *(Author's collection)*

Left: The grave of Massey's observer, Second Lieutenant Noel Vernham, at Aubigny Communal Cemetery, September 2019. *(Courtesy Suzanne Make)*

Below: Noel Vernham's engraved vesta case given by his widow, Violet, to Martin. *(Author)*

No. 10 British Red Cross Hospital (also known as Lady Murray's Hospital), the former Golf Hotel, at Le Trèport, where Massey was treated in France. *(Author's collection)*

His Majesty's Hospital Ship *Lanfranc*, which was torpedoed and sunk in the English Channel on 17 April 1917 with Massey aboard. *(Author's collection)*

A German UB II-class coastal U-Boat, the same type as the *UB-40*. *(Author's collection)*

Left: Kapitänleutnant Hans Howaldt, commander of the German submarine *UB-40* that sank the *Lanfranc*. *(Author's collection)*

Left: C Ward at the Welsh Hospital, Netley, Massey's first hospital in England after his shooting down and sinking. *(Courtesy Julie Green)*

Queen Alexandra's Military Hospital, Millbank, London, now part of Tate Britain. *(Author)*

The Furness Hospital in Harrogate, formerly the Grand Hotel, now Windsor House apartments. *(Author)*

Inset: Photograph of Massey walking with sticks published in the *Daily Sketch* on 17 January 1918 following the award of his MC at Buckingham Palace. The strain of walking and of coping with his injuries is clearly visible on his face. Above: Flight Lieutenant Martin Massey in early RAF uniform, circa 1922. Note the vertical 'wound stripe' on his left upper forearm. *(Courtesy Massey family)*

An Airco DH9A, or 'Ninak'. *(Courtesy Colin Moore)*

Martin (seated centre) with the personnel of C Flight, RAF College Cranwell while a flying instructor in 1928. The aircraft is an Avro 504N. *(Courtesy Massey Family)*

Massey (left, in suit) accompanying the Chief of the Air Staff, Sir John Salmond (centre), as his PA during a visit to the Italian Air Force, Naples, April 1931. *(Courtesy Massey family)*

Squadron Leader Martin Massey (front, centre) with the fellow students of his flying boat pilot's course at RAF Calshot, October 1931. *(Courtesy Massey family)*

A Short Singapore flying boat. *(Author's collection)*

Above: A Blackburn Iris III flying boat of
No. 209 (Flying Boat) Squadron.
(Courtesy Massey family)

Left: Fairey Gordons of No. 6 Squadron in
formation above the Egyptian desert.
(Courtesy No. 6 Squadron archive)

Above: Martin's wife, Peggy. Right: Peggy with their new-born son David at the Anglo-American Hospital, Cairo. *(Courtesy Massey family)*

A formation of No. 6 Squadron Hawker Harts. K4469 and K4471 were both damaged by Arab ground fire on 21 June 1936 during the First Battle of Bala; '71 was forced to land at Tulkarm with a holed radiator. *(Courtesy No. 6 Squadron archive)*

RAF Station Ramleh, Palestine, taken on 29 July 1936 at 1,000 feet by Pilot Officer Rampling.
(Courtesy Massey family)

A No. 6 Squadron pilot prepares for a sortie in the Ramleh operations room during the Palestine Emergency, 1936. Note the XX Call 'scramble' alarm button at right-centre of the map board. *(National Library of Congress)*

Massey's bullet-holed cigarette case which helped to save his life during the Second Battle of Bala on 3 September 1936. *(Author)*

Massey and Peggy outside Buckingham Palace for the award of his DSO in 1937.
(Courtesy Massey family)

backdated to the February, although it was only granted for a period of one year, perhaps because by the time of the award he was becoming fitter and overcoming his disabilities.[154]

As the weeks wore on, Martin slowly became stronger and at last regained some measure of independence and mobility, however slight. His father wrote that 'the lad is now convalescent, after many setbacks and sufferings, but his wounds appear to be finally healed and he can get about on crutches though still horribly crippled. There is however good hope that the next few months may restore the strength to his wasted limbs and that in the long term he will be slightly, if at all, crippled, though the left foot is much drawn and shrunk with the burns, and his legs, feet and thighs are all scar or very nearly so.'[155]

With Christmas and New Year celebrations imminent, Massey was spared another medical board at the end of December but was ordered to report to Major Highet at the Furness early in January 1918. In the meantime, however, his father expressed his delight that 'the children were home for the holidays and once more we were all together under the old roof as had last been the case when Martin was home on leave in Dec 1916.'[156]

The medical board examined Martin in Harrogate on the second day of the New Year, and, now satisfied that the gunshot wound to his left cheek and the laceration to his head were completely healed, the focus was on his burns: 'He has improved since the last board. The burns have now healed but the scars are somewhat thin. He has discarded the crutches and can now get about with the aid of two sticks. Recommended a further month's special leave.'[157]

Highet again assessed Massey as unfit for General Service for an 'uncertain' period, declaring that, even though his condition would not be a permanent one, he was still eighty per cent disabled at the time. No special medical treatment was deemed necessary, just the attentions of his own family doctor in Hilton. His father noted that 'he is still permitted to be at home with us and is making good progress'.[158]

Just under a fortnight later, on 15 January, Martin 'presented himself at Buckingham Palace and received the Military Cross at the hands of the King, HM George V',[159] which must have been a tremendous strain for him but doubtless an occasion he was determined not to miss. A photograph of him after the investiture, published two days later in the *Daily Sketch*, shows him stooped and walking with obvious difficulty, aided by two sticks. He is clearly in great pain and looks drawn and gaunt, far older than his twenty years.

By the time that Massey saw Major Highet again, on 6 February 1918, he had improved still further: 'The burns have healed but the scars are thin and tender and he is now able to get about with the aid of a stick. Recommended a further month's special leave ... directed to return to his home pending leave being granted.'[160]

Still eighty per cent disabled and assessed as unfit for General Service for the foreseeable future, Martin was prescribed 'massage treatment from his own doctor'. Remarkably, and contrary to the initial medical prognoses, he had gone from being completely immobile to being able to walk with just one stick in a matter of around two months; his determination to overcome his terrible wounds was extraordinary. However, Highet had by now reassessed the likelihood of Massey's wounds causing him long-term problems – one question on the medical board pro forma asked 'Are the effects of the injury permanent, or likely to be permanent?', to which Highet now responded 'Yes, to some extent.' It was an opinion that was to prove all too correct, since the damage done to the nerves in Martin's left leg by his burns later left him with 'rigid cavus deformity of [the] left foot', a condition possibly exacerbated by subsequent further injury, more of which below. Cavus deformity is an exceptionally high foot arch, drawing the front part of the foot downwards more than normal, tipping the arch upwards and the foot on to its outer side. He was also later to have skin grafts to his left foot to help with the burn scars.

Despite the improvement in his mobility, Martin Massey's war was over. He never regained sufficient fitness to allow him to return to front-line service during the First World War; instead he needed treatment for his injuries right through until the middle of 1919. By that time, the Royal Flying Corps had merged with the Royal Naval Air Service to form the Royal Air Force, and, now restricted to ground duties only, he was posted to the RAF's No. 16 (Training) Group in Yorkshire for staff work, the first of several such postings over the next two years, which were interspersed with further, regular, hospital treatment. He formally requested to resign his commission in the Sherwood Foresters and to transfer to the nascent RAF on 7 April 1920, which was approved on 1 August that year, backdated twelve months.[161] Now more or less fully mobile once more, Massey returned to playing sport, one of his great loves and, incredibly, he represented the RAF at rugby at scrum-half in the 1919–20 season, an astonishing achievement for a young man whose legs had been so terribly injured just two years previously. However, he found himself back in the doctor's surgery on 13 September 1920 when, while playing football, he collided with another player, which caused him to lose his balance and fall on his head, and in so doing to suffer concussion. The RAF doctor who examined him cautiously recorded the prognosis as 'uncertain',[162] but Martin fortunately recovered fully.

Even though he was back to playing competitive sport, Martin Massey was to endure what for a pilot must have seemed unendurable – flying a desk – until at last, in October 1921, the RAF's doctors were finally satisfied that he was fit to pilot an aircraft once more. The decision to keep him on in the service and permit him to fly again is an extremely surprising one since, at the time it was made, the British government was about to embark on a huge austerity drive designed to cut waste in public spending in the wake of the First World War. The so-called 'Geddes Axe' (named after the businessman appointed to head the Committee on National Expenditure, Sir Eric Geddes) hit the military hard, with the defence budget suffering a swingeing forty-two per cent cut in just one year,[163] so to allow Martin to stay in uniform when his long-term medical forecast was still uncertain and other, fitter, young men were being made redundant in droves was a remarkable choice. Someone was obviously looking out for him.

Back in late 1917 when he had been looking after his convalescing son, Ernest Massey had confided to his journal that 'about this time also my own health gave out and I realised that a long holiday was essential if I was ever to be fit again'.[164] Whatever was wrong with him seemingly did not improve for long, if at all, and he died on 23 September 1921, one month short of his 58th birthday. For Martin, the loss of his devoted father at no great age must have been devastating.

Chapter Four

Mixed Fortunes:
October 1921 – December 1933

Royal Air Force Station Spitalgate was situated just outside Grantham in Lincolnshire, and in October 1921 Martin Massey arrived there to undertake a 'course of eye training' (according to his RAF service record) with No. 39 Squadron, then resident at the base and operating the Airco DH9A. The DH9A, or 'Ninak'[165] as it was more familiarly known to its crews, was a single-engined biplane light bomber that had been introduced into service just before the end of the First World War, and remained the RAF's standard light bomber through until 1931. Quite what 'eye training' involved is not certain, but presumably was designed to ease pilots who had been away from flying for some time back into the cockpit – refresher training, as it would later become known. Massey's association with RAF Spitalgate and No. 39 Squadron lasted just three months until, on 24 February 1922, after embarkation leave at home, he found himself aboard a troopship at Southampton, bound for Iraq.

Martin, now holding the rank of flight lieutenant, joined No. 8 Squadron, also flying the Ninak, at RAF Hinaidi. Located just outside Baghdad, Hinaidi was the main British airfield in Iraq, featuring extensive barracks, a hospital, recreational facilities and a civilian cantonment. Probably to his great frustration, however, Massey was not posted to No. 8 Squadron as a full-time pilot, but rather as the squadron adjutant, a role of varied duties, mainly administrative. He was essentially the squadron CO's right-hand man, but there would have been the odd opportunity to get some time in the cockpit. One of the quirky, typically colonial features of life at Hinaidi was the Exodus Hunt, a full hunt with mounts and hounds (the latter being the local Saluki breed, rather than English foxhounds) that hunted jackal, instead of foxes, around the local area. On 29 October 1922

Martin was riding with the Exodus when he was thrown from his horse, once again suffering severe concussion as well as cuts to his face.[166] He was hospitalised for a short time until he was able to return to No. 8 Squadron, but a much worse injury was to come about not long afterwards. In the meantime, Massey joined another British institution when, on 29 November, he was initiated as a Freemason into the Baghdad Lodge. He joined and left several other lodges throughout his RAF career, depending on his posting location at the time, and remained active in Freemasonry for the rest of his life.[167]

At 4.30 p.m. on 11 March 1923, almost five months after his head injury sustained with the Exodus Hunt, Massey was roller skating at Hinaidi when the front wheels of his left skate came loose and parted company with the rest of the apparatus. He was thrown down on to his left leg, causing him, oddly, a 'severe fracture of the right fibula'[168] – the opposite leg. After the prolonged and painful recovery from his wartime injuries, he was immobile once more. So serious was the break to his lower right leg that he was unable to continue with No. 8 Squadron and was shipped home, officially 'supernumerary and non-effective – sick'. He had been back on an operational squadron for only just over a year, and Massey must have been wondering whether he was ever going to be fit enough to continue his flying career. The shattered fibula kept Martin grounded for four more months, but when finally he was out of plaster and traction, the news was good; the leg had repaired well but needed time and physiotherapy to strengthen the muscles. When he was at last considered to be fit to return to work, he found himself posted, on 15 July 1923, to adjutant duties once more, this time at the RAF's Marine and Armament Experimental Establishment (MAEE) based at a seaplane station on the Suffolk coast at Felixstowe. MAEE was a test unit, tasked with carrying out research and development work on sea-based aircraft and their associated equipment, including weapons and air-sea rescue apparatus. Massey stayed with MAEE until December 1927, almost four and a half years, interrupted only by a three-week flying refresher course with No. 24 Squadron's Ninaks at RAF Kenley in January 1924. A few months after the course, on 15 May, he attended a State Ball given by His Majesty King George V and Queen Mary at Buckingham Palace,[169] and in July 1925 he was made a member of the Royal Aero Club.[170] By the time that he left Felixstowe, it was more than ten years since he had served on a front-line squadron in a full-time flying capacity; for a 29-year-old decorated pilot, this must have been an immensely frustrating and trying time.

If Martin was hoping for a return to operational flying, it was not to be. On 12 December 1927 he began a course at the RAF's Central Flying School, then based at RAF Wittering on the border of Northamptonshire and Cambridgeshire, to learn how to teach – he was to become a flying instructor. Some four months later, in April 1928, he passed the instructors' course with a grading of A1, and arrived at the RAF College at Cranwell to begin almost two years of teaching the ab initio pilots there how to fly on the Avro 504N aircraft, a later variant of the tandem-seat biplane trainer that had first flown in 1913. Although not on a mainstream squadron, he was at least back in the air regularly again.

Massey's potential for advancement had by now been noticed, despite his lack of front-line duty since the end of the First World War. On 12 February 1930 he was selected to become personal assistant to the Chief of the Air Staff (CAS), who at the time was Air Chief Marshal Sir John Salmond. This was not a position that was awarded lightly – working in the outer office of the head of the Royal Air Force was a privileged and auspicious position, given only to highly competent, extremely motivated officers with a promising career ahead of them. Like Martin, Salmond was a veteran of the First World War, and he had also served during the Boer War earlier in the century; he had taken over as CAS just a month before Massey arrived on his personal staff. Sir John Salmond's older brother, Geoffrey, succeeded him as chief in April 1933 but lasted only twenty-six days in the job due to his untimely death, prompting Sir John to return for a short time until a replacement could be found.

One notable incident that occurred during Martin's tenure as the chief's PA was when, on 5 October 1930, the gigantic experimental airship, the R101 (at 777 feet long, the largest airship in the world at the time), which was designed and constructed under the direction of the Air Ministry, crashed in France while en route to India, killing forty-eight of its fifty-four passengers including the government's Secretary of State for Air, Lord Christopher Thomson. Given that Lord Thomson was Sir John Salmond's immediate superior, and that the Air Ministry was responsible for the planning and manufacture of the R101, there was naturally an official inquiry, held in public, which opened on 28 October.

But on 19 October, nine days before the Court of Inquiry convened and two weeks after the disaster, a film of the R101 was shown to Salmond by the Research and Technical Publications (RTP) department of the Air Ministry. Massey sent the film back to RTP once the chief had viewed it, writing a covering note that said, 'The R101 film which was sent personally to Sir John Salmond and which was demonstrated to him by your Department, is herewith passed to you for storage.'[171] Underneath Martin's minute returning the film is another, succinct and stern, note written by someone in the RTP department named Williamson that reads: 'This film is the personal property of Sir John Salmond and is not for public demonstration without his authority. It is not to be shown as on our charge in any way, nor is it to be mentioned as an Air Ministry film.' Below Williamson's entry is a further RTP missive, written almost twelve years later on 1 May 1942 by one H.D. Waley, stating that 'This box was found duly strapped up, but when I examined the contents of the tin inside it on 1/5/42 there was nothing there except a print from RAE [the Royal Aircraft Establishment at Farnborough] negatives 656 & 657 of the take-off and landing of a Gloster IVA & S6 Supermarine [both racing floatplanes, and nothing whatsoever to do with the *R101*] in June '31. I have placed a film found in another tin in the box.' It appears then that the *R101* film contained unofficial footage that the RTP department did not want made public for some reason, and therefore was in all likelihood not shown to the Court of Inquiry. Buried in the Air Ministry's vault, at some point in the next twelve years the airship film mysteriously disappeared and was replaced with completely unrelated still photographs.

Conspiracy theories aside, the early 1930s were an interesting and troubling time to be working in the Air Ministry, close to the hub of the British military and civil establishments. There was political turmoil in Germany, with Adolf Hitler beginning to achieve prominence and who would shortly become the German chancellor, bringing rearmament with him. During his time as CAS, Sir John Salmond read the writing on the wall and resolutely opposed the position that British politicians took at the Conference for the Reduction and Limitation of Armaments held in Geneva from 1932, which could have led to British aerial disarmament. As it was, the talks broke down in 1933 when Hitler withdrew from them. For a young career officer like Martin there was much to see and learn, and being close to the chief would do his prospects no harm assuming he did a good job, which he evidently did since he was promoted to squadron leader on 5 November 1930.

At last, almost a year later and most probably influenced by Salmond, Martin Massey returned to operational flying duties. On 4 October 1931 he went to the Seaplane Training Squadron, based at RAF Calshot on Southampton Water, to learn to pilot flying boats. Doubtlessly he had already flown such aircraft unofficially during his protracted stay as the adjutant at MAEE, which was perhaps a deciding factor in his posting. The course ran until the spring of 1932, after which he went to Portsmouth to attend the four-month-long Royal Navy Tactical Course, learning how the RAF's flying boats could interoperate with the Navy's ships and aeroplanes and act against hostile shipping.

Now fully qualified, on 28 August 1932 he joined No. 209 (Flying Boat) Squadron, then resident at RAF Mount Batten in Plymouth Sound. The squadron flew a mix of types during Massey's time with them, which was to last just five months. First, there was the Blackburn Iris, the largest aeroplane flown by the RAF up to that point, and operated solely by No. 209 (FB) Squadron. The Iris was an all-metal biplane flying boat, 67 feet long with a wingspan of almost 100 feet, powered by three Rolls-Royce Condor III engines mounted between the wings, above the fuselage. It carried a five-man crew, with its two pilots sitting in an open cockpit at the nose; there were three .303 machine guns and a bomb load of up to 2,000lb. Then, arriving at the same time as Martin, was the Short Singapore II, a newer design than the Iris (although still a biplane) that boasted four engines – two in a 'puller' configuration, and two in the 'pusher' position behind them. The Singapore was longer still than the Iris but with a slightly shorter wingspan and a crew of six – now, though, there was the luxury of an enclosed cockpit for the pilots – and it became the RAF's mainstay flying boat during the 1930s, even serving into the Second World War with the Royal New Zealand Air Force, with one accounting for a Japanese submarine during that conflict.

As mentioned, Massey's stay with No. 209 (FB) Squadron was a short one. Having proved himself a competent leader, and with operational, wartime experience behind him as well as his term as PA to the Chief of the Air Staff, he was selected to attend the RAF Staff College at Andover, joining his classmates of No. 11 Course on 23 January 1933, just one week before Adolf Hitler took power in Germany. The role of the college was (and still is, although the three services' individual staff colleges combined in 1997 to become the Joint Services Command and Staff College) to train suitable officers in the administrative, staff and policy aspects of Royal Air Force matters, in so doing preparing them for promotion to higher command appointments. The course lasted eleven months, its students graduating on 22 December that year. Martin's staff college chief instructor wrote of him while on the course that 'Sqn Ldr Massey is a sound, practical officer who has carried out his duties as senior student to my satisfaction. He is making good progress in his studies. In my opinion he will always be more practically-minded than studious, but he is certain to obtain great benefit from the course. Is already showing signs of considerable improvement.'[172] Massey's end of course report, written by Air Vice-Marshal Philip Joubert de la Ferté, the commandant of the college, said of his character: 'Quite firm. Full of common sense, reliable, industrious and loyal. Has been a little handicapped by an injury to his leg [he was obviously still being troubled by either his war wounds or the roller-skating accident injury, or both], but has taken a leading part in all activities of the Staff College and has been of great assistance to the staff.' The commandant remarked of Martin's general ability that he was 'As a staff officer, only average. As a commander, above the average. By dint of really hard work he has coped with the work given him, and has produced satisfactory results.'[173]

Joubert de la Ferté's observation that Martin had greater aptitude as a leader than as a staff officer was evidently taken into account when the students' subsequent postings were being considered. Rather than a headquarters desk job, he was selected for command of an operational squadron. Now, at long last, came an extended front-line flying tour, one which would bring Squadron Leader Massey his second taste of conflict.

Chapter Five

Egypt and Palestine:
January 1934 – January 1937

With staff college completed successfully, Martin Massey was set for a return to the Middle East colonies. He was given command of No. 6 (Bomber) Squadron, based at RAF Ismailia, which was approximately 2½ miles north-west of the city of the same name (known locally as the 'City of Beauty and Enchantment') in northern Egypt. RAF Ismailia had been opened in 1916, primarily to guard the Suez Canal on whose west bank the city and airfield was sited. No. 6 Squadron had made its home there in 1929, although the squadron regularly sent its Fairey Gordon aircraft on detachment to various far-flung desert airfields such as Ramleh and Haifa in Palestine, and Qasaba in Egypt. In fact, No. 6 Squadron kept one of its three flights, 'C' Flight, on permanent detachment at Ramleh (south-south-east of Tel Aviv), due to tensions between the Arab and Jewish populations and their British rulers – there had already been one serious uprising in Palestine in 1929, and it was not to be the last. Extensive use was made of air power in policing these desert colonies of the British Empire. Known as 'air control', the theory was that aircraft could cover large swathes of the country quicker and cheaper than could ground forces. As the RAF put it in 1930: 'The political administration of undeveloped countries inhabited by backward or semi-civilized populations rests, in the last resort, upon military force in one form or another. The term "air control" implies that control is applied by aircraft as the primary arm, usually supplemented by forces on the ground, which may be armoured vehicles, regular or irregular troops, armed police or tribal forces – according to particular requirements.'[174] Moreover, air control gave the fledgling Royal Air Force a showcase for its capabilities to an as yet unconvinced Army and Royal Navy.

Massey arrived at Ismailia on 22 January 1934 prior to formally taking over command of No. 6 Squadron on 1 February from Squadron Leader J.P. Coleman. The squadron had been the first in the Middle East to be equipped with the Gordon, a two-seat biplane light day-bomber, which had made its debut with No. 6 Squadron in June 1931. Martin's first significant assignment with his new squadron was to take part in the large RAF air display at Heliopolis, a suburb of Cairo. The two flights of No. 6 Squadron at Ismailia carried out formation flying practice daily up to 19 February, and then for the next three days flew to RAF Heliopolis for the air show, taking part in mass formations with three other Egypt-based RAF squadrons.[175]

Shortly afterwards, the almost daily routine of hosting guests began when the squadron was visited by a Mrs McAlery of *The Aeroplane* magazine, with Martin conducting her on a tour of the camp. Much of RAF Ismailia's life revolved around such visits, especially those by various British dignitaries such as government officials, civil engineers, scientists, military top brass and the high commissioners for Egypt and Palestine, who regularly transited through the airfield on their way to numerous meetings. Despite such interruptions, No. 6 Squadron still carried out its primary function of providing security for the Canal Zone; on 7 March 1934, for example, eight of the squadron's Gordons flew to Mersa Matruh in 'conditions approaching war-time conditions' on a fuel consumption test. Outbound, the flight lasted just over four hours, with the return leg, two days later, taking five hours. Joint exercises with the Royal Navy were also carried out, and when HMS *Resolution* visited Port Said, No. 6 Squadron flew height-finding and wireless communications exercises with the ship, which were apparently successful 'up to 9,000 feet'. The end of May saw the possibility of unrest in Palestine so 'C' Flight, at Ramleh, undertook a reconnaissance of all the Jewish colonies in the area 'for the purpose of inspecting and reporting on the roof markings'.

Like anywhere else, the operation of aircraft in the Middle East had its hazards, highlighted on 22 October when an Egyptian child ran into a taxying Gordon, piloted by Sergeant Dale, at Ismailia, killing the infant instantly. The squadron was also tasked on several occasions to help the Army hunt for missing soldiers and vehicles out in the Egyptian desert, as well as the occasional overdue civilian or RAF aircraft. In one such instance, a Dutch KLM airliner was reported missing on 20 December 1934 after taking off from Cairo en route for Baghdad. No. 6 Squadron assisted with the search, contributing two flights of Gordons, some eight aircraft in total. The lost aeroplane, a Douglas DC-2, was subsequently found wrecked in the Iraqi desert with its three passengers and four crew all dead, having crashed into the ground while descending in a rainstorm.

Massey had been in command of No. 6 Squadron for just six months when his next staff report was due. In his section of the report, dated 10 July 1934, the air officer commanding (AOC) Middle East, Air Vice-Marshal Cyril Newall (who would become Chief of the Air Staff in 1937) described Martin as 'an extremely pleasant personality, very keen and runs a good and contented unit'.[176]

The end of January 1935 saw No. 6 Squadron celebrate the twenty-first anniversary of its formation. A formal 'coming of age' dinner was held at the Mayfair Hotel in London on 1 February attended by 'the past and present officers of the Squadron',[177] which Massey attended as the incumbent commanding officer. Back in Egypt, 'C' Flight flew in from Ramleh to rejoin the rest of the squadron for the celebrations at Ismailia, which were held on 8 February (delayed due to the squadron's annual participation in the Heliopolis air display). The day was declared a 'holiday', although there was a formal parade, inspected by the senior air staff officer Middle East, Air Commodore G.R. Bromet, at which a short history of the squadron was read out. An open day followed, with around 400 visitors 'availing themselves of the opportunity to inspect the aircraft and general equipment'. That evening, celebration dinners were held in all three messes, concluding with an Anniversary Ball for all ranks, also attended by former squadron members.

On 16 May 1935, 'C' Flight at Ramleh was warned that 'considerable unrest' was expected in Iraq, and all aircraft were duly fitted with bomb racks in anticipation of hostilities. The aircrafts' guns were also inspected and tested in the firing butts, but tensions decreased and the bomb racks were removed on the 30th. The potential for insurrection was always there, though, either in Palestine itself or the neighbouring states, and in mid-June four aircraft from 'B' Flight flew to Ramleh for a reinforcement exercise with the detached 'C' Flight.

A month later, in July, it was once again time for Martin's annual staff report. Newall had by now been succeeded as AOC Middle East Command by Air Vice-Marshal Cuthbert MacLean, who wrote of Massey: '[He] is commanding his unit with distinct success, takes great interest in his station, he has the natural qualities of leadership, intelligence and application in his work.[178] I am very satisfied with his work.' August, however, brought frustration – the Gordons went through a refit programme to strengthen their tail fins, while the aircrafts' Armstrong-Siddeley Panther II engines were largely unserviceable due to 'anticipated failure of the master connecting rod assembly'. As a result, the monthly flying hours were severely curtailed.

The annoyances of the previous month were soon forgotten in early September 1935 when exciting news reached Martin Massey and the personnel of No. 6 Squadron. The squadron's Fairey Gordons were to be replaced by the faster and more manoeuvrable Hawker Hart light bomber, and an additional flight, 'D' Flight, was to be formed and equipped with the Hawker Demon, the fighter variant of the Hart. The Hart (designed by Sydney Camm, the man who created the Hawker Hurricane a few years later) sported a single forward-firing .303-calibre Vickers machine gun and a rearwards-facing Lewis gun, mounted on a moveable Scarff ring mount that was manned by an air gunner in the rear seat, and could carry up to 500lb of bombs. When it was introduced into service in 1930, the Hart was faster than every other type of bomber aircraft operated by the RAF and could also outpace most of its fighters. The Demon had twin forward-firing machine guns in addition to the rear Lewis gun and could also carry bombs, albeit at a reduced payload compared with the Hart due to the extra weight of the second Vickers and its ammunition. The initial party of groundcrew for the new 'D' Flight arrived at Ismailia on 11 September, with the first Demon pilots joining the squadron on the 19th. Shortly before the end of the month, a trainer version of the Hart was delivered to the airfield, and the remainder of the pilots began to convert on to the type from the Gordon. Once the aircrews were proficient on the new aeroplanes, the Gordons were sent to Nos 14 and 47 Squadrons based at Amman and Khartoum respectively and, by 16 October, No. 6 Squadron was fully equipped and operational with the Hart and Demon.

There were early aircraft casualties, though, probably caused by unfamiliarity with the new machines. For instance, on 14 October, Flying Officer Shute taxied a Demon on to a patch of soft sand, tipping the aircraft on to its nose and damaging the propeller. Another incident on the 30th saw Acting Pilot Officer Pinfold crash his Demon on landing. Fortunately both Pinfold and his gunner were unhurt, but the Demon was sent away for repair, the damage caused being greater than could be remedied at Ismailia. The squadron's association with the Hawker Demon was not to last long, however, and on 6 January 1936, 'D' Flight's five aircraft were sent to join No. 29 (Fighter) Squadron at Amiyra, while an equivalent number of Harts were transferred in from No. 45 (Bomber) Squadron at Helwan on the same day. No. 6 Squadron was back to being an all-bomber aircraft unit once more.

Another highly significant, but this time personal, event for Martin Massey occurred in January 1936, when, on the 16th of that month, he married Gertrude Elizabeth Mary Lutterell Hodges at the Roman Catholic Church of the Kasr-el-Nil British garrison in the centre of Cairo. Gertrude, known as Peggy, was nine years Martin's junior, and was from Brentford in Middlesex. She was a teacher and had been working at the RAF base school at Ismailia since September 1934, and she presumably had met Martin at one of the many social functions that were, and still are, central to the officers' mess life on an RAF station. After Martin had proposed, in accordance with the protocol of the time, given that this was to be a mixed-religion marriage (Martin was Church of England, and Peggy Roman Catholic), permission needed to be sought for the union. The Roman Catholic Chaplain to RAF Middle East Command wrote to the Church that 'it is my considered opinion that this is a most desirable alliance, and as Miss Hodges is "addicti"[179] in the terms of our faculties, I should be more than grateful if you would obtain the necessary dispensation from the Bishop'. The padre further confirmed that 'to my knowledge she has not contracted any alliance which would be an impediment to marriage'.[180] The bishop accordingly gave his permission for them to wed.

February 1936 heralded the first major deployment of the new aeroplanes when No. 6 Squadron carried out a practice move of the entire squadron to Qasaba landing ground (also known as LG11) on the Egyptian Mediterranean coast. LG11 was a temporary station for the squadron in the Western Desert, and such practice moves were vital in case air support to ground forces was needed in that part of the country. Three transport aircraft took the advance maintenance party from Ismailia at 8.30 a.m. on 6 February, arriving at Qasaba in the sweltering heat of midday. The first nine Harts followed shortly after, with another five joining them half an hour later. The next day was spent reconnoitring various advanced desert landing strips by air before the aircraft landed back at LG11 to be refuelled prior to the homeward leg to Ismailia. Poor weather prevented the groundcrew leaving in their transport aircraft until the following morning. Later in the month, long-range practice bombing sorties saw the squadron dropping bombs on an air weapons range in Sinai.

By the end of March 1936, trouble was once again brewing in Palestine. The Arab and immigrant Jewish populations in Palestine could never agree to share power, so the British ruled directly. As far as Great Britain was concerned, the country was strategically vital not only in protecting the route to India, but also because of the Iraqi oil pipeline that ran through Palestine to the Mediterranean ports. Unlike the revolt of 1929 when the Arab and Jewish communities had turned on each other, this time Arab hostility was focused on the government and British security forces. Six of No. 6 Squadron's Harts at Ismailia flew to Ramleh on the 27th of the month to carry out a reconnaissance of northern Palestine for the Army.

The survey was just in time for, in early April, rioting broke out in Tel Aviv and Jaffa, instigated by the murder of two Jews. Aimed initially at Jewish migrants, the rioters attacked settlers' property and crops before the Arab political leaders (the Arab High Committee) declared a general strike on 21 April to force the government to halt Jewish immigration and land sales to the migrants, and to attempt the establishment of a national constitutional government. The disturbances escalated into widespread civil disobedience, with the destruction of infrastructure and violence aimed at anyone connected with the government, be they Arab or Jew, becoming commonplace; assassinations, sabotage, bombings and attacks by massed groups of armed insurgents were rife. On 19 April, No. 6 Squadron was ordered to be ready to move to Palestine in accordance with the Armed Forces Internal Security Scheme then in place. For the next month, though, nothing much changed, and the squadron remained at Ismailia, carrying out its normal routine. On 22 April, Massey led a formation of nine Harts on a three-hour search of the Western Desert looking for Baron Eberhard von Stohrer, the German ambassador to Egypt, whose aircraft was reported missing the previous day. Von Stohrer was found, alive, by an aircraft of another squadron on the 23rd.

The situation in Palestine continued to deteriorate, however, and by the end of May, Massey and the bulk of his squadron had deployed to Ramleh, leaving only 'D' Flight back at Ismailia. In a statement to the House of Commons on 18 June, the Secretary of State for the Colonies, William Ormsby-Gore, outlined the British government's military response to the escalating crisis:

I have made it abundantly clear, in answer to questions, that the first essential is that order must be restored. It may interest the Committee if I give an account of the measures which we have now taken. In the last three weeks the security forces have been strongly reinforced. In normal circumstances the military garrison of Palestine, apart from the Air Force garrison, consists only of two infantry battalions, one Royal Army Service Corps mechanical transport company, and details of Royal Engineers for signal purposes only, and the Trans-Jordan Frontier Force, of which two cavalry squadrons and half a mechanised company have been stationed in Palestine. Reinforcements have now been sent to Palestine, including six additional infantry battalions, one Royal Army Service Corps mechanical transport company, two field companies of the Royal Engineers, one company of light tanks, and two sections of armoured cars.[181]

Air Headquarters Palestine and Trans-Jordan, which was running the RAF's contribution to the Palestine Emergency operation, issued orders to No. 6 Squadron on 29 May for 'the commencement of operations', under which the squadron was to maintain:

a) One aircraft standing by at 30 minutes' notice at the disposal of [Army] Officers' Commanding each of the four areas: NABREA, JEREA, SAFFREA, HAIFREA.[182]
b) One aircraft at the disposal of the Officer Commanding Armoured Car Detachment, Auja.
c) One striking force of three aircraft at 45 minutes' notice to operate in any area.

Further orders were given that 'machine gun fire from the air may be used without previous authority only in the following circumstances':

a) When persons are caught in flagrante delicto committing acts of violence (eg looting or incendiarism).
b) When an officer commanding a body of troops engaged with tribesmen asks for assistance to extricate him from a difficult position.
c) Against armed bodies of tribesmen which by reason of their numbers, appearance and movements are known to be intent on active aggression, or to be, or have been engaged in such aggression.
d) Against that house or those houses in villages (not towns or main centres) from which hostile rifle fire has been directed against aircraft or security forces.

What had started as a largely urban revolt quickly spread to the rural areas of Palestine. No. 6 Squadron's first operational sorties of the conflict came on 4 June 1936, not by means of armed intervention, but rather through the dropping of 5,000 propaganda leaflets on Arab villages. The leaflets carried messages or warnings to the local population, an example of which was Propaganda Pamphlet No. 4 (Blue), which read:

> Who pays for the strike and the lawlessness it produces? It is the poor and the sick who pay. Do you know that, before the strike, more than 350 poor Arabs underwent treatment each month for eye diseases in the hospital at Jerusalem but now, owing to the strike, less than 30 are able to come for such operations.
>
> It is the same throughout Palestine owing to the strike. Hundreds of poor Arabs who came for treatment to the hospitals in the towns and cities are prevented from coming. These poor persons are deprived of treatment and many who might have been cured are condemned to blindness and death. Who is responsible for this inhumanity? Those who are urging the useless continuance of the disorders.
>
> Put an end to the disorders and to all the misery which they bring. To continue them only prolongs the day when your grievances will be heard.[183]

Troops of the Cameron Highlanders carried out regular patrols on the Ramleh to Jerusalem road looking for Arab snipers, and Massey was given the additional task of supplying one aircraft on stand-by in support. Accordingly, trucks carrying wireless sets were sent out with the Camerons so that air support could be called in at short notice, an early example of air–land integration in the form of what would now be termed a 'forward air controller' that was later to prove so vital in the Second World War, and again in Iraq and Afghanistan in the twenty-first century. The RAF's radio network was less hierarchical than that of the Army (plus all its wireless sets were interoperable with the Army's, but the Army's sets could not 'talk' to the RAF's), meaning that signals reached the intended recipient far faster. An aircraft could be airborne within a matter of minutes of an emergency call being received and arrive overhead anywhere in Palestine within thirty minutes, often quicker.[184] The arrangement became common to all convoys thereafter.

On 10 June, word came from HQ British Forces in Palestine and Trans-

Jordan (HQ BFPTJ) that Palestine was to be divided into two operational areas, Northern Brigade (NORBRIG) and Southern Brigade (SOUBRIG), with each area hosting three infantry battalions. As a result, a change to air cooperation commitments was required, as outlined by Air Headquarters: 'Requests for reconnaissance or to co-operate with troops in operations may be made by Brigade or Battalion commanders direct to Ramleh repeating this HQ. Normally not more than two aircraft should be airborne in either Brigade area at any one time. In emergency, however, Brigade or Battalion commanders may request additional air support or reconnaissance.'[185]

No. 6 Squadron's operational tasks were therefore reorganised thus:

To maintain:
a) 1 aircraft standing by at 15 minutes' notice, and 1 aircraft standing by at 45 minutes' notice, at the disposal of Officers Commanding of each of the two areas.
b) One aircraft at the disposal of the Officer Commanding Armoured Car Detachment, Auja.
c) One striking force of three aircraft at 45 minutes' notice to operate in any area.
d) 1 aircraft standing by for cooperation with troops patrolling Jerusalem – Ramleh road, locating snipers.
e) Aircraft for pamphlet dropping.
f) Aircraft for photography.

In addition to its operational tasks, the squadron also carried out ground training to ensure its military skills were kept at a high level; that same day, Massey and seven of his fellow aircrew undertook pistol practice at Ramleh's 25-yard firing range, with Martin scoring 80 out of a possible 150, earning him a 'B' grading.[186] Now and again, passengers from the Army would be flown in the Harts' rear seats for the soldiers to get an aerial overview of their patrol areas. On one such occasion Captain McIntosh-Walker and Lieutenant Douglas of the Seaforth Highlanders were taken aloft around Nablus, but 'it is reported that neither of the passengers enjoyed very good health in the air'.[187] Not that the RAF was in any way deliberately attempting to make the Army officers lose their lunch, of course.

The squadron's first 'scramble' in support of ground troops came on 11 June, when a signal was received at 5.07 p.m. from 1 Seaforth Highlanders requesting urgent air action against a band of thirty armed Arabs who were attacking a convoy south of Bala on the Tulkarm to Nablus road. Three Harts took off at 5.25 p.m. and duly arrived overhead at the scene, whereupon the bandits promptly took cover in caves. Two British armoured cars fired red Very flares in the direction of the caves to indicate the position to the Harts, but due to the cover that the caverns afforded the rebels, only limited air action was carried out. Just five rounds from one forward machine gun and twenty-one rounds from a rear Lewis gun were fired into the cave entrances and at three Arabs seen fleeing towards Bala. No casualties were reported, and the aircraft were back on the ground at Ramleh by 6.50 p.m. It was not to be long, though, until No. 6 Squadron's Harts fired a greater quantity of shots in anger. Two days later, on the 13th, Flying Officer Theed took air action against a party of armed Arabs who were taking refuge in a tin shed close to Burqa. Theed took the unusual, but inspired, decision to climb to 6,000 feet in altitude and then cut his engine to glide silently towards the enemy to take them by surprise. He then opened fire on the shed, expending twenty-five rounds from the front gun and a further twenty-seven from the rear, killing one of the occupants in the process.[188]

As the days went on, more duties were allocated to the squadron. In addition to the tasks detailed above, they were now to provide escorts to road convoys and to protect trains, since several had reported being fired upon while en route to their destinations. Massey himself, as CO, paid visits to the headquarters of both brigade areas and HQ British Forces, as well as the battalion headquarters of the 2 Camerons, 2 Dorsets and 1 Seaforths, all in connection with plans for emergency calls for aircraft in the event of rebel roadblocks. Following his meetings, 'B' Flight was allocated exclusively to NORBRIG and 'C' Flight to SOUBRIG.

On 16 June, 8,000 leaflets were dropped over Jaffa, giving warning to the inhabitants that a portion of the old city was to be demolished by the Army to allow for the construction of a new road through a no-go area. Owners of the affected properties were told via the leaflets that 'the costs of these houses will be paid to the owners. Compensation will be paid according to valuation.'[189] This was probably not a fine example of a 'hearts and minds' campaign, but the Royal Engineers carried out the demolition task on the 18th, with No. 6 Squadron providing air cover and taking reconnaissance photographs throughout the day.

Later that evening, Flight Lieutenant Reynolds was on patrol in the Jaffa area when he received a signal requesting air support to British tanks at

Yazaur, between Jaffa and Sarafand. Reynolds arrived over the target some half an hour before the armour, so circled until the tanks arrived, whereupon his task was cancelled. He decided to stay on station in case he was called for again, watching as the tanks destroyed 'numerous roadside huts' in retaliation for an earlier killing of a Jew, the fatal shot having been fired from one of the huts.[190] Also that day, No. 6 Squadron's 'D' Flight arrived from Ismailia, bringing the squadron up to full strength, with nineteen aircraft now based at Ramleh. Consequently, Martin reorganised the flights' tasks, ordering 'A' Flight to provide on-call support for any tasks from HQ BFPTJ, with 'B' and 'C' Flights supporting their respective brigade areas and 'D' Flight covering the striking force and reserve role for all commitments. There were also two 'emergency call' aircraft on standby for immediate action when time was of the essence (patrols and convoys now routinely operated with an RAF wireless truck accompanying them) and any delay in allocating the task to the appropriate flight may have resulted in casualties. Massey also spent time visiting other squadrons in Palestine to discuss his arrangements, and how squadrons might best work with each other as well as the ground forces.

His organisational plan was to pay dividends when, on 21 June, Flight Lieutenant Clark was escorting the Tulkarm to Nablus road convoy when he saw the vehicles stop below him. Going down to investigate, Clark saw that the road had been barricaded with large stone blocks and that armed Arabs were attacking the convoy from both sides of the road, so he immediately opened fire with both his forward-facing machine gun and the Lewis gun in the rear cockpit, operated by his crewman, until all of the aircraft's ammunition had been expended (400 rounds from the Vickers and 172 from the Lewis) and he was relieved by another Hart. Clark arrived back at Ramleh with his aircraft holed in the upper wing. His relief was Pilot Officer Walker who carried on where Clark had left off, but his forward Vickers jammed soon after opening fire. Walker descended so that the rear Lewis could be brought to bear, but his aircraft was hit three times, causing him to force-land with damage to the engine, oil tank and water system. At the same time, the convoy troops under attack sent an 'emergency call' signal to Ramleh requesting the help of 'D' Flight's air striking force. 'Continuous air action' then took place until 7.00 p.m. that evening, with nine aircraft taking part. During the extended, hectic action against the insurgents (in what became known as the First Battle of Bala), three of the Harts were 'forced to land due to enemy rifle fire' at Tulkarm landing ground, and in total, six of the squadron's aircraft took thirteen hits between them:

K4461 (Flt Lt Tighe): 1 shot through bomb panel – fuselage side strut damaged. 1 through upper main plane – no damage.

K4478 (Flt Lt Clark): through fabric of upper main plane – no damage.

K4469 (Fg Off Theed): 1 through fairing of radius rod. 4 through starboard lower main plane – no damage. 1 through rear main spar lower main plane.

K4471 (Sgt Dale – Tulkarm): Radiator shot (1 shot).

K4457 (Plt Off Rampling – Tulkarm): 1 shot in oil pump.

K4462 (Plt Off Walker – Tulkarm): 1 in radius rod, radiator, radiator radius rod and oil tank.

After the rest of the squadron had landed back at Ramleh, the commanding officer of NORBRIG, Brigadier Beauman, signalled Martin to give 'sincere thanks for excellent and successful cooperation during today's action. Hope you will congratulate pilots concerned on my behalf.' Two of the three downed aircraft at Tulkarm were dismantled on the ground and taken back to base by road for repair, with the third able to fly back to Ramleh after it had been patched up in the field. Massey's squadron had acquitted itself well during its first major combat of the campaign, but the dangers of such operations had been starkly highlighted – to ensure that the rules of engagement were adhered to, pilots had to first fly within a few hundred feet of the ground to positively identify the guerrillas, thereby exposing the aircraft to ground fire. Fortunately, though, throughout the insurrection the rebels were generally poorly armed and had no automatic weapons; had they managed to obtain heavy machine guns during the Emergency, the British aircraft and their crews would have faced far greater dangers.

The air officer commanding RAF Palestine and Trans-Jordan Command, Air Vice-Marshal Richard Peirse, paid a visit to Ramleh on 22 June, briefing Massey and all available pilots on the current situation, and congratulating No. 6 Squadron on the work it had carried out up to that point, particularly that of the previous day at Bala. The situation in Palestine was evidently growing more serious, since Peirse announced that bombing sorties had now been approved by the Air Ministry, but with caveats:

1. Only 20lb bombs are to be used.
2. Bombing is only to be carried out in certain areas laid down by HQ BFPTJ.

3. In those areas, bombing is not to be carried out within 500 yards
   of a village or building of any kind. There are many sacred
   buildings and mosques in open areas which on no account must
   be damaged.[191] The religious fervour of the Arabs must on no
   account be aroused.

4. Bombing is only to be used where it is more effective than machine
   gun fire, i.e. against large armed bands.

Peirse took pains to point out to the assembled aircrew that Palestine was
the Holy Land, and that 'quite naturally bombing should only be resorted
to after very careful consideration and must then be employed with certain
restrictions to safeguard the civil population as far as possible'.[192] For the
time being, however, the squadron dropped nothing more lethal than
propaganda or warning leaflets (over 36,000 were dropped in one day
alone), although all air patrols were henceforth routinely carried out with
the Harts loaded with four 20lb high-explosive bombs. On 26 June, the
two 'emergency call' aircraft were despatched to Azzun after an urgent signal for air support. When they arrived on station, one of the pilots, Pilot
Officer Burns, saw a party of Arabs carrying a coffin, which they hurriedly
threw to the ground and commenced firing on the Harts, hitting one but
causing no casualties. The aircraft swiftly returned fire, killing three of the
funeral party.

By now, the 'emergency call' system had become known as XX Call, and
once a signal for immediate assistance had been sent by the ground radio
truck, it took precedence over all other radio traffic. What had started out
as 'a method of bringing early assistance to road hold-ups and limiting the
number of sorties as escorts to road convoys' had evolved into 'a means of
obtaining air assistance wherever required'. When the XX Call aircraft
arrived overhead, it was given further instructions via visual ground-to-
air signals, such as smoke and flares, to guide it on to the target. Such was
the success of the air striking force and the XX Call system that an Army
commander in Palestine later wrote that 'the role of the aircraft was to
locate and fix the enemy until infantry could close, or if the enemy broke
cover to pursue and destroy him. Cooperation between air and ground
forces reached a very high standard and the losses inflicted on the armed
bands were exceptionally heavy in proportion to their numbers'.[193]

An excellent example of this close cooperation came when a No. 6
Squadron pilot answered an XX Call and saw four Arabs who 'bolted into
a hut'. The pilot circled the shack to keep the rebels pinned inside until the

road patrol troops arrived, whereupon seven Arabs were arrested and taken away. The squadron Operations Book records that this was 'an example of good cooperation, where the pilot resisted the temptation to inflict a few doubtful casualties, but fixed the enemy in a position where ground forces could capture the whole gang'. The ready availability of air power meant that the ground patrols often did not need to use large numbers of troops, knowing that they could make an XX Call if need be. As a result, 'the knowledge of the rapid support they [aircraft] can bring has a very great morale effect on everyone concerned'.[194]

As the month of June 1936 came to a close, the RAF's contribution to the Palestine campaign was augmented by a detachment of six Harts from No. 33 Squadron (which had deployed to the Middle East in response to the Abyssinian Crisis that began in 1935), which joined No. 6 Squadron at Ramleh. That month, No. 6 Squadron flew close to 1,000 hours, almost double its peacetime levels, a work rate recognised by the high commissioner and commander-in-chief for Palestine and Transjordan himself, General Sir Arthur Wauchope. The high commissioner wrote to Air Vice-Marshal Peirse from Government House in Jerusalem on 23 June:

> My Dear Peirse
> I wish to express my congratulations to you on the organization, discipline, soldierly conduct and endurance shown by all Army units and Air Force during the last two months in Palestine.
> I shall be glad if the Royal Scots Fusiliers, The Loyal Regiment and Seaforth Highlanders may be informed how much I appreciate the soldierly qualities shown by these Battalions in the recent affrays which have led to considerable losses and captures of armed and lawless men.
> I ask you further to congratulate on my behalf the 6th Squadron RAF [sic] on the sound organization which enabled this Squadron to take such quick and successful measures to co-operate with Army troops in the suppression of these armed bands and to express my appreciation of the fortitude shewn [sic] by all when under fire.
> Yours very sincerely
> Arthur Wauchope

The covering letter from Peirse's outer office to Massey that accompanied a copy of Wauchope's missive expressed 'the Air Vice-Marshal's personal congratulations of the excellent work done by the unit under your command'.[195]

Early July saw a major search operation by ground forces in the Jerusalem area with the objective of locating and capturing two large Arab gangs operating in the district. On 5 July, cordons were placed across lines of communication, and villages suspected of harbouring the gangs were seized. Operation X, as it was known, was a huge undertaking, utilising four infantry battalions; a regiment of mechanised cavalry; over five sections of armoured cars; a company of tanks; a detachment of Royal Engineers; and six flights of aircraft. No. 6 Squadron contributed four of the flights, flying reconnaissance sorties in support, as well as maintaining XX Call aircraft at readiness and dropping supplies to the ground troops. The operation lasted from 9.30 p.m. on the 5th until 2.00 p.m. the following day, when the air element was stood down once the troops had reached their final positions.

The dramatic increase in No. 6 Squadron's flying hours brought major engineering challenges to the groundcrew. The Hart's Rolls-Royce Kestrel engines began to suffer camshaft drive failures, which threatened to ground the squadron entirely. The HQ Middle East engineer staff officer, Wing Commander Probyn, arrived at Ramleh on 11 July to assess the extent of the problem, and decided, with Massey's urging, that seven new engines were needed immediately, with a further nine to be sent in the near future. If the British were to be successful in the Emergency, it was vital that the air element be kept serviceable.

Bombs were first dropped by No. 6 Squadron on 13 July when one of the Harts was conducting a routine patrol in the NORBRIG area of operations and its pilot noticed twelve suspected enemy crossing a field of maize. Flying low to investigate, the aircraft was fired upon, so the crew took immediate retaliatory action, opening fire with their machine guns and claiming four casualties. Coming around for a second pass, the aircraft released four bombs and inflicted a 'probable' six more fatalities. Dropping bombs became a more frequent occurrence thereafter (although the bulk of the squadron's work was still the leafleting of Arab villages), with the favoured tactic for weapon delivery being dive-bombing from 1,000 feet.

On 19 July a Hart was on a routine convoy escort sortie, covering a column of vehicles from the Potash Company on the Jerusalem to Jericho road, when the trucks halted and began to fire Very flares, the signal for immediate air assistance. The pilot saw a band of fifteen Arabs firing on the convoy from nearby hills, so he and his air gunner promptly engaged them with both machine guns, claiming seven casualties. As the insurgents withdrew, the Hart bombed them but the crew saw no further fatalities caused. When he landed, the pilot counted four bullet holes through his aircraft, none of them serious. More action came on 26 July when an Army road convoy was 'heavily ambushed' on its way from Jaffa to Jerusalem; an immediate XX Call was made and two aircraft arrived on the scene within a few minutes. Working with a nearby patrol from the Dorsetshire Regiment, one of the Harts, flown by Pilot Officer Burns, pinned the insurgents down by strafing and dropping four bombs while the Army attacked on the ground. Twelve Arabs were killed, two from the air and the remainder by the British troops, and a number of prisoners were also taken. The commanding officer of the Dorsets, Major Woodhouse, afterwards wrote to Martin:

> Dear Squadron Leader
> I should be so glad if you would convey my deepest thanks to your
> pilot who was of such great assistance to my Coy [Company] at Bab
> El Wad today. He held the bandits until my men could get round
> them, also his bombing etc was most effective. Further, his
> movements guided my men. I also consider that he had a most
> difficult task in distinguishing my men from the bandits in very
> difficult ground.[196]

But not all air action against insurgents involved the use of lethal force. On one occasion, Pilot Officer Walker was flying a routine reconnaissance sortie near Zababibe when his Hart came under attack from a 'native' who 'flung stones at his aircraft from a catapult'. Walker decided that the appropriate course of action was to fire two flares from his Very signalling pistol towards the man, a tactic which 'seemed to frighten him as he bolted'.[197]

On 28 July Massey led air action by the squadron that saw its aircraft flying in continuous support of the Army for around nine hours. What had begun as an XX Call from a road patrol, answered by two aircraft at about 8.40 a.m., led to extended bombing and strafing of the enemy until early evening, by which time fifteen insurgents had been killed from the air. For his part, Massey fired fifty-seven rounds from his front Vickers and a further ninety-six from the rear Lewis. The use of bombs, naturally, significantly increased the numbers of casualties caused, with the monthly total for July 1936 estimated at thirty-seven.

On the early afternoon of 7 August, an XX Call reached Ramleh from a Seaforth Highlanders' ground patrol on the Nablus to Deir Sharaf road that had been ambushed by a large band of armed Arabs. Five Harts were scrambled to give immediate assistance, which they duly did, causing eighteen losses to the enemy. As ever, the low flying that was necessary to identify and engage the group put the aircraft in harm's way, and No. 6 Squadron experienced its first casualty of the campaign when one of the pilots suffered a 'superficial wound to his left thigh'. Once again, the squadron's actions elicited the praise and thanks of the ground commander who later signalled: 'Accept my congratulations on the energetic and successful action by your Squadron in yesterday's operation near Nablus. I was able by personal observation to judge the excellence of the air co-operation as well as effective offensive action. The excellent information dropped was invaluable to the Seaforth Highlanders.'

The squadron's biggest action (in terms of munitions expended) in the Palestine Emergency up to that point came three days later on 10 August. At around 4.00 p.m., a request for a reconnaissance of an area to the south of Radidiya was received, to try to locate an armed group. The aircraft tasked with the observation was fired upon from the crest of a hill, so the pilot promptly engaged the spot from where the shots had apparently come, and sent his own XX Call for backup. Two more Harts arrived some fifteen minutes later, with another joining in shortly afterwards on its way back from a routine reconnaissance sortie. Between them, the four aircraft fired some 874 rounds of ammunition and dropped 17 bombs, with 7 of the enemy seen to be killed, although that number was probably higher since the insurgents were taking refuge in wooded country where it was difficult for the aircrew to see them.

The situation in Palestine continued to worsen, and the security forces found themselves stretched ever further by the arrival of new recruits to the Arab cause from Syria and Iraq. To help cover more of the operational area from the air, Massey was ordered to detach one of his flights to Semakh in the north of the country. Accordingly, Martin and the commander of 'B' Flight, Flight Lieutenant Clark, flew to Semakh on 14 August to make the necessary arrangements, with the flight's Harts deploying to the air-field the following day. The groundcrew and their equipment travelled by road convoy, escorted by armoured cars. 'B' Flight would now cover the north of Palestine, with the remainder of the squadron taking responsi-bility for the central region. 'B' Flight went into action from its new home almost immediately, attacking a group of fifty armed enemy on the 20th in response to an XX Call, claiming twenty-seven killed before failing light ended their participation. Around this time, new Arab tactics were seen, whereby a rifleman would lie on his back to shoot at a passing Hart, and would then roll over on to his front, thus concealing his weapon from the pilot's view and making positive visual identification more difficult.

As the month came to its close, XX Calls continued and aircraft were again hit by ground fire. But political intervention came in the form of the foreign minister of Iraq, Nuri Pasha, who arrived in Palestine to talk with the Arab leaders in an attempt to get them to call off the strikes and disorder. Pasha asked that 'punitive action' by the British and domestic security forces be restrained during his visit, to which the British agreed, but on the understanding that 'this does not limit the action of troops against armed persons or armed bands'. August finished with No. 6 Squadron's claim of enemy killed estimated at eighty-four, more than twice that of the previous month.

On Thursday, 3 September 1936 at 9.17 a.m., two No. 6 Squadron Hawker Harts left Ramleh in response to an XX Call from patrolling troops near Bala, on the Tulkarm to Nablus road. Arriving overhead, the pilots saw that insurgents had barricaded the road and consequently dropped low to search for the rebels in the area indicated by the British soldiers. As they did so, one of the aircraft (serial number K4473) was hit by ground fire and was seen to glide down, with a dead engine but apparently under control, into a nearby wadi. Some three minutes after it touched down, the stricken Hart burst into flames. The second machine went to investigate and was itself hit five times, with one round piercing the engine's gravity tank and forcing the damaged aircraft to return to Ramleh. The rapidly escalating situation demanded further air action, and so Massey took off, with Leading Aircraftsman Donald Gibbs as his air gunner to assist, as soon as he heard what had happened. He arrived on scene at around 10.30 a.m., but fifteen minutes later, while engaging the enemy, a shot fired from the ground went through the thin fabric covering of the Hart's fuselage and hit Martin in the left knee. Without doubt in great pain and losing blood, he managed to force-land his aircraft at Tulkarm. Once more, Martin Massey had suffered lower limb wounds due to enemy action, but it could have been far worse – a cigarette case in the upper left pocket of his flying jacket, which was struck by another of the insurgent's bullets, fortunately prevented the round from entering his chest, possibly into his heart. Gibbs in the rear seat was unharmed. After he had been helped from his cockpit and given first aid, Massey was flown back to Ramleh in a Fairey

Gordon and was then admitted to the RAF General Hospital at nearby Sarafand.

Nine of Martin's aircraft were in action that day, with the operation lasting all day and the squadron claiming six Arabs killed. As the desert sun began to set, British troops finally reached the wreckage of the burned-out Hart that had come down in the wadi earlier, whereupon they discovered the bodies of its crew. The pilot was Pilot Officer Thomas Hunter, aged twenty-one, and the air gunner was Aircraftsman First Class Edward Lincoln, aged twenty-three, who became the first (and as it transpired, only) fatalities of No. 6 Squadron's Palestinian campaign. Both men were buried at dawn the following morning at Ramleh War Cemetery, not far from the airfield. The Second Battle of Bala had been a costly one for Martin and his squadron.

There are no records to show exactly how serious Massey's latest wound was, but reference to it (as 'GSW left knee') appears throughout his service medical history for many years after the event. The injury, then, obviously gave him some measure of debilitation afterwards, although luckily not enough to curtail his flying career. He was discharged from Sarafand on the 14th and sent on sick leave for two weeks, arriving back at Ramleh to reassume command of No. 6 Squadron on 30 September. In his absence, under the temporary leadership of Flight Lieutenant Tighe, the squadron had continued its frenetic air actions, and on one such occasion, 'B' Flight at Semakh claimed twenty-four Arabs killed during an XX Call. The rules of engagement had also changed, and aircraft were now authorised to strafe houses from which hostile fire was coming, and the use of much larger 112lb bombs was sanctioned against enemy forces. The bigger bombs were first used on 6 September against rebel forces occupying sangars and trenches at a location known as Point 771, near Nablus, being dropped from low level with a twelve-second delayed-action fuse. The attack was successful, with the enemy positions being destroyed. HQ BFFPTJ said later that: 'The air bombing of Point 771 on 6 September appears to have made more impression on the inhabitants of Nablus than any other recent event of this kind. A number of casualties in that action were inflicted on an armed band composed partly of local people, and the inhabitants could see and hear the action from their own doorstep. It is probable that this incident has done more to prevent local recruits from joining the gangs than any number of warnings could have achieved.' So much, then, for all the tens of thousands of propaganda and warning leaflets dropped.

More British troops had arrived to strengthen the presence in Palestine, with a full division coming from the UK augmented by further units from Egypt. Some of these extra forces deployed to the north of the country, placing greater demands on 'B' Flight, so another complete flight of Harts was sent to Semakh to reinforce them. On 24 September, the squadron lost another aircraft when, while chasing mounted Arab insurgents, it was hit in the radiator by rifle fire. The pilot, Pilot Officer Rampling, was seriously wounded, having taken rounds in his left thigh and wrist. The Hart crashed as the injured Rampling was attempting to force-land, but both he and his gunner fortunately escaped any further harm. Top cover arrived in the form of five more Harts, which continued the action against the enemy until dusk, by which time some forty-one casualties had been inflicted upon them, the highest amount claimed by No. 6 Squadron in a single day during the Palestine Emergency. To compensate for the deployment of the second flight of Harts to Semakh, further air reinforcements arrived at Ramleh on 28 September in the form of a flight of Hawker Audax aircraft from No. 208 (Army Cooperation) Squadron that had flown in from Heliopolis. The Audax was, like the Demon, a derivative of the Hart, but one specially adapted for working with the Army. Armed like its sister aircraft with forward and rear machine guns, it also featured a retractable hook for collecting messages from the ground and had the ability to carry two air-droppable 112lb supply containers.

September 1936 saw far fewer XX Calls than the previous two months, but an increase in the number of casualties claimed, totalling ninety for the month. Three reasons were cited for this:[198]

a) The enemy were working on a more organised basis.
b) Enemy attacks were less sporadic than heretofore, and that a greater force and concentration of numbers were being brought to bear by the enemy.
c) The efficiency of our intelligence system had increased.

The extra troops and aircraft, and the associated increased efficiency of the British military response to the Palestine Emergency, were obviously having the desired effect, so much so that the General Strike was called off on 12 October. Massey received orders that day that 'military action will be defensive and no active operations will be carried out except to meet cases of unprovoked attack and to effect arrests'. October therefore petered out with very little in the way of air action against the enemy being taken. Just five XX Calls were answered during the month, with weapons being fired and bombs dropped for the final time on 8 October. The number of flying hours dropped back down to peacetime levels. But for Martin, October 1936 was to be marked by another milestone, the birth of his and Peggy's first son, David, at the Anglo-American Hospital in Cairo on the 28th. As is so often the case for servicemen, Massey was not at home to be present at the birth – duty came first, even for such a significant event. David not only took the traditional family middle name of Martin, but also that of the family home, Hilton.

As November arrived, No. 6 Squadron was informed that it would soon be stood down from the Palestine operation and sent back to Ismailia. Martin Massey's outstanding leadership of his squadron during the campaign, along with his personal bravery and implementation of innovative air-to-ground cooperation tactics, was recognised with the announcement on 7 November that he had been awarded the Distinguished Service Order (DSO), a medal that, at the time, was not far short of the Victoria Cross. Further, he was also Mentioned in Despatches for his time in Palestine, his second acknowledgement for participation in that campaign along with the DSO. Letters of congratulation flooded in from friends and colleagues throughout the RAF and also from industry, including Rolls-Royce. Many also sent good wishes on the birth of David, with one correspondent commending Martin's 'synchronization' of the events. Along with Massey's DSO and Mention in Despatches, No. 6 (Bomber) Squadron also won three Distinguished Flying Crosses and one Distinguished Flying Medal, awarded to a sergeant pilot, during the Palestine Emergency. Throughout the campaign, from June to October 1936, the squadron had lost just two men killed; had flown 2,473 hours; had answered 47 XX Calls; had taken 2,450 reconnaissance images; had dropped 680,500 propaganda leaflets; had expended 18,757 rounds of ammunition from the front gun and 10,284 from the rear weapon; had dropped 217 20lb and 8 112lb bombs; and had claimed 230 enemy casualties. The use of air power, and particularly the XX Call system, during the campaign had been a decisive factor in the British success, highlighted in a War Office report written after the Emergency:

> The value of the Air Force, when arrangements can be made for it to be at instant call, has been most marked. Rebels hold the Air Force in such respect that on occasions it had the effect of driving them to cover or dispersing them before the troops could get in touch with them. When it came to striking the enemy in the hills it was usually

upon the bombs and guns of his aircraft that the [ground] commander would rely … the fact that in some months more than 50% of enemy casualties resulted from air action bears witness to their effect. There were few engagements in which aircraft and troops did not work together in very close cooperation – so close in fact that 'combined action' is probably a better description. Practically every case of a successful attack on armed rebels resulted from the combined efforts of air and land forces. Air provided the commander with his principal weapon of offence; local conditions of ground and policy combined to make it an especially effective weapon in Palestine.[199]

There is a perception, even today, that between 1918 and 1939 the RAF forgot how to support the Army, but No. 6 Squadron's contribution in Palestine more than disproves that; the squadron had certainly lived up to its motto, 'Oculi Exercitus', translated as 'The Eyes of the Army'.

Martin's annual staff report of 1936, written once more by Air Vice-Marshal MacLean, called him an 'able and painstaking commander who possesses very sound judgement and useful powers of command; he enters fully into the games and social life of the airmen of his station. A very good type.' A later, interim, report penned by the AOC Palestine and Transjordan commented: 'As this officer was only under my command in Palestine for three and a half weeks, I feel unable to assess his character in detail. He was however here long enough for me to form a general impression of his great zeal and fine operational leadership. He behaved most gallantly and was awarded the DSO.'[200]

By 19 November, 'A', 'B' and 'D' Flights were back in Egypt at Ismailia, leaving 'C' Flight alone again at Ramleh; the squadron's status quo had been restored. On the 23rd, 'D' Flight was disbanded and its Harts were sent to other squadrons. Martin took some well-earned leave from 3 to 30 December, and was fortunate to be away from Ismailia when scarlet fever broke out in the camp, enforcing quarantine on the station personnel and preventing much of the flying programme from being carried out. But good news reached him on New Year's Day 1937 – he was promoted to wing commander, and was to proceed back to the UK for posting in his new rank. His command tour of a flying squadron had, without question, been both eventful and successful, and it seemed that, now aged thirty-nine, his star was on the rise.

Chapter Six

Third Strike and Out:
January 1937 – June 1942

The newly promoted Wing Commander Martin Massey was not to go immediately to a new post, since his arrival back in England heralded a further period in hospital – perhaps his return to duty following his recent knee wound had been too soon. From 5 February to 10 April 1937 he was officially listed as 'supernumerary – sick', after which he was sent home on sick leave until early July.

Once he had recovered, a posting finally came on 10 July, to the head-quarters of No. 5 (Bomber) Group, a new group of RAF Bomber Command that was being formed at RAF Mildenhall in Suffolk under the command of Air Commodore William Callaway. Bomber Command itself was relatively young at the time, having been formed barely a year before. The new No. 5 Group was an offspring of No. 3 Group, born, like Bomber Command, as a result of the RAF's expansion period of the mid-to late 1930s as a direct reaction to German rearmament. New aircraft, a massive support network, new training facilities, aircraft and aero-engine factories, storage facilities, armaments factories, flying schools, and a range of new airfields were all sanctioned during this period. To pay for it all, the RAF's budget, which included research and procurement, rose from £17.5m in 1934–35 to £74.5m by 1938–39. Establishing an entirely new bomber group would take all the skills of capable and experienced officers, so Massey, with his recent success in Palestine behind him, was an ideal choice for such a demanding staff role. His 1938 annual report,[201] written by Callaway, called him 'a very thorough and sound officer with an unusual capacity for work. He is level-headed, indefatigable and imperturbable. Would be a good staff officer in time of war or in emergency. He is tactful and has been of great assistance in training an inexperienced Group HQ staff. Recommended for Imperial Staff College.'[202] Martin had obviously developed from the student described by the RAF Staff College in 1933 as better suited to command than staff work into an able, multi-talented officer, highlighted by his recommendation for Imperial Staff College, the senior establishment to the RAF Staff College that prepared students for the very highest service appointments.

After just one month at Mildenhall, the No. 5 Group HQ moved to St Vincent's Hall, a nineteenth-century Gothic revival mansion in Grantham, Lincolnshire, and assumed responsibility for the airfields, squadrons and aircraft that were allocated to it. To begin with, No. 5 Group's aircraft were a mixed bag of Bristol Blenheims, Avro Ansons and Hawker Hinds, the latter being yet another derivative of the Hart that Martin knew so well from his time with No. 6 Squadron. Of the three types, only the Blenheim carried any real, modern, offensive threat. Clearly, if Britain was to keep pace with German aviation technology, then biplanes such as the Hind were simply not going to deliver the capability that the RAF so badly needed. In an attempt to close the gap, a variety of new, twin-engined medium bombers were introduced in the run-up to the Second World War, with types such as the Vickers Wellington, the Armstrong-Whitworth Whitley and the Handley-Page Hampden all entering service during the expansion period.

By the time that war with Germany came, for a second time that century, on 3 September 1939, No. 5 Group's six operational and two reserve squadrons were all equipped with the Hampden, flying from five airfields across southern Lincolnshire. Just one week after the outbreak of the war, Martin found himself working for a new superior when Callaway was succeeded as air officer commanding (AOC) of the group by Air Vice-Marshal Arthur Harris, later to become the head of Bomber Command itself. But more importantly, while at Grantham there also came a new addition to the Massey family when Martin and Peggy's second son, baptised John Ernest, was born on 27 July 1939.

War brought with it the need for energetic and dynamic commanders throughout the Royal Air Force, and someone of Massey's undoubted talents could not expect to remain as a staff officer at a headquarters for long. His 1939 annual report, compiled by Group Captain Thomas, senior air staff officer at No. 5 Group, said that he was 'a very hard-working and thorough officer of wide experience. Gives of his best to the Service. Careful of detail. Possesses sound judgement. Strong character. Calm. Easy to work with.'[203] Martin was once more recommended for Imperial Staff

College but future events were to determine that he did not attend, otherwise he could perhaps have reached as high a position as Chief of the Air Staff – he certainly had the potential and the credentials. Almost incredibly, he was promoted to group captain on 12 February 1940, just over three years since his previous elevation in rank and with just one tour as a wing commander under his belt. Happily, with the promotion came a new job, meaning a return to a direct involvement with aeroplanes and the occasional opportunity to fly.

Group Captain Martin Massey arrived at RAF Abingdon, five miles south-west of Oxford, on 6 February 1940 to begin his handover with his predecessor as station commander. A week later, having settled his young family into the nearby village of Boars Hill, Massey formally took command of the station, which had been in existence for eight years, having opened in 1932. In the early months of the Second World War Abingdon had been home to several squadrons of the ill-fated Fairey Battle light bomber but was now a medium bomber station with two squadrons, Nos 97 and 166, both equipped with the Armstrong-Whitworth Whitley, a large twin-engined aircraft, in residence.

Entering RAF service in 1937, the Whitley was used from the outset for night operations and was a mainstay of Bomber Command during the war's early years until superseded by more modern, and therefore more advanced and capable, designs. But despite being effectively obsolete at the beginning of the war, the Whitley held the distinction of being the first Bomber Command type to penetrate German airspace (which it did on the very first night of the conflict dropping 5.4 million leaflets over Germany), and of carrying out the first British bombing raid against Italy.[204]

RAF Abingdon's two squadrons were due to be merged to form No. 10 Operational Training Unit (OTU) on 2 April 1940, with the responsibility of converting trainee aircrew on to the Whitley before posting to front-line squadrons, and this was to be the focus of Martin's early period at the station. In addition to the Whitleys, there was also a resident flight of Avro Ansons, which were used to give novice wireless operators, air gunners and navigators their basic training before transitioning to the larger aircraft. In all, Massey's new station was home to some fourteen Whitleys and eighteen Ansons[205] and, along with that of RAF Abingdon, came the command of the OTU itself. Further, Massey also held responsibility for Abingdon's satellite airfield at nearby RAF Stanton Harcourt and, later, for another training unit that arrived in January 1941, namely No. 1 Blind

Approach Training Flight, that taught prospective Whitley pilots how to land in the dark using an automatic radar landing system. By any measure, Martin certainly had his work cut out because the RAF required forty fully trained, operationally ready Whitley crews to graduate every month from the OTU to meet the demands that the war was placing on the rapidly expanding Bomber Command, a responsibility that was entirely his.

And aside from the training output came the day-to-day tasks involved in the running of a large RAF station, including the welfare, discipline and morale of its sizeable population. Such was the intensity of the training regime at Abingdon that some of the OTU's instructor pilots were logging as many as 100 flying hours per month.[206] Accidents were inevitable under such pressure and with novice crews, yet were relatively few compared with other units – during Martin's time at Abingdon (almost two and a half years), No. 10 OTU lost twenty-six Whitleys, five Ansons and one Miles Magister.[207] These amounts may seem large nowadays, but Massey's chief instructor at No. 10 OTU, Tom Sawyer, was a highly experienced pilot who wrote that 'our Whitleys stood up to the demands made on them very well, for which much credit must be given to the maintenance staff and ground crews. Although the rate of accidents at OTUs seems to have been quite high generally … I cannot remember it being so at Abingdon.'[208]

One local geographical feature in particular claimed several unwary aircrews and their Whitleys, namely the ridge of high ground at Boars Hill, which lay in the path of the Abingdon circuit to the north of the airfield, and was where the Massey family lived. At least one aircraft, though, was lost due to being shot down when, on 5 July 1941, a Whitley (serial number Z6667) crashed at nearby Chiselhampton during a training sortie. There is evidence to suggest it was the victim of a German night fighter on an intruder mission, but other sources hint that it could have been hit by friendly anti-aircraft fire. All six members of the crew perished. Deaths caused by No. 10 OTU's flying training activities were not restricted to RAF personnel, though. On 4 May 1941, one of the unit's Whitleys, N1467, developed engine trouble while over the northern side of Oxford, and the aircraft came to ground. First hitting the bank of the River Cherwell, the Whitley then slid along Linton Road, only stopping when it smashed into the farmhouse at Cherwell Farm. The stricken machine destroyed the house before exploding in a pall of black smoke, the resulting fire setting off the bomber's machine-gun ammunition – the sound of the explosion was apparently heard all over the north of the city of Oxford. The three crewmen aboard died in the crash, and the occupants of the cottage, Mrs

Frances Hitchcox, her husband Joseph and son Kenneth were all injured. Joe, who was sunning himself in a deckchair in the garden at the time, and Ken, who was shaving in the bathroom, miraculously both survived but, sadly, 62-year-old Frances died in Oxford's Radcliffe Infirmary the following day.[209]

Martin was evidently running a very tight ship and had become a popular station commander; Sawyer called him 'dear old Herbert Massey',[210] and Maurice Driver, a Fleet Air Arm observer who was later imprisoned with Massey at Sagan, felt that he was 'just the right sort of person to be commander of a British airfield and a number of bomber squadrons'.[211] So great was the success of Massey's command of Abingdon that he was awarded not one but two Mentions in Despatches in recognition of the job that he was doing. The first came in the New Year's Honours list of January 1941,[212] and the second on 24 September the same year,[213] meaning that Martin now had three 'Mentions' to his name. The great and the good came to the station to inspect Massey's work, and during his time at RAF Abingdon he hosted His Majesty King George VI, Her Royal Highness the Duchess of Gloucester, and the 'father' of the RAF, Marshal of the Royal Air Force Lord Trenchard.

Around a year after Massey took command of the station, the enemy brought the war to Abingdon. On 12 March 1941 a lone Luftwaffe night raider dropped sixteen bombs on the airfield, putting it out of action temporarily. One Whitley was damaged and several bombs fell close to the bomb dump, thankfully not causing any secondary explosions. The Germans paid a repeat visit on the 21st, when several offices belonging to No. 6 Group (later renumbered No. 91 Group), whose headquarters were at Abingdon, were wrecked.[214] The Luftwaffe was not to have it all its own way, however, and in June 1941 No. 10 OTU's Whitleys were ordered to undertake their first operational sorties, dropping propaganda leaflets over enemy territory. Such missions, codenamed 'Nickel', were generally given to crews as their final training 'exercise' with the OTU before being posted to a front-line squadron, taking them over France where the skies were more benign than those above Germany and so giving them vital experience and a boost to their confidence. Martin flew on Nickel sorties whenever he could even though, as station commander, it was not in his remit to do so, another example of the leadership that he showed to the men under his command. Actual bombing raids by OTU crews were rare at that time, but Abingdon-based Whitleys did attack enemy airfields at Orleans and Tours on 30 November, and some raids against German invasion barges on the Dutch coast were also carried out.[215] By that time, the number of aircraft resident at the station had risen still higher, and there were now around forty-eight Whitleys and eighteen Ansons, bolstered further by the arrival of a flight of Westland Lysanders to act as target tugs for the trainee air gunners and local ground-based anti-aircraft gun crews.[216] Massey's sphere of responsibility was growing ever larger.

On 16 May 1942, Martin Massey was called for an interview at the Air Ministry in London. There, he was informed that he had been selected to command a new unit – no doubt as a result of the success that he had brought to his role at Abingdon – namely No. 110 (Heavy Bomber) Operational Training Unit that was due to be formed at Alamogordo in New Mexico, USA. This new OTU, along with ten others to be based in the Americas,[217] was intended to train British and Commonwealth aircrew to fly four-engined heavy bombers that were due to be supplied to the RAF by the United States, specifically the Boeing B-17 Fortress and the Consolidated B-24 Liberator. The scheme was one of huge proportions – the number of staff needed was estimated at around 17,000 personnel, and approximately 730 aircraft would have to be retained in America for the training commitment. The entire programme, apart from the pay and transportation costs of the RAF personnel involved, was to be financed through the US Lend-Lease act. Arrangements were made with the Americans to have the first three OTUs in operation in August 1942, with the remainder open before the end of that year. The day after his meeting, and almost certainly after a night's reflection, Massey wrote the following confidential request to his commanding officer, the air officer commanding No. 91 Group:[218]

Sir,
I have the honour to submit the following application with reference to my posting to command No 110 (Heavy Bomber) OTU in New Mexico, America.

It seems from my interviews at the Air Ministry yesterday that the Royal Air Force Commanding Officer of this and other OTUs in America will be required to take more direct charge of flying training than in home OTUs. On this account, and since I have only carried out Nickel operations, may I apply for an attachment to an Operational Squadron for further operational experience on actual operations before my posting abroad. If possible, I would prefer an attachment to a Stirling Squadron.

I have the honour to be,
Sir,
Your obedient servant
H.M. Massey
Group Captain

His request no doubt caused his AOC some anxieties, since, despite the logic behind Martin's reasoning, senior RAF officers were formally discouraged from flying on operational sorties, even though several of them had, unofficially, done so. The 'ban' was mainly for security reasons because senior officers were privy to sensitive information that could be compromised if they were captured and interrogated, but was also intended to prevent the loss of precious, hard-earned experience. However, many such officers felt that the risk was worth taking so that they could experience at first hand what they were asking their crews to put themselves through, thereby increasing their credibility with their men. Also, a desk-bound pilot was often itching to have one last 'go' at the enemy. Such was the RAF's concern over the issue, that on 30 May the senior air staff officer of HQ No. 3 Group Bomber Command wrote to the station commanders within the Group:[219]

AIRCREWS
1. On more than one occasion during the last year this Group has been unfortunate enough to lose crews containing a high percentage of key personnel, in many instances a Squadron Commander accompanied by his Station or Squadron Navigation Officer, Gunnery Leader, etc.
2. It is appreciated that there is a rather natural tendency for these key personnel to get together and have a crack at some tempting target, but there is no doubt that the Squadrons cannot really afford to take the risk of having all their eggs in one basket.
3. In view of the above the Air Officer Commanding wishes Station and Squadron Commanders to guard against this in the future.

The above memorandum does not amount to a direct order, but the intent is clear. And while Martin did not have current operational experience, he certainly had a thorough knowledge about the RAF's bomber crew training system. Despite the concerns, though, Massey's request was approved by his AOC, and he was subsequently attached to No. 7 Squadron at RAF

Oakington in Cambridgeshire (part of No. 3 Group, to whom the above 'banning order' was directed), a squadron that, as he had requested, operated the Short Stirling heavy bomber.

In the late spring of 1942, the by-now head of RAF Bomber Command, Martin's former AOC at No. 5 Group, Air Marshal Sir Arthur Harris, sanctioned a short series of raids against Germany that were to be undertaken with unprecedented numbers of aeroplanes, the idea being to overwhelm the enemy air defences (what the British called the 'Kammhuber Line' after the Luftwaffe officer who established it) through a prolonged stream of aircraft over the target area. The raids were to feature 1,000 aircraft on each night, targeted against specific German cities. In addition to the sheer physical damage that such a large number of bombers could achieve was the psychological and propaganda effect on the German population (not to mention the American and Soviet audiences), and a morale boost to the domestic populace, with the British media crowing about the might that the RAF could wield against the enemy. Harris was also keen to demonstrate to his political masters that Bomber Command alone had the means of taking the war to Germany.

The first of the so-called 'thousand-bomber raids' took place on the night of 30/31 May that year, flown against Cologne.[220] Operation Millennium, as it was code-named, gathered as many bombers as the RAF could muster, mainly twin-engined medium types such as the Vickers Wellington, but also larger aircraft such as the Short Stirling, Avro Manchester, Handley-Page Halifax, and the small numbers of Avro Lancasters that were entering service at the time. But if the promised force strength was to be achieved, then many of the aircraft and crews would have to come from training units and hence were not yet fully ready for combat. To help make up the numbers, No. 10 OTU contributed twenty-one Whitleys from Abingdon to the raid, and in a remarkable feat of logistics and engineering, Bomber Command accordingly despatched 1,046 aircraft that night, with 890 of them actually reaching the target. The raid was a spectacular success, setting Cologne ablaze and destroying 3,330 houses with around 9,000 others damaged; some 45,000 people were made homeless. Thirty-six factories were also completely destroyed, and a further 200 damaged to a greater or lesser degree. Additionally, significant damage was done to the city's transport system. Over 450 German lives were lost, both civilian and military.[221]

Bomber Command losses that night numbered forty aircraft, an attrition rate of around 3.8 per cent. Remarkably, considering their crews' lack of combat experience, all of Abingdon's Whitleys returned home, although one crash-landed at RAF Manston in Kent on the homeward leg. No records exist to show if Massey took part in the raid, but given that he was by now at Oakington (which contributed Stirlings to the aerial armada) and that the opportunity was just what he had been looking for, it seems likely that he did so.

A second 1,000-bomber raid was planned for the night of 1/2 June 1942. The target this time was to be Essen in the German industrial heartland of the Ruhr (or Happy Valley, as the British aircrews ironically dubbed it), home to the vital steelworks of the Krupp company. In all, Bomber Command (once again augmented by the OTUs and Coastal Command) was able to muster 956 medium and heavy aircraft for the attack which, when supplemented further by some Bristol Blenheim light bombers, meant that the total came to 1,004 aeroplanes. Just over half the force was made up of Wellingtons, with a sizeable contribution by Hampdens and Whitleys. Of the 'heavies', there were 127 Halifaxes; 77 Stirlings; 74 Lancasters; and 33 Manchesters.[222] No. 7 Squadron at Oakington was again to be part of the raid and, in accordance with his wish for more operational experience, Martin Massey joined the operation as second pilot in one of the squadron's Stirlings.

The Short Stirling was the RAF's first four-engined bomber aircraft, and therefore the service's first truly strategic heavy bomber. It was a huge aeroplane at a shade over 87 feet in length, making it almost 20 feet longer than its successors, the Halifax and the Lancaster. Capable of carrying a bomb load of up to 14,000lb, and with a maximum range of 2,000 miles,[223] the Stirling represented a step-change in capability for RAF Bomber Command when it entered service in August 1940 with No. 7 Squadron. The aeroplane was designed for a crew of seven, comprising the pilot; a co-pilot; a navigator/bomb-aimer; a wireless operator (who also acted as a gunner in the nose turret); a flight engineer; and two further air gunners, one for the mid-upper turret and one in the tail-gun position. As the war progressed, though, it became apparent that a specialist bomb-aimer was required since the navigator had more than enough work to do due to the long distances involved, and that increasingly complex bomb sights needed expert operation. To that end, the co-pilot was generally not carried on operations, and a bomb-aimer would take his place in the crew, thereby freeing the navigator to concentrate on getting to and from the target.

Reputed to have few vices in the air, the Stirling was generally known as a delight to fly, being surprisingly manoeuvrable for such a large aircraft and often able to out-turn enemy night fighters such as the Junkers Ju-88 and Messerschmitt Bf-110. However, an Air Ministry stipulation that the aeroplane's wingspan should be limited to 100 feet or shorter (to allow for fitting several machines into a standard-sized hangar for servicing) meant that its operational ceiling was restricted to around 17,000 feet, which proved to be a handicap (the Lancaster had a larger wingspan despite being a shorter aeroplane, so could fly as high as 24,500 feet) as it placed the aircraft within range of enemy anti-aircraft guns. On take-off or landing, though, the Stirling was somewhat less forgiving than while airborne. Take-off meant feeding power to the engines correctly otherwise the aircraft would swing uncontrollably to the right, while landings could produce a sudden stall, dropping the huge aircraft to the ground like a stone. Both characteristics often collapsed the Stirling's lanky undercarriage, leading to the aeroplane being written off.

No. 7 Squadron had been the first to take the Stirling to war. On the night of 10/11 February 1941, three aircraft took off from RAF Oakington to attack oil storage facilities at Rotterdam. Dropping fifty-six 500lb bombs, the raid represented the RAF's first use of a four-engined heavy bomber in anger. The following April, Stirlings paid their first visit to Berlin, the 'Big City'. The RAF's Stirlings shouldered much of Bomber Command's burden until 1943 when the more advanced Halifax and Lancaster took over in earnest. The last bombing sortie carried out by the type was on 8 September 1944, but by then the Stirling had taken on a new lease of life as a glider tug, seeing action in that role on D-Day, as well as during Operation Market Garden (Arnhem), and Operation Varsity, the airborne element of the crossing of the Rhine.

Martin's pilot for the raid on Essen was to be Flight Lieutenant Norman Winch of No. 7 Squadron, an experienced flyer who already had a Distinguished Flying Cross and at least thirty operational sorties to his name. He had also had two lucky escapes from Stirling crashes – one on 31 October 1941 and another on 12 April 1942, both on landing. Martin had apparently personally selected Winch's crew to fly with, presumably because of their great experience, for his fact-finding mission. For the sortie that night, Winch's crew was made up of Pilot Officer Geoffrey Booth, the navigator, from Stockport; Sergeant Evan Williams, the wireless operator/air gunner who, despite his Welsh-sounding name, was from London; Warrant Officer Brian Iverson, the flight engineer, also from London; Flight Sergeant Ray Boag, an air gunner from New Zealand operating the mid-upper gun turret; and Flight Sergeant John Hankin, another Londoner, the rear gunner. This was to be Winch and his team's last mission before being sent for a well-earned rest away from operations. Since Martin was on board (listed officially as 'second pilot'), the usual bomb-aimer was left behind to accommodate him, so one of the other crew members would have taken on that role, most likely Booth, the navigator. Geoff Booth was a pre-war regular who determinedly wore the observer's brevet rather than the later navigator's badge on his uniform and, as an observer, he would have been trained in bomb aiming as well as navigation.

When the briefings were over and the crew had been fed, they donned the cumbersome flying clothing that was necessary to keep them from freezing at altitude in an unheated aircraft. A crew bus then took them out to their waiting Stirling, serial number N3750 and code letter D-Dog, parked out on one of Oakington's twenty-eight hardstands, just one of eighteen aircraft from No. 7 Squadron detailed for that night's operation. Once the crew had settled themselves into their assigned cramped positions within the confines of the bomber's fuselage, Winch, with Martin Massey alongside him in the cockpit, began the procedure for starting the aircraft's four Bristol Hercules XI engines. Once the flight engineer, Warrant Officer Iverson, was satisfied that each motor was performing correctly and that all his gauges were reading as they should, Winch released the brakes and slowly taxied the lumbering Stirling, laden with fuel and bombs, towards the runway threshold to await its turn in the queue to get airborne. N3750 left the ground at 11.07 p.m. on 1 June 1942[224] and, after clawing its way into the Cambridgeshire night sky, turned on to its easterly course towards Germany and Essen, taking its place among the gathering mass of British aircraft.

Many years later Norman Winch related to Pino Lombardi, writer of *Short Stirling: The First of the RAF Heavy Bombers* (and who passed the story on to this author), that on the outbound journey, Martin spent time with each crew member of N3750 at their respective stations, talking to them and quizzing them about their roles, their training, and what their experience had taught them. He was apparently especially interested in the navigation of the bomber and what the gunners could see from their turrets. Massey was clearly gathering as much information as he could from a veteran crew prior to his forthcoming posting to New Mexico.

Some hours later, over the target, things were not going well. The weather was not as good as forecast due to a sudden build-up of haze and cloud and, as a result, the bomber stream had been dispersed widely during its outbound journey. Also, the marking of the target was somewhat haphazard, with marker flares dropped well short of the city; one aircraft reported seeing target markers over Duisburg, some ten miles to the west. Instead of a concentrated attack, the British aircraft dropped their bombs far and wide, so much so that the Germans apparently did not even realise that Essen was the intended target, prompting Reich radio to report 'widespread raids over western Germany'.[225] Debriefed on return to their home bases, many crews were unsure as to whether they had in fact bombed Essen or other built-up areas because of the cloud cover – so scattered was the attack that 14 other German towns were hit that night. Only 11 houses were destroyed in the centre of Essen itself, with a further 184 damaged in its southern suburbs. As for the Krupp works, no damage was reported to its factories by the company.[226] Bomber Command lost 37 aircraft that night (3.2 per cent of the total despatched), with 149 airmen killed and a further 46 taken prisoner.[227]

Nothing more was heard back at RAF Oakington from Norman Winch after take-off,[228] but at around 2.30 a.m. on 2 June 1942, a time (and position) that indicates that the aircraft had released its bombs and was on the homeward leg, N3750 crashed into the grey North Sea waters of the Westerschelde, just off Vlissingen on the southern Dutch coast, the only aircraft from No. 7 Squadron to be lost that night (although one other was hit by flak but managed to return to Oakington safely).

Exactly what happened to the Stirling is uncertain; Winch thought that it had been hit by enemy anti-aircraft fire,[229] but there is an extremely strong probability that it was in fact shot down by a German night fighter. Oberleutnant[230] Doctor Horst Patuschka, a thirty-year-old Luftwaffe pilot who hailed from Kahla in Thuringia, was on patrol in his Junkers Ju-88C of III/Nachtjagdgeschwader 2[231] from his home base of Gilze-Rijen in the southern Netherlands, one of eleven aircraft from his unit launched to hunt for British bombers that night. He was operating under the guidance of a coastal Freya radar station, code-named 'Hamster', which was part of the German *Himmelbett*[232] night fighter control network, integral to the Kammhuber Line. 'Hamster' directed Patuschka on to a radar contact, which he engaged and shot down. He later identified his victim as a Wellington, but no aircraft of that type came down either in the location or at the time that he reported; however, both those pieces of information match the loss of N3750.[233] Shortly afterwards, Patuschka attacked a second British bomber, this time definitely a Wellington and possibly that from No. 305 (Polish) Squadron, which managed to limp home but stalled and crashed while attempting a landing on one engine.[234] Spotting a stalking night fighter in the dark was incredibly difficult, so if Winch or his crew never saw the Junkers, it could explain why he thought they had been brought down by flak.

Norman Winch later said that Martin was surprised to have to bale out,[235] but he acted quickly, exiting the crippled Stirling through the forward escape hatch. Warrant Officer Brian Iverson was on hand to 'bundle him out' if he wavered, but there was to be no hesitation or indecision – Massey went straight out into the night air. For Martin, it must have been a considerable effort to escape from the Stirling given his previous injuries, especially as it was obviously severely damaged, possibly on fire, and therefore difficult for Winch to keep under some sort of control. As he was the aircraft's captain, Norman Winch was the last to leave, remaining at his controls for as long as possible to keep the aeroplane in the air, thereby ensuring that everyone else had got out before he took his turn. 'His parachute opened and he swung twice before hitting the ground and breaking a leg',[236] which seems to indicate that the Stirling was at a fairly low altitude by the time that he jumped. Flight Sergeant John Hankin, the rear gunner, was also wounded, but there are no details of his injuries. Martin Massey was badly injured once again, this time in the left foot that had already been damaged from the burns of 1917. Some accounts attribute his wounding to shell splinters when the aircraft was hit, while others suggest that it was the result of a heavy landing in the dark after his parachute descent. Considering the harm caused and the subsequent years of trouble that the injury gave him, it was most likely the former. But whatever the reason, for a man already living with the results of his injuries from being shot down in 1917, his left knee wound from Palestine in 1936, and the serious break of his right leg in the roller-skating accident of 1923, more trauma to his lower limbs was excruciating. The injuries to these three men notwithstanding, all seven members of the Stirling's crew baled out of the stricken bomber successfully and lived to tell the tale, surely a testament to Winch's skill and bravery as a pilot.

One by one, the British airmen were recovered by the Germans from the Netherlands countryside and taken into captivity, although news of their safety and detention inevitably took time to reach England. Martin was at first listed officially as 'missing', which no doubt caused Peggy and their sons a good deal of anguish until they heard that he was in fact a prisoner of war. At some point between arriving at Abingdon and being shot down, Martin and Peggy had decided to take out a long-term lease on a small house (which they eventually bought, and that Peggy described as 'this dear little cottage') in the village of Croyde on the North Devon coast, presumably using it as a retreat away from the pressures of life at the station whenever they were able. Plus, Croyde was a safer location than the high ground of Boars Hill next to Abingdon that seemed to attract aircraft like a magnet. Peggy was walking on the beach at Croyde with the children when she received the news that her husband was alive and had been taken prisoner.

Ironically, an agreement between Britain and the United States to cut drastically the number of American-manufactured aircraft to be supplied to the RAF was signed on 21 June (only a week before the advance parties for the first of the new OTUs were due to sail for America and just under three weeks after N3750 was shot down), thereby significantly reducing the need for the training of British aircrews in America. No. 110 OTU, Martin's intended new command, was therefore never formed,[237] and his very reason for being on the Essen raid in the first place (although he did not know it at the time, of course) was nullified. Now, though, he was about to start a very different tour of duty, arguably the most challenging, in terms of leadership, of his entire military career.

Chapter Seven

Prisoner and Accused:
June 1942 – October 1943

Group Captain Martin Massey was the first RAF officer of his rank to be incarcerated as a prisoner of war during the Second World War. Following his capture in Holland, he was first taken (along with the other crew members of N3750) to Dulag Luft,[238] a transit camp at Oberursel, to the north of Frankfurt, where newly captive RAF personnel were sent to be collected, registered and interrogated before being moved on to a permanent camp. Here, Martin was allocated the prisoner of war (POW) number of 553. As mentioned above, not long afterwards the news of his imprisonment reached Peggy, and now that she knew where he was, she was able to write, sending her first letter to her husband on 28 June 1942.[239] She told him of her 'joy and relief … to know that you are alive and not too badly hurt [this was to prove not to be the case] – I think my heart was nearer being broken than you'll ever know – and now my dearest I send you all my love and David's and John's'. The children were obviously at the forefront of their concerns and Peggy told Martin to: 'never worry; always know that until your return my whole life will be spent for you and the boys, with the thought of our eventual reunion. I have everything to work and live for. … David every night in his prayers says "please God keep Daddy safe" and he adds "dear Guardian Angel take care of Daddy" … they are both so fit and so full of life. Johnnie says the same in his prayers too – they are too young to realise anything, but for me to look at them and know that they still have a Daddy is wonderful.'

She also wrote that she was gathering things to send him, particularly photographs, clothing and cigarettes, and was doing everything she could to get them to him but that there might be a delay since everything had to go through the Red Cross. They were all having to get used to a very new way of life.

Once the registration process at Dulag Luft was completed, the Stirling crew was split up and sent off to different camps. The flight engineer (Iverson), mid-upper gunner (Boag) and navigator (Booth) went to Stalag[240] 357 near Fallingbostel, while the wireless operator (Williams) went to Stalag Luft VI[241] near Heydekrug in what is now Lithuania. Massey, Norman Winch and the rear gunner, John Hankin, were sent to their new home, a POW camp named Stalag Luft III in Silesia, then part of Germany but now in western Poland (it is interesting to note that the three crew members who had been wounded were kept together); Berlin was around 100 miles away to the north-west. Located in a forested area on the southern tip of the town of Sagan, the camp was new, having only been opened in late March 1942 to ease the overcrowding at older camps caused by the ever-increasing numbers of Allied aircrew that were being shot down over occupied Europe.

During Massey's time at Stalag Luft III the camp and its population were to grow ever larger, but when he arrived in June 1942 there were just two compounds within the camp boundaries; the East Compound kept around 400 officer prisoners, while the senior NCOs (SNCOs), numbering some 873, were confined in the Centre Compound. Since it was new, the camp had been designed with the deterrence of escapes in mind, therefore the barbed-wire boundary fence was set some distance away from the accommodation huts to discourage tunnelling, and the huts themselves were raised above ground level for the same reason. That said, the whole compound was built close to a busy railway to provide easy access to the camp for arriving prisoner transport, but which also offered would-be escapers a nearby opportunity for a quick getaway.

As it was a camp for aircrew prisoners, Stalag Luft III came under the jurisdiction of the Luftwaffe. The guards were generally Luftwaffe anti-aircraft gunners on rest from the Eastern Front,[242] but the main administrative personnel were permanent staff. Overseeing the camp was its commandant, Oberst[243] Friedrich von Lindeiner, or to quote his full, grandiose, name, Friedrich Wilhelm von Lindeiner genannt von Wildau. In June 1942, von Lindeiner was sixty-one years old and had been a career soldier, having joined the German Army in 1898, an archetypical product of the Prussian military tradition. Active service in Germany's colonial wars in East Africa and then the First World War followed, with von Lindeiner being decorated for bravery in both conflicts; he was awarded one of Imperial Germany's highest decorations, the Pour le Mérite (or

Blue Max). Although he was a patriot, he was no Nazi and had refused to join the party, but in 1937 von Lindeiner came out of retirement and accepted a position in the Luftwaffe and joined Hermann Göring's personal staff. When he was offered the chance to run the camp at Sagan, he likely saw it as a way to serve his country without giving direct support to the Nazis.

Von Lindeiner's deputy at Sagan was Major Gustav Simoleit, a pre-war professor of history, and below Simoleit was Hauptmann[244] Hans Pieber. The commandant's philosophy for running the camp was one based on a common respect; he understood that the prisoners' lot was not a happy one, and tried to make life as bearable as possible for them. Together with Simoleit (known as a decent and fair man), von Lindeiner ensured that intellectual and cultural pursuits were promoted at the camp, and classes in a variety of both practical and academic subjects (including German) were taught, and with plays ranging from Shakespeare to bawdy farces also put on by the prisoners. There was an ulterior motive to all this activity, though, since the more occupied the prisoners were, the less likely they were to put their efforts into escaping, or so the Germans hoped. Simoleit later recalled that von Lindeiner tried his best to 'make the hard lot of the thousands of prisoners endurable and to reach his aim of a coexistence and cooperation based on mutual understanding and estimation'.[245]

Most prisoners (or Kriegies, as they called themselves, from the German word for POW, *Kriegesgefangenen*) found the English-speaking von Lindeiner to be a fair man, albeit an upright and correct military one, which could make him appear a little remote, and many remember him as an old-school 'officer and gentleman', which perhaps made him an anachronism during the era of the Nazis. Eric Williams, one of those who escaped from Sagan using the famous 'Wooden Horse' later described von Lindeiner as 'a gentleman himself'.[246] Both Williams and another Sagan Kriegie, the author Paul Brickhill, recall that von Lindeiner would still give a proper salute and a 'good morning gentlemen' to motley inmates who were garbed in shabby, threadbare uniforms, were unshaven due to a scarcity of razor blades, and who could not return the compliment (except with a polite nod) since they were invariably bare-headed and the British do not salute without wearing a hat. Some prisoners even felt a degree of affection for the commandant, with the relations between captors and captives at Sagan, fostered by him, arguably better than at any other camp in the German POW system.

But there was another side to the commandant's personality, highlighted by a senior American captive, Lieutenant Colonel Albert P. Clark. Clark testified upon repatriation in May 1945 that von Lindeiner often promised more than he could (or would) deliver in terms of improved conditions, that he possessed a violent temper that he struggled to control, and was prone to launching into lengthy rants during meetings with the senior Kriegies.[247] A US Army Air Force report[248] into life and conditions at Sagan, written shortly after the war, confirms Clark's evidence, stating that although the commandant was 'courteous and considerate at first sight, he was inclined to fits of uncontrolled rage'. The report further said that von Lindeiner 'upon one occasion … personally threatened a POW with a pistol', but did, however, concede that he was 'more receptive to POW requests than any other commandant'.

While the welfare of the Stalag Luft III inmates was ultimately von Lindeiner's responsibility, there were other methods by which their interests were represented. Above all was the Geneva Convention of 1929, which outlined the legal status of captives and how they were to be treated by the belligerents. That said, the Germans only followed the Geneva Convention in the camp when its provisions coincided with their own policies. Then there was the Protecting Power, which exists during times of war to represent another sovereign state in a country where there is no diplomatic mission. Since Great Britain obviously had no embassies in Germany, its interests were covered first by the United States, and then, after the American entry into the war, by Switzerland. Among its other commitments, the Protecting Power guaranteed the protection of prisoners held in enemy territory, and had the right to enter the camps and interview the prisoners, in private, regarding their grievances and to make representation on their behalf to their captors. Next there was the International Red Cross and the YMCA, both of whom were also entitled to visit the camps to ensure the spiritual and physical well-being of the POWs. The Red Cross provided information about prisoners, such as where they were being held and the extent of their injuries (if any), back to Great Britain, and most famously organised the distribution of Red Cross parcels. The parcels, containing many prized items such as food, toiletries and tobacco, supplemented the meagre rations provided by the Germans and were a great source of morale improvement when they arrived at the camps.

Massey himself felt that the International Red Cross was a more effective organisation than the Protecting Power, and considered that their influence over the Germans was greater than that of the Swiss legation.

The Protecting Power's authority was limited in that even though they may have agreed with a Kriegie's grievance, they had no way of forcing the Germans to do anything about it. The aforementioned US Army Air Force report backs Martin's opinion, stating that although the mere existence of the Protecting Power had a beneficial effect, 'direct interview was the only satisfactory traffic with the Protecting Power. Letters usually required six months for answer – if any answer was received'.[249] Prior to an inspection of the camp by the Swiss, the Germans would usually grant a few concessions to the prisoners to make themselves look more benevolent. Excuses for a variety of poor conditions were then offered to the visiting delegation before its representatives held meetings with the senior Kriegies and then the commandant. The outcome of a visit usually amounted to some minor concessions from the Germans. For their part, the YMCA established a scheme known as War Prisoners Aid to support prisoners of war by providing such valued items as sports equipment, books, musical instruments, art materials, radios, gramophones, and eating utensils. Von Lindeiner wrote highly of the YMCA, stating that 'to honour their work to the fullest is impossible to do in words; it was an expression of deepest human concerns'.[250]

On a day-to-day basis, without the permanent presence of the above international organisations at the camp, the prisoners' interests were represented by the highest-ranking POW, known as the senior British officer, or SBO. When Massey arrived at the camp, the SBO was Wing Commander Harry Melville Arbuthnot Day, a larger-than-life character who had been a prisoner of war for over two and a half years, having been shot down in October 1939, just a month after the outbreak of war. 'Wings' Day, as he was more usually known, was a former Royal Marine who had won the Albert Medal[251] during the First World War when his ship was torpedoed and he had courageously rescued two men who were trapped below deck. Later, he became a pilot in the Fleet Air Arm before transferring to the RAF. At the outbreak of the Second World War, Day was over forty years old when his squadron was deployed to Metz in France, but as the commanding officer he naturally chose to fly its first operational sortie of the war, a reconnaissance mission across the German border. His Bristol Blenheim light bomber was attacked and shot down near Birkenfeld by enemy fighters, killing his two fellow crew members and landing 'Wings' as a prisoner of war.

Day was not the sort of man to accept defeat or incarceration lightly, and by the time Massey arrived at Sagan he had already tried to escape several times from other camps and would carry on doing so right through to the end of the war. He possessed a personality that seems to have polarised opinion of him among his fellow Kriegies. Alex Cassie, for example, described him as a 'formidable character', called him 'intolerant', and expressed relief that he had not served on Day's squadron.[252] Maurice Driver had known Day at a previous camp (Stalag Luft I, Barth) where it seems that several prisoners grew suspicious of him since he appeared to be too close to the Germans – Driver went so far as to call it 'collaboration' – although this opinion appears to have subsided over time.[253] Day also had a reputation, both before capture and afterwards, as a heavy drinker, and Cassie considered that being shot down had actually saved 'Wings' from being killed by excessive alcohol consumption, presumably since although drink produced by home-made stills was available among the prisoner population at Sagan, it was in lesser quantities than would have been accessible to him at home. Day's drinking perhaps goes some way to explaining one description of him as 'volatile, and he could swing from a mood of high bonhomie to one of frosty aloofness'.[254] Such variations in temperament were also apparent to Paul Brickhill who wrote of Day that 'he was capable of a sort of austere introspection and then it would vanish in a mood of turbulent gaiety. He could be steely and frightening, and then sometimes that wry mouth of his would relax in a gentle smile.'[255] Another prisoner, Leonard Hall, remembers him as being known to many of the Kriegies as 'Pricky',[256] no doubt due to his unpredictable nature. Others, though, admired him, with Sydney Dowse calling him 'a good character … a jolly chap – a bit "hairy-scary" … very popular',[257] and in some circles an aura, bordering on hero worship, grew up around him, probably fuelled to an extent by Day himself.

Martin Massey's arrival at Stalag Luft III heralded the end of Day's role as SBO since Martin outranked him, yet Day's biographer, Sydney Smith, himself a Kriegie at the camp, says that Massey 'told "Wings" that he wished to be Senior British Officer in name only, and asked "Wings" to continue to run the camp and deal with the Germans'.[258] This story is repeated in other accounts by former inmates and various authors and seems to have become accepted as fact. Some say that Massey delegated authority to Day because his leg wounds were so debilitating, and one even goes so far as to say that Martin 'ordered'[259] Day to continue in the role. But it seems that this was not the case – given Massey's strength of character, he was simply not the sort of man to give in to his pain, wallow in self-pity and entirely relinquish his responsibilities to someone else. More likely, he saw 'Wings' as a very welcome and valued assistant (they knew each other well having served in the Middle East together in the 1930s and were of a similar age) and probably listened closely to his counsel during the early part of Martin's time at Sagan given Day's long experience as a prisoner; indeed, Massey would have been foolish not to have done so. Other testimony than Smith's points to the reality, such as that from Alan Bryett, one of the Kriegies, who said that Massey was 'ably supported'[260] by 'Wings', and that the camp was run by them both, rather than solely by Day. There was obviously some form of informal dual responsibility, at least initially until Massey had learned the ropes and which probably lasted around four months to October 1942 when Day was transferred to another camp. Indeed, in von Lindeiner's own memoirs (detailed below), when writing of his dealings with the senior British officer, Day warrants no acknowledgement at all, whereas Massey features at length. Further, the official history of Sagan makes no mention of any such shared responsibility arrangement, but instead lists Massey as SBO from June 1942, when he first arrived, replacing Day in the role.[261]

More evidence can be found in the handwritten personal dedications of two first-edition books, both presented after the war to Martin, the first of which is a copy of Paul Brickhill's *The Great Escape*. Brickhill was himself a prisoner at Stalag Luft III and signed his book 'For Martin Massey – The Boss! With vivid memories and warmest regards'[262] – he seems to be in no doubt that it was Martin who was in charge. The second volume is a copy of Sydney Smith's biography of 'Wings' Day, dedicated not by the author but by Day himself, who wrote on the flyleaf 'Martin Massey; a friend from the early theatre in Egypt. A tower (Yorkshire[263]) of strength to a southerner (Kent and Hamp[shire]).'[264] This is perhaps the most telling evidence, as for a man of 'Wings' Day's undoubted self-assuredness and volatile character to call Martin a 'tower of strength' is a remarkable plaudit and arguably tacit acknowledgement of where the real responsibility for the role of SBO did actually reside. Losing the 'top dog' status of SBO after so long probably rankled with Day, and might go some way to explaining the origins of the tale of Massey delegating authority to him – Day was the source of much of Sydney Smith's biography of him. When von Lindeiner died in 1963, 'Wings' wrote to Delmar Spivey, who had been a senior American officer at Sagan later on in the war, to break the news to him. In his letter, Day said that 'I suppose that I had more to do with him than any other POW',[265] a typically vainglorious presumption that, as we shall see, was not true. As a final point on the subject, in all the many existing photographs showing the SBO interacting with the commandant, the Red Cross, the Protecting Power and visiting Luftwaffe dignitaries – be they held in either the UK or US National Archives, the Imperial War Museum, the RAF Museum at Hendon, personal collections, or by the International Red Cross – it is Massey who is pictured, not Day.

Another forceful personality was resident at Sagan when Martin arrived, in the form of Douglas Bader. Like 'Wings' Day, Bader refused to sit back and accept imprisonment and, despite famously having no legs, he made it his personal mission to escape or, failing that, to cause the Germans as many problems and as much disruption as he could. Also like Day, Bader's character divided opinion among his fellow Kriegies. While some admired his spirit, others felt that his troublesome behaviour, and the resulting punishments for it, brought unwelcome attention and hardship upon all of them. One inmate, Maurice Driver, said that Bader was 'rather difficult to get on with; he was a very arrogant person … a man who was extremely determined always to have it his own way'.[266] Two months after Massey's arrival, Douglas Bader was removed from Stalag Luft III and sent to the infamous Colditz POW camp following another unsuccessful escape attempt.

Unlike a normal RAF career posting, which is usually negotiated between the officer concerned and the service's personnel management system, the job of SBO at Stalag Luft III was not one that Martin had asked for, nor had been trained for, or that he had been selected for; it had been thrust upon him by fate, albeit a fate of his own making. His first task was to get to know the German commandant and the way he ran his camp. The two men had much in common as they held the same equivalent rank, and were both decorated veterans of their respective country's colonial conflicts and the First World War. Both had been seriously wounded during those earlier wars, and the health of each had been undermined by their injuries. Von Lindeiner had tried unsuccessfully to be retired on medical grounds more than once, and here was Massey, in pain and walking with great difficulty, aided by a stick. Both were somewhat older than the men they commanded (Massey was still the junior man by over fifteen years, however), and both were held to be officers and gentlemen through and through. In their respective positions, they were probably the perfect match, and one RAF prisoner, John Dominy, later said that 'all in all, Sagan was a remarkable camp, for it contained men who were the best of their respective warring races'.[267]

Martin's new-found command saw him responsible for the administration of the East Compound, assisted by an adjutant, who at that time was Squadron Leader Bill Jennens, a man respected by captives and captors alike. He was further helped by an interpreter, Squadron Leader Sidney Murray. The Germans provided the SBO with an office, supplied with furniture, stationery and a typewriter,[268] and Massey held a weekly meeting with the senior representative from the SNCOs' Centre Compound, Sergeant James 'Dixie' Deans and his deputy, Warrant Officer Ronnie Mogg, both of whom were, like 'Wings' Day, long-serving and experienced Kriegies.[269] Deans was one of the younger SNCO prisoners, but nonetheless had been elected to the role of compound representative by his peers and was known as a firm but fair leader. Von Lindeiner said of Deans that he 'knew how to treat his men with tact and a firm hand'[270] – a typical senior NCO, in fact.

Martin organised teams of prisoners to deal with welfare, entertainment, games, education and the distribution of Red Cross parcels and clothing,[271] to the extent that von Lindeiner later commented that the 'POWs had established a form of self-rule under a British senior officer',[272] and he was apparently content to allow the status quo to continue rather than take a heavy-handed approach. When a matter arose from the prisoners that needed representation to the commandant, Massey would request a meeting with him, accompanied by Sergeant Deans if the issue involved an SNCO, bringing to von Lindeiner's attention any complaints or alleged breaches of the Geneva Convention. Martin was also the prisoners' conduit to the neutral international organisations, and as such he was responsible for dealing with correspondence and visiting delegations from the Red Cross and the YMCA, and for making representation to the Protecting Power when necessary.[273]

One such occasion was in the winter of 1942 when the Germans stopped the issue of Red Cross parcels in retaliation for attempted escapes (prisoners were supposed to receive one parcel per man per week). This move was contrary to the Geneva Convention since it constituted a reprisal, so Massey arranged for a report, written by one of the Kriegies who happened to be a qualified dietician, to be sent to the Red Cross, copied to Berlin. The report stated that the stoppage of parcels meant that each prisoner's calorific intake was too low to maintain his health sufficiently (the daily German food ration allocated to a prisoner typically amounted to under 2,000 calories[274]). Consequently the Germans relented, with the result that at Christmas that year, each prisoner received around five parcels.[275]

Martin became a familiar figure to all when he was moving around the East Compound, with Paul Brickhill recalling ironically that 'when he could move, he hobbled with a stick, his foot swaddled in an old flying boot, a picturesque condition'.[276] The boot was of 1940-pattern RAF issue, calf length and made of dark brown suede with a sheepskin lining, a wide-opening front-entry zip and a flexible rubber sole. It was far more comfortable for his wounded left foot than a shoe or stiff leather flying boot, and was destined to become (along with the walking stick) a Massey trademark during his time at Sagan. He developed a particular way of talking to his captors – not being particularly tall, Massey would tilt his head back and look down his nose at them, in an act of defiance and authority.[277] In his dealings with the Germans as SBO, the prisoners were, in general, delighted with the way that Massey conducted himself and represented them and 'were considerably cheered up to see 'The Old Man' limping across the compound on his way to argue a point with the Germans'.[278] Alex Cassie considered him 'very conscientious … he was a man of great conscience … a very devout man … I liked him very much; I admired him', and felt that he did 'a very good job'.[279] Another prisoner, Sydney Dowse, recalls that he was 'very nice, a very pleasant man, not as robust as Day, but a much calmer sort of man'.[280] Maurice Driver considered Massey to be 'a real military-type man. He was an honest man; he was a person of strong personality but he didn't inflict his personality on other people in the way that Bader did.'[281] Charles Clarke, who had been a Lancaster bomb-aimer before being shot down and sent to Sagan, remarked that 'Massey was our Senior British Officer – an amazing man.'[282]

Martin's approach to his role was typical of him, mirroring the efficiency and dedication with which he had run first No. 6 Squadron in the Middle East, and then RAF Abingdon and No. 10 OTU. Yet another Sagan Kriegie, Leonard Hall, remembers Stalag Luft III as 'a remarkably well-run camp, with a first-class Senior British Officer, Herbert Massey … a great character … he was a real Commanding Officer. I had total confidence [in him]; you obeyed him … it was a full Service atmosphere – I say that in the best possible sense.'[283] The atmosphere of discipline and order that Martin brought to Sagan is confirmed by John Hartnell-Beavis who wrote that Sagan was 'very well organised, as prison camps go',[284] and also by Alec Ingle, a Typhoon fighter pilot who arrived at Stalag Luft III in 1943 – he said that it was 'a highly organised RAF camp; it was organised to the Nth degree, absolutely first-rate … that camp was so well organised, it wasn't true … the whole thing was highly organised'.[285] Further testament comes again from Charles Clarke, who remembered that 'we were a disciplined bunch. I think we were exceptional in a way. I mean, the Senior British Officer was the *Senior* British Officer in every way – our first one was Massey.'[286] But perhaps the quote that best sums up the attitude that most of the prisoners had towards Massey and the way that he ran things comes from Alan Bryett, who called him 'very wise; clever … a father to all of us … he was very good … a highly respected man who gave the orders for the whole of the camp'.[287]

Of course, no human being is universally popular – Alex Cassie did say that Martin could come across as 'a bit pompous', and that although Cassie himself 'thought he did his job very well, a lot of people didn't',[288] but in all of the available interviews and written evidence of former Kriegies sourced for this book, no direct, first-person quote has been found to support this statement. In fact, Cassie's comment is the only one that even hints at some element of dissatisfaction.

As for the camp commandant, von Lindeiner considered that although Martin possessed an 'obstinate vigour' when dealing with him, he was a 'most outstanding personality … he was the typical conservative and correct Englishman who stood up for the rights of his comrades in a most emphatical manner. I believe that I can say that he and I had a respectful trust in each other.'[289] Although this mutual respect was, from von Lindeiner's perspective at least, later to be broken, it was exemplified when Martin, upon hearing that von Lindeiner's Berlin home had been bombed, expressed his concern and regret for the loss. Occasionally he would approach the commandant for help with prisoner matters, such as soliciting his support for persuading the Kriegies to attend Sunday church services in greater numbers. He also asked von Lindeiner to discipline any prisoner who was insubordinate to Massey under German military law so that he did not have to do so himself under RAF King's Regulations, which would have blotted the man's service record. Von Lindeiner felt that he did not have the authority to do so unless it was German orders that were being flouted, which Massey undoubtedly knew to be the case, but his request highlights again the consideration and concern that he had for his men, even the recalcitrant ones. The two senior officers were, in the words of Paul Brickhill, 'within the limitations of war … friends. Even if von Lindeiner had been a petty tyrant, Massey would have tried to keep on reasonable terms for the concessions he could worm out of him for the camp, but as it was, it was an association based on mutual respect.'[290]

All of this is not to say, though, that Massey went out of his way to make the Germans' lives easier. He could still be a thorn in their side, exemplified by the way in which *Appell* – the twice-daily roll-call – was conducted. In theory, the prisoners were to parade on the camp's sports field in neat and silent rows to be counted, with Martin at their head. But in practice 'the parade was a complete farce, purposely made so by the prisoners. They never formed up properly, but kept moving around and creating disturbances. The sick prisoners [who were supposed to be in their rooms] slipped from one room or barrack to another and were counted twice. The Germans carried out a superficial count as well as they could under the impossible circumstances but rarely attempted to take a second count, usually accepting the count falsified by the [British] Adjutant or falsifying their own count.'[291]

It is easy to imagine Massey allowing himself an inward smirk as he stood, correctly at attention and apparently innocently, facing the exasperated Simoleit and Pieber, well knowing what chaos was being created in the ranks behind him. He also encouraged less overt nefarious activities. As an example, Martin suggested to one Kriegie, a Canadian named Kingsley Brown, that he might consider becoming involved with propaganda work, given his former civilian occupation as a journalist. Brown readily agreed, and was astonished to discover that the scheme involved attaching brief notes written on tissue paper (declaring 'Hitler Kaput' and the like) to bees, which would then, so it was hoped, fly the messages out of the camp to the local German populace.[292] In February 1944, Martin asked one of the prisoners to have plans prepared for the construction of a radio transmitter,[293] presumably to be able to make contact with the Allies. By the following May, the majority of the parts had been gathered for assembly, dependent only on acquiring an amplifier, which was sourced from the camp cinema. For some reason, however, the transmitter was never completed.

Martin Massey's role as SBO involved far more than just the up-front administrative parts of the job that were visible to the Germans and the neutral international organisations. He well understood the desire of many of his men to escape, and he knew that a good number of them were, like 'Wings' Day, inveterate escapers. As Eric Williams put it: 'to us, escaping was a sport',[294] and some prisoners felt it was their duty to get away, even in the absence of any official British policy. Of course, by no means all of the Kriegies wanted to escape, and many were happy to sit out the rest of the war in the relative safety of a POW camp, having 'done their bit'.

Massey knew that his own chances of escaping were all but impossible given the extent of his wounds and the lack of mobility that they afforded him, but that did not stop him being fully involved with the escape organisation at Stalag Luft III, albeit in an executive, rather than active, capacity. The Sagan Escape Committee, known as the X Organisation, had been running since the camp first opened to control and coordinate all escape activities and attempts, and to allocate the required resources to any approved scheme. The committee members held individual responsibility for clothing; wire-escape schemes; security; tunnels; tunnel security; maps; intelligence; and forgery. The X Organisation had Martin's full support, and he attended their weekly meetings to listen to, and comment on, what was being planned.[295] All new Kriegie arrivals at the camp 'were assembled in the theatre, where the Senior British Officer explained to them the existence and rules of the Escape Organisation, and how it would help them'.[296] Martin also stressed the need for complete secrecy regarding the X Organisation, forbidding any overt reference to it or any of its members.[297] A similar organisation was established by the SNCO prisoners in the Centre Compound, and Massey decreed that a member of it would go to the officers' compound to learn how the X Organisation functioned. Consequently, a similar-looking officer and SNCO prisoner swapped identities and compounds for two weeks.[298]

The head of the X Organisation would naturally have needed to be a strong and charismatic leader, and in October 1942, just such a man took over the reins as 'Big X' when 'Wings' Day and a group of like-minded perpetual escapers (including the then 'Big X', Lieutenant Commander Jimmy Buckley, RN) were 'purged' from Stalag Luft III and transferred to a different camp. Squadron Leader Roger Bushell was a well-built, athletic, South African-born lawyer, a fighter pilot with a typically forceful personality. His Spitfire had been shot down on 23 May 1940 over France and he was taken prisoner, eventually arriving at Sagan after stopovers in other camps. Like Day (who he knew well from previous camps), Bushell was an experienced and persistent, if so far unsuccessful, escaper. Alex Cassie recalls that his 'presence filled the room, and sometimes there wasn't proper room for him and 'Pricky' Day ... he was an ominous-looking man'.[299] As befit his temperament, Bushell had very strong opinions on a variety of subjects and was 'not at all backwards in expressing them; whatever you felt about the opinions and what effect they had on you meant nothing to him at all. I didn't find him an agreeable character; I didn't find him likeable ... he didn't inspire me with anything except distaste', said

Fleet Air Arm observer Maurice Driver.[300] Alan Bryett found Bushell a 'very taciturn man; a man who said very little, who always looked rather grumpy and irritable and didn't communicate with anyone at all unless he was directly talking to them and then he was just asking questions to which he wanted the answer and that was the end of it'.[301]

But whatever the individual Kriegies' personal opinions of him, there was no doubt that Bushell's leadership of the X Organisation would be thoroughly dedicated, energetic and enthusiastic, and it was welcomed by many of those who wanted to break out of Sagan. Alex Cassie said that 'one felt that the whole thing was in safe hands and things would be organised properly'.[302] Managing such dynamic and egotistical personalities as Roger Bushell and 'Wings' (or 'Pricky') Day, who evidently sometimes clashed, would have been a test of Massey's own leadership skills, but the situation was eased by Day's transfer, prompting Massey to appoint Bushell as the new 'Big X'.[303] Martin obviously saw in Bushell a man of almost fanatical desire to escape and one who would get things done, but his decision to hand him the role is overlooked in most accounts of the Great Escape, which seem to imply that Bushell took over from Buckley by some form of divine right. As one source put it, 'it was natural that Bushell should take over escape activities'.[304] Natural it may have been, but it was still Massey's choice to give him the job.

Before Bushell's arrival, there had been several escape attempts from the East Compound, none of which had been wholly effective. Perhaps the one that came closest to success was from a tunnel through which three prisoners managed to get clear of the camp in the summer of 1942. They had intended to steal an aircraft from the nearby Sagan airfield but could not find one suitable, so instead they attempted to walk to Stettin on the Baltic coast where they would hopefully board a neutral ship. They were discovered sheltering under an upturned stolen rowing boat and returned to Sagan. There had also been four schemes to walk out of the camp using a variety of disguises (the first of which involved Day and others dressed as Germans); six attempts to get through or over the perimeter wire; and one so-called 'transport' scheme, whereby a prisoner hid in a laundry basket to be driven out of the camp on a lorry loaded with soiled linen. Similar efforts were also made by some of the SNCO Kriegies from the Centre Compound.

Punishment for re-captured prisoners was inevitable and, once back at Sagan, they were placed in solitary confinement – the 'cooler' – for varying lengths of time depending on their record as a repeat offender. Restrictions on food rations could be imposed on the individual while in the cooler, and, if the Germans' patience had been particularly tried, reprisals against the entire prisoner population were sometimes carried out. These mass measures included closure of the theatre, forbidding inter-compound games and sports, and the confiscation of Red Cross parcels (although this particular practice ceased after Massey's intervention in the winter of 1942).[305] Despite the penalties, though, the escape schemes continued with both Massey's and Bushell's full approval since they contributed hugely to the morale of the prisoners. The mood of the camp lifted when attempts were being planned, but would drop noticeably during periods of inactivity.[306]

Sport, too, was important to the Kriegies' well-being (and was often used as cover during the preparation of an escape to mask noise and to distract the guards' attention), and in January 1943, Massey was invited, as SBO, to formally open a new ice rink built by the prisoners. Skates were provided by the YMCA, and the inaugural event was an ice hockey tournament between two teams of Canadian prisoners, followed by the British versus the Americans. Apparently the British won by a single goal.[307]

From the early spring of 1943, the demographic and the structure of the camp began to change. The SNCO Kriegies were moved out to another camp and replaced by American aircrew prisoners, and a newly built compound, called the North Compound, was opened in the March of that year to accommodate the swelling numbers of British officers. When they first arrived, the American prisoners had very little, so Massey made sure they were provided with whatever items of food, clothing and toiletries could be sourced from the British POWs' own Red Cross parcels, and immediately helped them to settle into the routine of the camp. He also arranged for an American officer to represent the new arrivals at the senior Kriegies' meetings with the camp commandant. His accommodating approach towards the American captives was never forgotten by them.

Following an 'advance guard' of British prisoners who were moved into the new North Compound from the East Compound came transferees from other camps, one of whom was 'Wings' Day, fresh from yet another attempted getaway from a POW camp at Schubin, in northern Poland. Martin Massey was one of those moved into the North Compound, becoming its first SBO, and, one month later, he took on the position of SBO for the entire, enlarged, camp. But Day's biographer, Sydney Smith, says that when Day arrived back at Sagan from Schubin, Massey 'asked "Wings" to carry on as before in charge of the executive side of the job and of all the usual contacts with the Germans',[308] an account that is again at odds with the recollections of the other Kriegies already quoted above, as well as those of von Lindeiner and the official history of the camp,[309] and is probably a further example of the aggrandisement of Day by Smith and others who idolised him. One account says that Massey took over as senior British officer as late as the time of the Great Escape (the following March, almost a year later), and only then because Day was one of those 'going out in the escape',[310] which is plainly incorrect. There would have been no reason for Martin to have simply abdicated a role he had been performing solo for the past six months (if we accept that he had previously employed Day in a close advisory capacity), and moreover one that he had obviously been accomplishing extremely well. Furthermore, there was by now another group captain, Richard Kellett, at the camp, so if Massey had wanted to hand over responsibility, he would most likely have done so to an officer of equivalent rank rather than one below him. Also by this stage, Martin had an American counterpart, Colonel Charles Goodrich of the US Army Air Force, who undertook the role of senior American officer for the US prisoners.

Martin Massey's foot injury from being shot down in the Stirling was not healing properly. Twenty-five years' worth of war and sporting wounds, exacerbated by incarceration, the associated restricted diet and lack of specialist medical care, were all taking their toll on his lower limbs. He needed surgery, so on 28 May 1943 he was admitted to a hospital camp to get the treatment he required.[311] Stalag IX-C was a POW camp for mainly Army prisoners close to Bad Sulza, a town between Erfurt and Leipzig, that had under its administration a large POW hospital known as Reserve-Lazaret 1249 IX-C. Located in the town of Obermassfeld to the south-west of Erfurt itself, the hospital was housed in a three-storey stone building that had once been an agricultural college and later a hostel for the Nazi 'Strength Through Joy' workers' leisure programme. Although commanded by a German Army doctor, the facility was staffed by Allied medical personnel who had themselves been captured, mostly at Dunkirk and in the North African desert campaign. Despite being eligible for repatriation as non-combatant protected personnel, the doctors and orderlies had selflessly chosen to stay on in German captivity instead, to care for the wounded prisoners.

By the time Massey arrived there, Obermassfeld held almost 200 patients and boasted two operating theatres, wards, a plaster room and an X-ray room. Given the difficult circumstances under which they worked (the Germans could barely afford to spare scarce medical supplies, so POW hospitals were a low priority; however, the Red Cross were able to provide basic medicines, spectacles and occasionally artificial limbs), the service provided by the hospital staff was little short of miraculous, and many life-saving operations were performed there, including burns treatment, eye surgery, plastic surgery, neuro-surgery and orthopaedic procedures. One British Kriegie doctor at Obermassfeld said that the range and types of operation that he carried out there gave him far greater surgical experience than if he had not been captured and had remained with his unit behind Allied lines. The incredible work undertaken by one of the surgeons, Major John Sherman, was highlighted years later by a medical orderly called Bert Martin: 'The extraordinary accomplishments of Major John Sherman, who minus the essential tools initially, set to work skin grafting the scores of burnt airmen who came into his care. Pre-war he had been medical officer of the Cadbury's factory at Bournville and it would seem his insights into the skills of transplanting must have been limited. Yet he achieved remarkable results and many ex-airmen lived on to appreciate his timely intervention to, at least, prevent the grossest of distortions and disfigurement which must have been their fate otherwise. Apart from those who have expressed gratitude for his surgical intervention, he has remained unrecognised over the years.'[312]

According to von Lindeiner, it was he who had arranged for Massey to be treated at Obermassfeld, something that was only organised, he wrote, 'with great difficulty'.[313] After Martin had been there for around two months, von Lindeiner said that he received a telephone call from the German commandant of the hospital who informed him that Massey was 'under suspicion of inciting his fellow prisoners to mutiny'.[314] Von Lindeiner was asked if he considered Massey to be capable of such activities; if so, then military legal proceedings against him would be instigated. Martin's integrity and character were vouched for by the Sagan commandant, but von Lindeiner says he was again contacted several days later by his opposite number at Obermassfeld who asked if he would take Massey back. After 'serious consideration', he says that he agreed (even arranging for transport to collect and return Massey), a decision he stated was helped by a letter he had received from Martin's wife Peggy thanking him for his help in having Massey admitted to the hospital, but one he says he later came to regret, after the Great Escape.

This whole story seems completely ridiculous, however. Mutiny is arguably the most serious of all military crimes, punishable by death if proven by court martial, so considering Martin Massey's rigid sense of duty, leadership, correctness and bearing, it is utterly inconceivable that he would have promoted a course of action that would have placed his own life, and moreover the lives of his fellow patients (if found to be complicit) at risk. In fact, evidence exists to show that, far from urging rebellion at Obermassfeld, Martin continued in the same caring leadership role that he had carried out at Stalag Luft III. On 11 October 1943, 27-year-old Leading Aircraftman Charles Quilliam, a patient at the hospital, died of complications from a ruptured appendix, having already been badly injured while in the Western Desert with No. 30 Squadron, where he had been taken prisoner. The following day, Massey wrote a letter to Quilliam's mother:[315]

> Dear Mrs Quilliam
> I want to send you my sincerest sympathy in the loss of your son.
>
> I have been a patient in the hospital here with him for some months and frequently I have had talks with him. We easily found common ground for I also am in the Regular Air Force and, like him, have served in the Middle East.
>
> Although he had been seriously wounded and had spent a very long time in bed he always maintained a happy outlook, and showed that he had a wonderful spirit. Also, I was always very much impressed by his great interest in his Service, and he was hoping that, even although he had lost a limb, he might be allowed to continue to serve in the Royal Air Force in some capacity.
>
> Yes! Most certainly he was a great little man and in our small community here we shall miss him. God bless him and may he rest in peace; he had done his duty.
>
> Yours sincerely
> H.M. Massey
> Group Captain
> Royal Air Force

Mrs Quilliam wrote back some months later (due to the delays in POW mail getting through), after receiving the news.[316] In her letter to Major Sherman (by now senior RAMC doctor at the hospital), she expressed her 'many thanks for your kind letter and sympathy', and also her shock since her son had never told her that he was so ill. She added that 'after receiving

Major Henderson [the previous senior doctor] and Captain [sic] Massey's letters, I can see now how ill he really was, and how everything possible was done for him … I send my most grateful thanks to Major Henderson and all who did their utmost for my dear son'.

Martin's obvious rapport with, and concern for, Quilliam is heart-warming and typical of him, the more so considering the gulf in their respective ranks, and is surely not representative of the behaviour of a mutineer. Furthermore, a hospital full of seriously wounded men is hard-ly the ideal place to instigate an uprising; if Massey had really wanted to do that, then why not back at Sagan where the inmates were physically – not to mention mentally – more robust? Certainly, prisoners did try to escape (sometimes successfully) from Obermassfeld on more than one occasion, but 'mutiny' is a different matter altogether. Moreover, von Lindeiner's account of the timeline does not add up since, according to the Germans' own patient admissions record for the hospital,[317] Martin stayed at Obermassfeld for just a few days short of six months (a fact supported by the letter to Mrs Quilliam, written in October, five months after Martin arrived there), yet von Lindeiner says he reluctantly took him back at Sagan after less than half that period. There is also a further anomaly to the story, which will be discussed in a following chapter. The mutual trust and respect that Massey and von Lindeiner shared at that time is beyond doubt, and again it is extremely unlikely that Martin would have compromised that close relationship and his own reputation by committing such an act, especially if von Lindeiner had worked so hard to have him admitted to the hospital in the first place, as the commandant claimed. Whether or not von Lindeiner fabricated the tale will never be known for certain and, if he did, nor will his motives for doing so. Most likely, he was preparing the ground in his memoirs for an attempt at shift-ing a proportion of the blame for the deaths of the Great Escapers in Massey's direction by casting doubt on his integrity, more of which is also to follow in the next chapter. Suffice it to say, there is no mention of this highly implausible allegation anywhere other than in von Lindeiner's own account.

Massey was discharged from Obermassfeld on 24 November 1943[318] and arrived back at Stalag Luft III shortly afterwards, immediately step-ping back into his position of overall camp SBO, which had been occupied by Group Captain Douglas Wilson of the Royal Australian Air Force during his sojourn in hospital, while 'Wings' Day had filled in as SBO of the North Compound.[319] Even if von Lindeiner's memory had confused

Wing Commander Martin Massey DSO MC in full dress uniform, 1937.
(Courtesy Massey family)

An Armstrong-Whitworth Whitley Mk V, the type operated by No. 10 OTU at RAF Abingdon.
(Author's collection)

Group Captain Martin Massey (front group, centre) escorts His Majesty King George VI during a visit to RAF Abingdon. *(Author's collection)*

Massey with Marshal of the Royal Air Force Lord Trenchard (with walking stick) at RAF Abingdon. *(Courtesy Massey family)*

A Short Stirling, the RAF's first four-engine strategic heavy bomber. *(Author's collection)*

The crew of No. 7 Squadron's ill-fated Short Stirling N3750. The photograph was taken immediately post-war after all seven men had been repatriated from their respective POW camps and reunited. Rear row L-R: Geoffrey Booth (Navigator); Evan Williams (Wireless Operator); Brian Iverson (Flight Engineer). Front row L-R: Ray Boag (Air Gunner); Norman Winch (Pilot); Martin Massey; John Hankin (Air Gunner). *(Courtesy Pino Lombardi)*

Above left: Oberleutnant Doctor Horst Patuschka, the Luftwaffe night fighter pilot who more than likely shot N3750 down in the early hours of 2 June 1942. *(Author's collection)*. Above right: Oberst Friedrich von Lindeiner-Wildau, the Commandant of Stalag Luft III, Sagan. *(Courtesy Massey family)*

Massey at Dulag Luft, shortly after being shot down in June 1942, before being sent to Sagan.
(Courtesy Massey family)

Massey (centre) with 'Wings' Day (left) and Sergeant James 'Dixie' Deans (right) at Sagan.
(Courtesy Massey family)

Martin in conversation with Hauptmann Pieber at Stalag Luft III. *(Courtesy Massey family)*

Martin Massey (with crutches) attends a prisoners' football match at Stalag Luft III during a visit by the International Red Cross on 15 September 1942. *(ICRC)*

Massey with an official of either the Red Cross or the Protecting Power, von Lindeiner (second from right) and (left) Major Simoleit. On the right is Massey's adjutant, Squadron Leader Bill Jennens.
(Courtesy Massey family)

Massey with Herr Gabriel Narville, an official of the Protecting Power and, on the right, Wing Commander Bob Stanford-Tuck. *(Courtesy Massey family)*

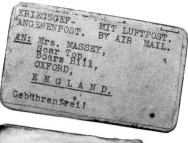

Above: Martin (left) making a point to von Lindeiner (centre) and Simoleit (right) at Sagan. Note Massey's characteristic walking stick and flying boot on his injured left foot. *(Courtesy Massey family)*

Right: A set of 'trench art' RAF sweetheart wings, made at Sagan and sent by Martin from the camp to Peggy. *(Author)*

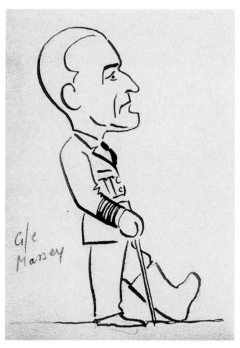

Caricature of Massey drawn at Sagan by fellow Kriegie Ley Kenyon. *(Courtesy Ben van Drogenbroek)*

Squadron Leader Roger Bushell - 'Big X'. *(Author's collection)*

Reserve-Lazaret 1249 Stalag IX-C at Obermassfeld, the POW hospital where Massey was treated and allegedly accused of inciting mutiny in 1943. *(ICRC)*

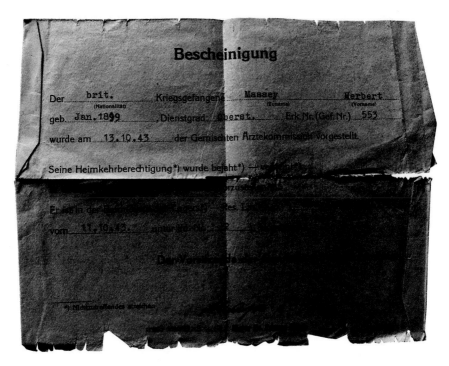

Massey's repatriation certificate issued by the Mixed Doctoral Committee at Obermassfeld, dated 13 October 1943. *(Courtesy Massey family)*

Martin (front row, fifth from left) with other repatriates, some of them amputees, at Annaburg. *(Courtesy Massey family)*

Martin (right) with Flight Lieutenant Vincent 'Paddy' Byrne at Stalag IV/DZ Annaburg, awaiting repatriation. The two men knew a great deal of detail about the Great Escape and its aftermath and were rushed home for debriefing. Note the black diamond on both men's upper left sleeve, sewn on at Sagan to commemorate the murdered Great Escapers. *(Courtesy Massey family)*

Left: Doctor Robert Schirmer of the International Red Cross (left) pictured on the dockside at Marseille in front of the *Gradisca*. Schirmer approached Martin for details of the shootings of the Great Escapers prior to Massey boarding the ship. Below left: Allied military repatriates crowd the deck railings of the *Gradisca* as she leaves Marseille bound for Barcelona, 16 May 1944. *(ICRC)*

The German hospital ship *Gradisca* alongside at Marseille docks on 16 May 1944 before departing for Barcelona with Massey and over 1,000 other repatriates aboard. *(ICRC)*

Above: The US-chartered Swedish ship *Gripsholm* awaits departure following the transfer of Allied repatriates from the *Gradisca* at Barcelona on 18 May 1944. This picture was taken from the deck of the *Gradisca*; the warehouse used to facilitate the POW exchange is to the left. Right: British medical orderlies await permission to take a disabled serviceman aboard the *Gripsholm* for the journey home. *(ICRC)*

Massey in a reflective mood at home after repatriation. The scar from the gunshot wound of 4 February 1917 is clearly visible on his left cheek. *(Courtesy Massey family)*

Martin and Peggy share tea at Croyde after his repatriation. He still wears the flying boot on his injured left foot. *(Courtesy Massey family)*

A sketch map of Stalag Luft III North Compound drawn by Martin Massey as part of his evidence to the RAF Board of Inquiry into the murders of the 50 escapees from Sagan. *(Crown Copyright)*

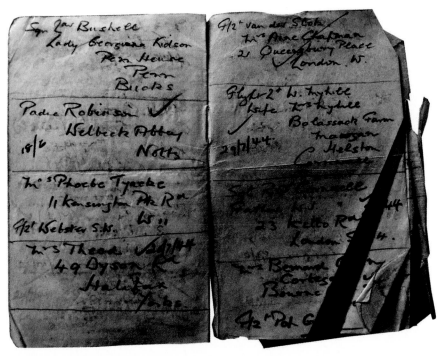

Martin's notebook of names and addresses of the friends and relatives of British POWs, compiled at Sagan, whom he promised to visit after repatriation. The pages are only around two inches high and are gossamer-thin to enable the notebook to be hidden. He has marked off those he has visited with a tick and the date. Roger Bushell's details are at top left (Lady Georgina Kidston was an old flame), and those of Bram van der Stok, one of only three Great Escapers to make a home run, are at top right. *(Courtesy Massey family)*

Air Commodore Massey (seated front, centre) with the officers of the RAF Selection Board at Ramridge House, Andover in 1948. *(Courtesy Massey family)*

Air Commodore Herbert Martin Massey CBE DSO MC 1898-1976 Senior British Officer at Stalag Luft iii Sagan who authorised 'The Great Escape' was born here

Hilton and Marston History Group

The commemorative Blue Plaque at Hilton House unveiled in 2016. *(Courtesy Helena Coney)*

Martin and his wife Peggy outside Buckingham Palace again, probably after the investiture of his CBE in 1950 (Peggy appears to be holding the award in its box and is probably wearing his Caterpillar Club brooch on her left lapel). Note how he holds his wounded left foot, in what looks to be an orthopaedic shoe.
(Courtesy Massey family)

the dates, would he really have allowed Martin to resume the SBO role if he had indeed been accused of inciting mutiny at Obermassfeld? It seems unlikely – he could simply have kept Wilson on in the job instead.

A month before Massey's return to Sagan, the Kriegies there had scored a major success against the Germans. Three British officers escaped from the camp on the night of 29/30 October, using a tunnel dug from beneath a home-made gymnasium vaulting horse (built by the prisoners from Red Cross parcel packing cases) under the wire of the East Compound. The so-called 'Wooden Horse' escape has since entered Second World War POW folklore, with a book and a film produced about the story post-war. All three men succeeded in reaching Britain, providing a major fillip to the morale of the prisoners back at Sagan, but 'Big X', Roger Bushell, was already hatching a far bigger, even more ambitious, plan.

Chapter Eight

Barefaced Murder:
October 1943 – March 1944

Roger Bushell's idea for a mass breakout from Sagan took root in the winter of 1942/43, before the move into the North Compound. Sensing an opportunity to begin tunnelling from the new compound as soon as it was opened, he assembled a team of experts around him, all hardened escapers, and began to formulate the plan. Three tunnels, code-named Tom, Dick and Harry, were to be dug, all starting from huts within the North Compound with the aim of getting 200 prisoners away – it was a scheme of unprecedented proportions. Paul Brickhill says that Bushell took the proposal to Massey who 'listened with satisfaction' but urged caution on Bushell's part; 'Big X' was too well known to the Germans as a serial escaper and would be watched closely, so Martin apparently warned him to stay in the background as the brains behind the plan rather than as a worker.[320] Martin gave his complete support to Bushell's idea, telling him 'I'll see you have the whole camp behind you. Let me know of anything or anyone you want and I'll make it an order.'[321]

Reconnaissance of the North Compound before it was flooded with Kriegies was the first task on the list, so Bushell asked Martin for his help. Massey duly suggested to von Lindeiner that 'a few POW working parties might go over and help in the new compound',[322] to which the commandant agreed. The 'working parties' of course consisted of Bushell and his accomplices who surveyed the area, paced out distances, and assessed angles. As the details became clearer, Bushell went to Martin 'every day … and they talked over the master plan'.[323] Massey's full backing of the escape scheme is confirmed by Alan Bryett who said that 'it was [Bushell's] vision completely, encouraged I think I must say by Wing Commander Day, and encouraged by Group Captain Massey; I mean, those three at the top had all agreed it. Group Captain Massey or Day could have vetoed the plan right from the start, but the enormity of it [was] known by the people at the top, and the risks of it were known by the people at the top as well'.[324]

As far as Bryett was concerned, the main threat to the operation was the discovery of the tunnels, but the question of knowing the broader hazards, and any warnings thereof, of an undertaking of such magnitude is an important one when considering Massey's role in the Great Escape. As previously mentioned, the punishment for failed escape attempts was solitary confinement for the individuals concerned (with the very worst, most persistent, offenders being shipped off to Colditz) or restrictions of privileges for the wider prisoner population. There had been some shooting incidents at the camp, though, since the guards' orders (according to Martin) allowed them 'to fire into the camp for what you might call minor disobedience of orders'.[325] In January 1943 von Lindeiner had written formally to Massey following a prisoners' riot (which had apparently injured some of the guards) to warn him that 'the officers' barracks will be closed at 1730 henceforth. The [guard] towers around the officers' compound will get reinforcement and mechanical weapons [presumably meaning automatic weapons]. Everybody will be shot at without warning who leaves barracks after 1730. Should a stray bullet get into a hut, this would be to the debit of those who cannot submit to a discipline which is beyond question for officers according to German ideas.'[326]

In the main, shootings had occurred when Kriegies had tried to retrieve balls beyond the inner 'warning' fence – a low fence on the compound side to keep prisoners away from the main fence – which was forbidden. None of those shot at were wounded, however.[327] But there were a few more serious firing episodes, one of which involved Martin directly. Shortly before the move to the North Compound, one of the prisoners, a Royal Navy officer named John Kiddell, had apparently suffered a nervous breakdown and was causing Massey 'great anxiety'.[328] Massey appealed to von Lindeiner to have the man repatriated on medical grounds, but for some reason the German authorities refused to grant the request. On the SBO's insistence, he was removed to isolation and, not long afterwards, the Red Cross visited the camp and the unfortunate Kiddell's mental health was discussed. He was subsequently moved into the camp's sick quarters, but he managed to climb out on to the roof, clad only in his pyjamas, whereupon he began to shout. A patrolling guard ordered him back inside, but Kiddell jumped to the ground instead and ran to the main security fence and began to climb. The sentry opened fire at close range, and killed him.[329] Kiddell was clearly not in control of his faculties, so whether or not he can be classed as being shot and killed while attempting to escape is debatable, but the incident does show a willingness on the part of the guards to pull the trigger if they felt it necessary.

In another case, on the night of 29 December 1943 a sentry fired 'a number of shots into one barrack without excuse or apparent purpose' hitting an American, Lieutenant Colonel John D. Stevenson, in the process. Although seriously wounded in the left leg and hospitalised for the next six months, Stevenson did not die but was left 'somewhat crippled'.[330] Massey also recalled another American prisoner being shot, without warning, and this time killed for not being inside his hut during an air raid, which was against regulations.[331] The unfortunate airman was Corporal Cline C. Miles, a kitchen orderly, who was standing in the cook-house doorway, facing the inside. He was hit by a guard's bullet in the right shoulder, the round exiting through Miles's mouth, killing him instantly.[332] On another occasion, a prisoner was spotted outside his hut after curfew and was shot in the stomach five times – incredibly, he survived.[333] Such incidents were fortunately rare, however, and, thus far at least, were confined to within the camp's boundaries. Despite their infrequence, though, Massey did take up the issue of the shootings 'continuously' with the Protecting Power to try to get them stopped. He later said that the Protecting Power had 'endeavoured to get out orders [to prevent sentries from opening fire] and have not been able to get them'.[334] Notwithstanding his objection to the guards' orders, Martin did acknowledge that he and the other Kriegies were well aware of the German rules of engagement (allowing them to open fire) and that the shootings within the camp had therefore been legitimate.[335]

Von Lindeiner wrote in his memoirs that he, along with other POW camp commandants, was given a verbal order (which he refers to as 'Step III') at a meeting early in 1944 from the German Army High Command, on Hitler's instruction, which specified that British and American POWs who were recaptured after escaping were not to be returned to their camps immediately, but instead would remain in the custody of the Gestapo. The High Command would then decide who should be returned and who would be kept on as guests of the Gestapo. Von Lindeiner further stated that a so-called 'bullet decree' from the Gestapo, stating that all escaping prisoners (with the exception of British and American POWs who were to be handed over to the Gestapo) were to be taken to the Mauthausen concentration camp and shot, was 'not then, or later, given to us'.[336] The

Sagan commandant professed to have been profoundly disturbed by Step III since it flew in the face of the honourable military traditions with which he had been imbued – he wrote that it 'filled me with deep worries'. His concerns prompted him to call a meeting with Simoleit and Pieber, at which he swore them to 'absolute secrecy' about the order and told them that he could not, on his honour, countenance following such a command, so he must therefore have realised, or at least suspected, what the implications of the order were – those who remained with the Gestapo were extremely unlikely to have been allowed to live because that was simply not how that despicable organisation operated.

What he says he did next is extraordinary: he held a meeting with Massey and the other senior Kriegies, plus the camp's clergy and doctors, but not to inform them of Step III or of his concerns about it; instead he warned them that he was anxious that any escaping prisoner would be at risk of reprisals from the German civilian population because of the deaths and damage being caused by the Allied bombing of the country. When he spoke of this meeting in his testimony to the 1947 war crimes court (at the trial of those accused of the murders of the recaptured Great Escapers), it was in somewhat matter-of-fact terms – he said that he was 'uneasy' about the order because he thought that the prisoners might 'get into difficulties or that they might be sent to a stricter camp', but he thought that mass execution was 'impossible'. When asked by the judge advocate specifically if he had been given any notification from higher authority that 'more stringent measures would be taken against prisoners if there was a mass escape', his response was a confusion of words about prisoner transport and handcuffs. Yet in his memoirs, written years later once he had had time to reflect on the events of the escape, his role in it, and his treatment at the hands of the German military authorities (more of which below), von Lindeiner paints a far more vivid picture of the meeting. He seemingly appealed to the assembled senior POW representatives: 'I therefore beg of you, the rightful representatives of the men incarcerated here in Stalag Luft III, to exert your influence in such a manner as to discourage escape attempts of any kind … I beg of you to think of the mothers, women and children of your friends, whose happiness will be in jeopardy if some young hotheads try something foolish … I beg of you to take my words seriously and act accordingly.'[337]

In closing, he said that within the confines of the camp, he was responsible for the lives of the prisoners and would protect them, but that outside of the wire, he was powerless. The full text of the rather lengthy speech that von Lindeiner says that he gave is a masterclass of drama and rhetoric, quoting such wild claims as children on their way to school being gunned down from the skies by Allied airmen. If he did indeed give the speech verbatim, and with passion, as quoted in his memoirs, then his performance would have been worthy of an Academy Award. The commandant also wrote that 'at the time I made this speech, nobody even dreamed that Adolf Hitler would ever issue such orders as the shooting of 50 escaped and recaptured POWs',[338] which is an unusual, not to mention contradictory, statement given that he knew of Step III before the meeting, which is why he convened it.

Did the meeting, though, ever actually take place? Neither Massey nor 'Wings' Day (who would have surely been present as a senior prisoner) make any mention of it in their later testimonies, and no record of it appears either in the aforementioned US Army Air Force report into Sagan (the senior American officer would also have been in attendance) or the British official history of the camp. If we accept that it did happen and that von Lindeiner did not make any specific mention of Step III or of his fears about it, then as far as Massey and the others present would have been concerned, it was simply a warning about possible violence from rogue elements of the general public, not about being detained and possibly executed by the Gestapo. Such cautionary advice would probably not have come as a great surprise to the Allied prisoners anyway, given that British civilians had apparently sometimes carried out similar acts against downed Luftwaffe aircrew during the Blitz in 1940.[339] Von Lindeiner then went on to say that, because he seemingly had a sense that something big was being planned by the Kriegies, 'to explore all possible avenues of preventing a major disaster, I finally visited the most influential personality amongst the British POWs, Group Capt Massey, and talked at length and rather seriously with him. I reminded him that after two years of working together he should know me well enough to give my warnings the attention they deserved, and I repeated with emphasis the warnings given earlier to the POWs.'[340]

But again, it is doubtful that this second, supposedly lengthy, meeting ever happened since Martin makes no reference to it (or of being given any kind of warning whatsoever direct from the commandant) in his sworn testimony to the subsequent RAF Board of Inquiry, and nor does von Lindeiner himself mention it at the war crimes tribunal. If it did occur, then von Lindeiner by his own admission once again chose not to take Massey into his confidence and tell him explicitly about Step III; instead he merely repeated 'the warnings given earlier' about possible harsh treatment by the German public. Von Lindeiner perhaps felt that he could not tell the assembled senior prisoners about Step III at the first meeting as to do so would have been contrary to his orders, but surely he could have confided in Martin, in private and man to man. It seems very strange that he did not, given the mutual trust and respect that existed between them and his professed desire to avert a 'major disaster'; had he done so, Martin Massey would most likely have taken the direct warning seriously and either stopped the Great Escape or at least have drastically scaled it back.

As it was, in the absence of any specific, explicit, warning from the commandant or any of the other senior German security staff about Step III, and given the relatively benign nature of punishments for escaping up to that point, Massey could not have known exactly what risks those who would attempt the Great Escape would be facing. For a man with his sense of duty, integrity, and loyalty to his men, it is implausible that he would have knowingly and willingly sanctioned a plan that had a good chance of sending them to their deaths. It could be that von Lindeiner thought that the inference from what he had said was sufficient, but whatever the truth, in his memoirs he used Massey's apparent disregard of his 'serious warning' as the basis of his assertion that Martin had 'broken the mutual trust that I thought we had for each other'.[341] In his final treatise on the subject, he said: 'I was rather deeply hurt when I found out later that Group Capt Massey not only knew every detail of the plan of his subordinates [did von Lindeiner seriously expect the SBO to be ignorant of what was going on?] but also approved their actions. I believed that he, being responsible for the well-being and future of so many young men, would stop them from going through with this senseless, if not childish, adventure. How bitterly I was deceived.'[342]

These statements, coupled with von Lindeiner's fanciful account of Massey's alleged 'mutiny' while at Obermassfeld, cast doubt on his own integrity, and would appear to be an attempt to distance himself from culpability for the Great Escape and association with the Nazi war crimes committed in the wake of it. The language he uses is excessively passionate, and it would be highly improbable that an officer of proud Prussian military heritage, upright and stiff, would have repeatedly 'begged' the senior Kriegies to intervene, for example. To paraphrase Shakespeare, von Lindeiner 'doth protest too much', it seems.

At around the same time that Step III was issued, one of the German senior NCO guards, Unteroffizier[343] von Schilling, allegedly told a prisoner,

Flight Lieutenant Sedgewick Webster, that 'the Commandant was very
worried that there might be a mass escape and that if this took place, he
would be compelled to act in a manner that he would regret as an officer
and a gentleman'.[344] Von Schilling told Webster that the commandant had
recently attended meetings regarding escapes, and that 'he implied that he
had been told that if there was any escape the consequences would be very
serious, not only for the prisoners who escaped but for the prisoners left
behind', and that he (Schilling) had been asked by the commandant to get
the message through to the prisoners. Another Kriegie, Flight Lieutenant
John Grocott, said that he was told by a different guard that if another mass
escape occurred, 'very drastic action would be taken', and that 'if there is
another escape, there will never be another'.[345] Massey later declared that
Grocott's information had never reached him, and he made no mention
of hearing anything from Webster either (Grocott confirmed that the
message to Webster 'was intended for the SBO; I do not think it actually
got that far') and that, in any case, 'I do not attach much importance to the
threat mentioned by Grocott as threats of a like nature had been made in
the past both directly and indirectly with a view to dissuading prisoners
from attempting to escape. I never got the impression that the [German]
High Command had decided on any sudden change of policy towards
escaping.'[346]

Some commentators have used the exchanges between Webster, Grocott
and the German guards as further evidence that the prisoners were warned
of the dire consequences of a large breakout, but this suggestion does not
entirely stand up to scrutiny. Firstly, since Step III was a verbal, rather than
written order (presumably because it was unlawful) from the German
High Command to its senior officers, then the German NCOs could not
have seen and read it. Secondly, von Lindeiner said that he had sworn his
staff officers to secrecy about Step III, so they would not have passed word
down the chain of command against his instructions and it is highly
unlikely that, having demanded an oath of silence from his officers, he
himself would then have bypassed them and given details of the order to
his NCOs. And, as discussed, if the commandant had wanted a warning
to reach the SBO, he could simply have told Massey himself rather than
rely on 'Chinese whispers'. There was also no reason for the guards to have
been told of the content of the order since it did not directly affect them,
and they would not be carrying it out since they were responsible for the
internal security of the camp, not for hunting escapees outside the wire.
Grocott stated that 'the message came from the Commandant, saying that

if there was another escape, that he, as an officer and gentleman, would very much resent having to put into force punishment that would be put into force [sic]',[347] a sentiment backed by Webster's account, but von Lindeiner would not have been required to put Step III 'into force', since it placed matters into the hands of the Gestapo rather than his. Furthermore, it seems odd, given Webster and Grocott's evident belief in what they were told by the Germans (Grocott said that 'I feel absolutely convinced that he [the German NCO] knew of something of this nature which would be put into force'),[348] that neither of them seems to have gone to any great lengths to ensure that Martin received the information. More likely, as Massey averred, these were throw-away comments from the guards to the prisoners designed to put them off escaping, which after all was their job.

One further statement on the subject, this time from 'Wings' Day, is also worthy of mention. Day testified shortly after the war that 'I remember while I was at Sagan before the [Great] escape, the Commandant, with whom I was usually on good terms, said more than once that we should avoid making a "mass escape" because the Gestapo would come and would take over the whole camp. He had often said this since the "big walk-out" escape in 1943.'[349] The 'big walk-out' was a mass escape attempt in June 1943 at Sagan when almost forty prisoners, escorted by some disguised as German guards, tried to get away while on their way to being deloused. Day also mentioned a large-scale attempt he had been involved with at Schubin after which the Gestapo had indeed then arrived and 'taken over' the camp, but only for one day. So, von Lindeiner had himself evidently been using the threat of Gestapo involvement as a disincentive to escaping for almost a year before Step III was ever communicated to him. Little wonder, then, that such warnings as there had been attracted scant attention from the prisoner population. As one of the Great Escapers, 'Jimmy' James, wrote: 'Nobody thought seriously, if indeed they thought at all, of the possible, or probable, consequences of a mass escape on this scale.'[350] James also said that 'it is doubtful if knowledge of the contents of the two Gestapo orders would have made any difference [to the Great Escape]',[351] which again implies that the Kriegies had not been warned of Step III, but in any case such an assertion and any associated decisions were not his (or even Bushell's) to make – they were Massey's, and as already discussed above, the SBO would probably have taken a very different view had he been made aware of Step III and the 'bullet decree'.

Work on digging the three tunnels began by mid-April 1943. Each was to be large and elaborate, with the idea that if one was discovered the Germans would search no further given the scale of what they had found, thinking that such a huge project could not possibly be repeated elsewhere in the camp. Everything about the tunnels was a triumph of ingenuity and problem-solving, from the sheer length of each tunnel to the miniature railway lines to transport the spoil from the tunnel face to the entrance; the way the spoil was then disposed of; the ventilation system; the lighting system (the German electricity supply was tapped to provide electric lighting, with margarine lamps as backup); and the shoring-up of the tunnel walls to prevent collapses. And then there were all the other activities that would go along with the engineering, such as security, intelligence gathering, fake documents, clothing, food, money, map-making – everything the 200 would need once they had exited the tunnels. It was a massive undertaking, all of which has been covered in great detail in other books.

By July, the Germans had begun building another new camp compound where the exit to Tom was planned to be, so time was of the essence. All efforts were put into Tom to get it finished before the new compound was opened, so Harry was sealed up, and Dick was used as a repository for the spoil from Tom.[352] On 10 October, Tom was some 285 feet long and progressing well when it was discovered and subsequently partly destroyed by the Germans. Harry then became the focus of the scheme, with the discovery of Tom apparently succeeding in decoying the guards' attention, as had been Bushell's original intent. Work continued on Harry for a short while until it was closed up temporarily – there was little point in completing it before the following spring when it would be used (escapes were rare in the deep cold of the Silesian winter) – in case it was discovered or collapsed in the meantime.

Tunnelling began again in earnest in January 1944, but there was a setback. A satellite camp of Stalag Luft III, some three miles west at Belaria, was opened to accommodate the overspill from Sagan. Some of the main architects of Harry, including its chief engineer and security officer, were among the first batch of 500 from Sagan who were sent to the new camp, so others had to step into their shoes. Finally, though, Harry was ready. The construction work was completed by 14 March 1944 when the tunnel had reached 345 feet long and a vertical shaft reached up from it to within 9 inches of the ground above.[353] With still a few tasks to be finished here and there, the date set for the escape was 23 March, when the moon would next be favourable. As it was, a fall of snow postponed the operation for twenty-four hours.

Those who were to go were chosen, Massey recalled, by ballot – with 160 in the main party and another 40 in reserve,[354] – although he apparently personally vetoed the selection of two experienced tunnellers since he wanted to retain their expertise for future escapes.[355] Paul Brickhill recalled that Martin gave those selected a 'final warning' just before they went, telling them that 'if you are caught, some of you may not be treated very well. I do not think that the Germans would dare to take extreme measures as you are protected by the Geneva Convention, but do please avoid any provocation.'[356] In view of what von Lindeiner had told him and the other senior prisoners about possible mistreatment by German civilians (again, accepting that the commandant did actually give such a caution), Massey evidently gave as strong a warning as he felt was needed, but obviously did not believe that it was necessary to call the breakout off.

The first men out of the tunnel broke the surface at around 10.30 p.m. on 24 March 1944 and headed for the cover of the woods. At 4.50 a.m. on the 25th, a shot was heard by those still waiting their turn in Harry – the game was up. In all, seventy-six men had got away before the escape was detected (inevitably, 'Wings' Day was among them) but four others were arrested at the tunnel exit. The first few were recaptured the same day, and from then on over the next few days, most of the others were also caught, with the last one apprehended on 8 April. Only three made 'home-runs' (none of whom were British), but a few, including Bushell, managed to travel several hundred miles from Sagan before they were discovered. For the seventy-three who were subsequently recaptured, Step III was enacted and they were handed over to the Gestapo. Fifty of them were executed – murdered. The first group was shot on 29 March, and the last on or around 6 April.[357] Roger Bushell was one of those killed, but 'Wings' Day was sent, along with a small band of others, to the concentration camp at Sachsenhausen, just north of Berlin. Unsurprisingly, he broke out of there too, only to be caught once again.

At Stalag Luft III on 25 March, the morning after the night before, Massey recorded that there were the usual additional post-escape *Appells* and extensive searches, but during the course of the day 'the Gestapo came down and practically took over the running of the camp'.[358] The Gestapo's first targets were the camp's guards, who were investigated for evidence of any collusion in the escape. The first news that the prisoners heard about those who had been picked up locally outside the wire came after four or five days, via the more benevolent of the guards, although at that stage

only names were given – there were no reports of any deaths. But on 6
April, all that was to change. Hauptmann Pieber visited Martin in his
quarters shortly before 11.00 a.m. and was evidently in a state of some dis-
tress when he told the SBO that the commandant wished to see him
immediately. Massey knew Pieber well, and asked what was wrong, but
Pieber said that he was unable to comment, conceding only that 'the matter is the most terrible that I have had anything to do with since I was in
Prisoner of War camps'.[359] Massey summoned his interpreter, Squadron
Leader Sidney Murray, to accompany him, and when they arrived at the
commandant's office they were received by an Oberstleuntant[360] named
Erich Cordes[361] who had been second in command of Sagan for some weeks
and was placed temporarily in command of the camp since von Lindeiner
had been relieved of his post on the 26 March, the day after the breakout
had been discovered. Massey later said that he heard that von Lindeiner
had had 'a nervous breakdown owing to his interrogation by the Gestapo
and had been confined to his room awaiting court-martial'.[362]

The formality with which Massey and Murray were received by Cordes
did not bode well (there was no welcoming handshake as had been customary with von Lindeiner) – something was obviously wrong. Cordes
told Martin that he had to give him some information about the escape
from his higher authority, and that he proposed to read it out verbatim so
that Massey had the exact wording of the High Command statement.
Cordes then proceeded, in German with Murray translating, to read the
report aloud: 'The prisoners of war are to be informed of the following
statement orally and on the notice-board as well: In the course of an
enterprise to recapture British Air Force officers, who had escaped in a
large number, some of them offered resistance on being arrested. After
recapture, others tried again to escape on the transport back to their
camp. In these cases, the firearms had to be made use of. 41 prisoners of
war were hereby shot.'[363]

Massey, stunned, asked for a copy of the report but Cordes refused, saying he was not authorised to give one but would try to obtain permission.
Martin asked for more information regarding the circumstances of the
shootings, and whether all were dead or some wounded, but Cordes
refused to answer any questions, apparently on the orders of his higher
authority, only repeating what was in the statement. All he would say was
that all had been killed – there had been no woundings. Cordes did, however, concede to giving Massey a list of the names of the dead as soon as
he could, and to allow him to write to the Protecting Power direct, rather

than through the German High Command, which would have taken weeks for the letter to get through to the Swiss authorities. Martin also said that he required to be informed of what had happened to the corpses so that he could arrange for burial and the return of their personal effects.[364] He later stated that he had discovered (from conversations with 'various members of the Commandant's staff') that Cordes had been told of the shootings by telephone as early as 4 April and had been ordered then to inform the SBO, but had refused to do so until he had been given written confirmation.[365]

Massey and Murray returned to the North Compound in a state of shock, apparently joined by a 'shaken' Pieber, who asked them to believe that the Luftwaffe had had nothing to do with the killings, and wished not to be associated with them.[366] Martin then immediately called a meeting of his senior prisoner team, and after having informed them of what Cordes had just told him, he then decided to address the wider Kriegie population. Gathering the room leaders in the camp theatre, he told them 'the bare facts' as he knew them, and ordered that the whole camp should go into mourning, with the stoppage of all games and entertainments.[367] He understood that the worst thing that could now happen was for the prisoners to allow their emotions to get the better of them and cause trouble in the camp, which, with the Gestapo now running the show, might well lead to further bloodshed. He emphasised to them the importance of maintaining discipline throughout the camp and ordered that all contact with the Germans should be limited to essential communications on official matters.[368] This order was taken literally by the inmates, and they would 'merely stare them in the eyes and say nothing',[369] with only Massey and his adjutant, Bill Jennens, speaking directly to the Germans.

Paul Brickhill remembers that Massey's announcement about the shootings was met with a 'stunned silence' and a degree of disbelief; 'most of us thought the whole thing was a bluff, that the 41 had been moved to another camp and that we, believing they were dead, would be intimidated into stopping all escape activity'.[370] This notion would wane with most of the Kriegies in time, but would persist among a small group of them. Another of those present in the theatre, John Hartnell-Beavis, later wrote that Massey's announcement was met with 'an amazed gasp throughout the hall. The news was stunning, almost unbelievable. We had anticipated a few casualties, but 43 [sic] was over 50%.'[371] Hartnell-Beavis also recalled Massey saying that 'the Kommanadant [sic] wishes me to express his sympathy and assures me that the news was as great a shock to him as it is to us',[372] but such sentiments are not confirmed by Martin or any other commentator. That evening's *Appell* was conducted in silence by the prisoners, with none of the usual misbehaviour; it was a small act of defiance on their part. The following day, the 7th, was Good Friday, and a memorial service was held both at *Appell* and later on in the theatre, with each prisoner wearing a black diamond sewn on to the upper left arm of their tunic as a mark of respect for the dead.

While the camp absorbed the dreadful news, Martin Massey went about his sombre duties as senior British officer. He first wrote to the Protecting Power on 6 April, as Cordes had permitted, giving them the 'information I had obtained from the Commandant and requested them to make full enquiries concerning the circumstances of each individual shooting and requesting them to notify the British Government of the whole occurrence'.[373] Then he asked Cordes that any bodies of the dead that were returned to Sagan be buried in the camp cemetery, but this request was refused as it was against regulations, even for the corpses of German civilians and soldiers.[374] Next, he wrote a second letter to the Protecting Power on the 7th, this time 'suggesting to them that they should visit the camp to make enquiries into the circumstances [of the shootings]',[375] stressing that even if they did not get any information from the Germans, then the fact that they had at least made such a visit would help 'in view of the strained tension' in the camp. Massey said that he wrote this second letter 'because I did not know what might happen in the camp since it seemed obvious to me and to everyone with whom I discussed it that the shooting was a case of barefaced murder'.[376]

He then wrote one further letter, asking to be granted an interview with the head of the Luftwaffe, Herman Göring. Massey's rationale for this request was that, since the prisoners were in the custody of the Luftwaffe, they therefore fell under Göring's jurisdiction as the Luftwaffe's supreme commander, and that 'I, as Senior British Officer, was filled with the gravest misgivings about the whole occurrence and felt justified in asking for information from the highest authority, and for Göring's own view on the whole matter as from one soldier, though enemy soldier, to another.'[377] Whether or not Göring ever saw the letter is not known (but doubtful), although Cordes did show Massey a covering note on file a couple of days later that seemed to confirm that the request had been sent to the Luftwaffe headquarters in Berlin. Martin pressed daily for more information from the commandant, but nothing more was forthcoming. However, he did sense that the Luftwaffe was extremely worried about the shootings, saying that 'up to a point this was natural as the Germans had known some of the prisoners who had been shot for a long time. It went, however, further than this. They appeared concerned by the fact that the shooting on such a scale must have been carried out contrary to any established practice or principle followed by those in charge of prisoners of war. They endeavoured to impress that it was a Gestapo affair carried out under the Gestapo code and had nothing to do with the Luftwaffe. The key point of all discussion on the matter was that there had been no woundings and no-one, either German or British, believed that anything such as described in the German High Command letter could have happened without there having been a few woundings.'[378]

Massey decided that a committee should be formed by the prisoners to gather and record any and all evidence about what had happened, probably with a view to passing on a file to the Protecting Power in due course. Just as he gave that order, though, came surprising news that was to have severe repercussions for the Germans in the years to come.

Chapter Nine

Repatriation and Retribution:
March 1944 – June 1945

The terms of Article 72 of the 1929 Geneva Convention allowed for the negotiated repatriation of prisoners of war, stating: 'Throughout the duration of hostilities and for humane considerations, belligerents may conclude agreements with a view to the direct repatriation or hospitalization in a neutral country of able-bodied prisoners of war who have undergone a long period of captivity.'

Britain and Germany did discuss swaps of able-bodied prisoners under the Article, but none ever took place. However, successful repatriations of seriously ill or wounded POWs, and of protected prisoners such as doctors, medics and padres (as well as civilian internees), were conducted under the supervision of the International Red Cross, with four such exchanges taking place during the Second World War. For those prisoners who were considered as disabled and unable to fight further, their cases were first referred by their respective POW camp commandant to the German High Command, and then to a medical commission, known as the Mixed Doctoral Committee, consisting of two doctors from the Protecting Power and one from the Germans, which would make the final decision. The individual patients' cases were put before the committee by one of the Allied POW doctors.

Martin Massey's lower limb wounds, a culmination of the three traumas he had suffered in as many conflicts, marked him as potentially eligible for repatriation. Towards the end of his hospitalisation period at Obermassfeld, his case was presented to the Mixed Doctoral Committee on 13 October 1943 and authorisation for him to return home was granted,[379] whereupon he was returned to Stalag Luft III on 24 November to await a date to go home to England. The committee's decision, therefore, casts further doubt on von Lindeiner's tale of Massey being indicted for mutiny while at the hospital. If he was fit and able enough to incite uprising, and therefore considered to be a sufficient danger to the Germans, then the chances are that the German High Command would have vetoed the application before it even reached the Mixed Doctoral Committee – such behaviour would surely have jeopardised his chances, and they would not have allowed him to go home. Furthermore, von Lindeiner makes no mention of the committee's consideration of Martin's case, or their decision, in his version of events, and (as we have seen above) according to him, Massey had already been back at Sagan for almost four months at the time that his case was presented. In fact, he never alludes to the repatriation at all in his memoirs. A final point to consider is that the German doctor representative on the committee was most probably the commandant of Obermassfeld, who would have been unlikely to sanction the repatriation if Martin had indeed caused him the problems that von Lindeiner alleged.

Repatriation was not a simple case of choosing prisoners and sending them home since these were reciprocal arrangements meaning that similarly entitled German POWs and civilians were to be sent in the opposite direction. Complicated safe passage travel plans through neutral countries and dangerous international waters, using neutral transport, needed to be made to the satisfaction of all parties by the Red Cross. Such arrangements took time, and so Martin was selected as part of the second POW swap programme, set for the spring of 1944.

Massey was told on 8 April 1944, just two weeks after the Great Escape and only two days after being informed of the shootings, that he would be leaving Sagan within the next few days, along with other British and Allied prisoners who were to be returned home. Those who were to be repatriated were briefed by the evidence committee that Massey had directed to be formed, and were told to commit to memory everything for the authorities back in Britain.[380] At the time, the names and precise number of those who were alleged to have been shot were still not known, so between them, they memorised the list of the eighty thought to have got out. On 11 April, Massey was told that he was to leave Stalag Luft III that day, so he immediately convened a meeting with the other senior British prisoners and the senior American officer. He gave them his file of evidence knowing that it would be impossible to take it with him since the Germans would never allow it, and briefed them on everything that he knew and had done thus far. The gathering was interrupted by one of the German staff officers who was angered because he had apparently only given Massey permission to bid farewell to his comrades, not to hold a meeting, and had therefore 'betrayed a trust'.[381] Martin accordingly stood up, shook hands with each of those in the room and left, perhaps a little confused since he had earlier been granted permission by the commandant to hold a meeting with the senior Kriegies.

Massey and the group of other returnees were sent to a *Heilag*,[382] Stalag IV/DZ, at Annaburg, about twelve miles north of Torgau and a little over thirty miles south of Berlin. Conditions at Annaburg were a revelation after Sagan, with mostly a single, sprung-mattress, bed per bedroom rather than dormitories; good washing and bathing facilities; and a well-stocked canteen.[383] Most likely, the Germans were trying to create a good impression for the Red Cross and those about to go home. There would be a delay while the last few travel details were finalised, though, and in the meantime they kicked their heels at Annaburg for almost a month. Early in May, two medical officers who were due to be repatriated as protected personnel, a Major Matthews and a New Zealander, Captain Hetherington, arrived from Sagan armed with fresh information from the first of the recaptured escapees to have been released from solitary confinement there. They gave Massey a list, delicately inscribed on thin cigarette paper hidden inside a dummy cigarette, of the names of forty-seven men (six more than Massey had previously been told) then known to have been shot.[384] Martin already had with him several messages, some containing code (the deciphers for which were hidden inside his shoelace[385]), from prisoners back at Stalag Luft III for relatives, that he had promised to deliver once he got home. Knowing that these notes would be scrutinised by the Germans if found, and not wanting to risk the discovery of the codes, he was doubtful that he could smuggle the list back to Britain undetected and so instructed his fellow returnees to memorise the names instead.

Concealing secret messages on prisoners being sent home was nothing new for Martin as he had previously arranged for such notes to be taken out by others who were repatriated on an earlier exchange in 1943. One of those men was Sergeant William Legg, whose wounds were heavily bandaged. Massey asked Legg if he would secrete the missives under his dressings to which he bravely agreed, undoubtedly well aware of the consequences should they be discovered. Legg was successful in his mission, however, and all the messages were delivered safely.[386]

Captain Hetherington had also brought a message from Massey's re-placement as Sagan SBO, Group Captain Douglas Wilson (who had deputised for him while he was in hospital at Obermassfeld), which said that there was still a feeling among a minority of those back at Stalag Luft III (mainly the longer-term prisoners) that the executions had not actually happened, and that a false story had been concocted by the Germans simply to instil fear in the inmates and to deter them from making further escape attempts.[387] There was news, too, that a party from the Protecting Power had visited Sagan on 17 and 18 April and had been told what had happened by the commandant and the new SBO. Prior to their arrival, the Swiss delegation apparently knew nothing about the incident, therefore Massey's letters to the Protecting Power had either not got through (perhaps not sent or had been intercepted by the Gestapo), or the visitors had not yet been informed of the shootings by their head office since they had been in Paris prior to travelling to the camp – the former is more likely. In the light of that information, Martin then made a second application to see Göring, presumably on the basis that if his letter to the Protecting Power had not reached the intended recipient, then nor had his request for interview with the Reichsmarschall. However, he was told that, since he was no longer SBO at Sagan, his original bid had been rejected and he would not be able to submit another for the same reason.[388]

Finally, at 3.00 p.m. on 13 May 1944, all the transport arrangements were in place and the prisoners left Annaburg by train, destined for Marseille, where they arrived at 2.00 a.m. on the 16th after a brief stop in Stuttgart to collect twenty-nine civilian internees who were also being sent home.[389] Waiting for them at the quayside was a German (formerly Italian) hospital ship, the *Gradisca*, which took Massey and his compatriots (and the passengers from three further repatriation trains) aboard for the onward journey. While the relevant paperwork was being processed, Massey was approached by an official of the International Red Cross in Geneva, Doctor Robert Schirmer, who asked for details of the alleged shootings – presumably the Red Cross had been informed of them by the Protecting Power after their visit to Sagan on 17–18 April. Schirmer told Martin that he thought that his organisation might be able to make demi-official enquiries through 'sympathetic' contacts in the German Foreign Office. Martin gave all the details that he had, as well as reciting the list of the forty-seven names and the circumstances by which each of those killed were suspected to have met their deaths.[390]

In perfect Mediterranean weather and on a flat-calm sea, the *Gradisca* steamed out of Marseille harbour at midday that same day, bound for Barcelona in neutral Spain. Massey's thoughts were no doubt drawn to his last experience of being aboard a hospital ship back in April 1917, which had not ended well. His voyage this time was untroubled, though, and the *Gradisca* docked in the harbour of the Catalan city at 11.00 p.m. that night. Moored close by was another hospital ship, the *Gripsholm*, a Swedish cruise liner chartered by the US government to transport repatriates, which had brought the German POWs to be exchanged from New York via Algiers and had arrived in Barcelona just an hour before the *Gradisca*. A large warehouse on the dockside was used to facilitate the prisoner exchange, and in all, 1,043 British, Commonwealth and American nationals (979 disabled servicemen, protected military personnel and merchant seamen, plus 64 civilian internees) were swapped with 900 similarly categorised German prisoners. Martin and the other repatriates then boarded the *Gripsholm*, which sailed at 4.45 p.m. on 19 May, having unloaded, in addition to her German human cargo, 1,600 tons of Red Cross parcels bound for Allied POWs in Germany. The *Gripsholm's* next port of call was Algiers, where she arrived on the afternoon of the 20th to drop off 200 of her passengers,[391] mostly Commonwealth personnel who would continue on to their respective countries via different means.

Massey was among them; he was disembarked to be flown home immediately, presumably because of the information he had about the escape and subsequent events, news of which had now obviously reached Britain, again probably via the Protecting Power. The need to debrief him, as the former SBO of Sagan, was paramount.[392] He boarded an aircraft and finally arrived in the UK on 22 May 1944, almost two years after being shot down over the Netherlands. With him on board the aeroplane was Flight Lieutenant Vincent 'Paddy' Byrne, a fellow captive from Sagan who had feigned insanity for a year in order to be repatriated, so could therefore technically be classed as a successful escaper. Byrne had been tasked, along with Roger Bushell, with gathering intelligence about the Germans by MI9[393] and to pass what they discovered back to Britain via coded messages.[394] As a close friend and confidant of Bushell, Byrne knew a great deal of detail about the Sagan mass breakout, so was also rushed home with Massey to be similarly questioned.

The RAF wasted no time in opening an investigation into the alleged murders of the escapees, and Massey was interviewed at the London District Assembly Centre on the same day that he arrived home. The interview, or 'interrogation' as the transcript calls it, focused on the facts from the time that Massey was called to see the Sagan commandant on 6 April, his reaction to the news of the shootings, and his letters to the German and Swiss authorities in the days immediately afterwards until he left for Annaburg. Massey told his interviewer that he believed that 'the 47 officers shot had been murdered', based on his sense that the Luftwaffe was blaming the deaths on the Gestapo and distancing themselves from the events, and the fact that all British POWs knew the futility of forcibly resisting arrest (and the consequences thereof) and would therefore not have done so. He further said that he knew of no instance when an escapee from Sagan 'had done so [resisted arrest] in the past'.[395]

In addition to covering the details of and the events surrounding the escape, Massey also used the discussions to highlight the plight of the older prisoners at Sagan, stressing his 'great keenness'[396] that they should be repatriated on grounds of their age. He said that he had written to the Protecting Power back in March on the subject, and asked that his memorandum be hastened.

Further, Martin told the RAF about the Reverend Father Philippe Goudreau, a civilian French Canadian Catholic priest who had been interned after the ship on which he was travelling, the *Zamzam*, had been sunk by a German surface raider in the South Atlantic (off Cape Town) on 17 April 1941. The *Zamzam* was a neutral vessel and was carrying only civilian passengers, most of whom were missionaries on their way to carry out God's work in Africa. Miraculously no lives were lost, and all those aboard were rescued by the ship that had attacked them, the *Atlantis*. Taken first to Bordeaux, Goudreau later volunteered to serve as Padre to a British POW camp and had accordingly been sent to Stalag Luft III. Fluent only in French when he arrived at Sagan, Massey said that Goudreau now spoke good English and had been of 'very great value indeed', and asked that he be appointed 'honorary RC [Roman Catholic] Chaplain to the Camp; it would afford him much gratification. He has no money of course, and is paid out of the General Fund'.[397] Like Massey, Father Goudreau was dogged by poor health and had apparently been offered repatriation several times but he turned down the opportunity on each occasion, choosing instead to remain at the camp and minister to the Kriegies. Eventually he became too ill to continue and was sent home.[398]

Both of these interventions by Martin again highlight his humanity and his continued deep concern for the welfare of his former charges, even though they were by now far away, still in captivity, and no longer his responsibility.

With this initial part of the investigation over, the next matter of importance was to assess and treat Martin's wounds. To that end, he was sent to the RAF's No. 1 Personnel Holding Unit at Morecambe, which had requisitioned the nearby Midland Hotel as a hospital, including a burns unit, in 1940. He was to spend time at Morecambe and in hospital at the RAF Medical Rehabilitation Unit (MRU) in Loughborough, on and off until September 1944, the demands of interviews regarding the Great Escape notwithstanding.

Whenever possible, he also carried out the promises he had made to those left behind at Stalag Luft III and visited their relatives, travelling around the country to bring news and comfort to families and friends so desperate for word of their loved ones. He had compiled a small notebook back at Sagan containing the names and addresses of those to be visited, written on gossamer-thin paper just a couple of inches high, which he had successfully smuggled out of Germany along with the aforementioned coded messages. For those he did not manage to visit he wrote instead, and one Kriegie, Alex Cassie, recalls being 'really moved'[399] when he later learned that Massey had sent a reassuring letter to his relatives in Scotland, and considered that Martin 'must have done this for so many people', as was indeed the case. One of the more prominent prisoners at Stalag Luft III was Major John Dodge, who, like Bader, Bushell and Day, had been a constant source of trouble to the Germans through his repeated escape attempts. An American by birth but a naturalised British citizen, Dodge had joined the Royal Navy during the First World War before transferring to the British Army. He had rejoined the Army for the Second World War and had been captured in France in 1940. 'The Dodger' was one of the fortunate Great Escapers who had avoided execution, most probably because he was related by marriage to Winston Churchill, instead becoming one of the small group who were sent to Sachsenhausen concentration camp upon recapture. Martin wrote to Dodge's wife, Minerva, on 29 July 1944 from Loughborough:[400]

Royal Air Force MRU Loughborough

Dear Mrs Dodge
I think of hope. I formed a great friendship with your husband whilst I was a prisoner of war. We were in the same Compounds together in Stalag Luft III for some time. Let me tell you of the great work he has done and I've no doubt is still doing, amongst our young aircrew laddies out there. He was in a sense something of a father to them all (to us all) and everyone had a very great regard for him. He has

shown tremendous interest and done excellent work in organising debates, lectures, talks etc but in point of fact he interested himself in most everything that was going on in the Camp. I was repatriated a little time ago and he and I arranged that I should write to you. Please treat this very much as a first letter just to make contact. And let me assure you above all things that you need have no worries about him. He was in excellent health and he learnt from the earliest days the secrets of overcoming trials and tribulations of prison life – to keep oneself occupied and to live a community life in concord with all. Now please if you have any special questions you would like to ask me – do write and I will do my best to answer them.

My kind regards

Yours sincerely

H.M. Massey

Group Captain RAF

Although Massey knew when he wrote the letter that Dodge had not been murdered, we do not know if he was aware by then that Dodge was at Sachsenhausen. He probably was not, since, if he had been, Martin may not have been so confident in his reassurances to Minerva about her husband's well-being. As it was, he was to be proved right since John Dodge survived the war. Martin also wrote to Roger Bushell's parents, although not until 13 February 1945, telling them that: 'His name will ever live in my memory as one of the greatest men of his generation that I have known. He was a great officer, an outstanding leader of men, quite fearless and he had a very fine brain, and for what it is worth to you I say those few brief words as the Senior British Officer of Stalag Luft III.'[401]

On 29 May 1944 a Court of Inquiry was convened at RAF Weeton, a training base and RAF hospital in Lancashire, under the presidency of Wing Commander M.C. Leslie, with its terms of reference being 'to investigate from repatriated officers, as far as possible, the shooting of Air Force personnel at Stalag Luft III'.[402] Massey and those who had travelled with him from Sagan were called as witnesses. Martin was sworn in first, and was asked about the personalities involved in the Sagan escape committee and how the escapees themselves were selected. He was then asked if he knew the names of any of the Gestapo men who had arrived at the camp after the escape, perhaps the first indication that the British were intending to track down and prosecute the culprits after the war. Massey then testified as to what had happened in the immediate aftermath of the breakout. He said that for a day or two nothing seemed untoward, with the usual round of post-escape searches, an increased number of *Appells*, and the stoppage of privileges, all of which were to be expected. Indeed, it was his impression 'that things were not so bad on this occasion as I would have expected following such a big escape'.[403] He next told the court about his meeting with Pieber and the commandant, Cordes, on 6 April when he was informed of the shootings, his subsequent letters to the Protecting Power, and his application for a meeting with Göring himself. He restated his conviction that he could imagine perhaps the odd case of someone being shot and possibly killed for resisting arrest, but that the numbers involved this time were 'inconceivable'. The court president then asked him if 'that fact bears out your opinion that it was barefaced murder?', to which Massey simply replied 'Yes.'[404]

Martin was then asked whether he had any knowledge of how the prisoners were transported to their deaths, where they were taken, what they were wearing, and if they were all taken to be shot together or in smaller groups. His answers were sketchy since much of what he knew had reached him second- or third-hand, and only after he had left Sagan – he could only speculate. Over the next few days, the court heard evidence from eleven other repatriates. Massey was re-called as a witness on 2 June to clarify a few points and answer some more questions that had cropped up from the testimonies of the others. The president evidently wanted to look further into the question of whether the alleged killings had actually taken place, given that some of the prisoners back at Sagan had expressed doubts. He asked Martin, pointedly, 'What is your personal opinion as to whether the 47 prisoners named by the Germans as being shot were in fact shot?' Massey's response perhaps shows that he too had an element of doubt, albeit an extremely small one: 'I very much hesitate to give an opinion but I will say that I still retain a grain of hope that they may still be alive.'[405]

Martin concluded his testimony with a request to the court that the International Red Cross be approached for them to conduct an investigation, as he held them in a higher regard than the Protecting Power, based on his experiences of contact with them at Sagan and with Doctor Schirmer at Marseille. He went on record as saying:

I have been impressed by the influence that the International Red Cross has with the German Authorities. It seems to me that they adopt a more business-like method than the Protecting Power, and their personnel are generally of a higher standard. They seem to me to have contacts with the German government and means of investigating conditions in prison camps which do not appear to be made use of by the representatives of the Protecting Power. I do not want to belittle the activities of the Protecting Power but I do consider that an investigation by the International Red Cross, if it could be conducted without giving offence to the Protecting Power, might be productive of useful results. In comparing the activities of the Protecting Power with those of the Red Cross, I have not overlooked the fact that they visit the prison camps for different purposes.'[406]

Lastly, Massey insisted that the record of the inquiry be classified as 'Top Secret', and that it should 'in no circumstances' be communicated to either the Protecting Power or the Red Cross since it contained sensitive information that, if it reached the Germans, 'would not only prejudice the activities of the prisoners but would also possibly endanger their lives'.[407] Giving evidence to the Court of Inquiry had clearly been emotionally painful for Martin; writing on 8 June 1944, Sir Arthur Street, the Permanent Under-Secretary of State for Air, said that 'I saw Massey yesterday; he is still very much shaken.'[408]

After the findings of the court were released to the military hierarchy and the government, the Foreign Secretary, Anthony Eden, made a statement to the House of Commons on 23 June. By that time, official word had been received from the Germans that fifty, not forty-seven as first thought, British airmen had been shot. Eden's speech[409] named Massey as one of those from whom statements had been taken, and affirmed that he was the 'senior officer for the whole camp and the prisoners' representative'. Much of what the Foreign Secretary then said was drawn directly from Massey's evidence to the Court of Inquiry. After outlining the known facts, Eden stated that 'it is abundantly clear that none of these officers met their death in the course of making their escape from Stalag Luft III or while resisting capture ... there were no wounded as would have been inevitable if the shootings had taken place during an attempt to resist capture. ... From these facts, there is only one possible conclusion – these prisoners of war were murdered.' The speech concluded with a solemn commitment that '[HM government] will never cease in their efforts to collect evidence to identify all those responsible. They [the government] are firmly resolved that these foul criminals shall be tracked down to the last man … when the war is over, they will be brought to exemplary justice.' The British newspapers were now able to report the story to the public, and Martin's photograph duly appeared on the front page of the *Evening Standard* as the man who 'brought the news home from Stalag Luft III', under the headline 'Fifty Officers Murdered in "Cold Act of Butchery"'.[410] Another newspaper report into the story remarked that Massey was 'one of the elderly men of the RAF. He is 46, which is very old for active service in the air.'[411]

The Germans, though, on hearing of Eden's speech, were quick to deny what had happened. A typically distorted and obfuscating article, billed as a 'German note to England' and headlined 'Energetic Repudiation of Eden', appeared in the Nazi Party's newspaper *Völkischer Beobachter* on 24 July 1944 proclaiming:

British prisoners of war broke out of various camps in Germany in large numbers in March this year.

Measures undertaken to return the prisoners were a complete success. In the course of this it came to light that a carefully planned action [of sabotage] had been prevented, which had been partially prepared in collaboration with forces abroad. Because of resistance to arrest or attempts at flight, the German security forces were compelled to make use of their firearms whilst recapturing the prisoners who had escaped from one prison camp. In this action, a number of prisoners of war lost their lives.

The German government informed the English government of these occurrences via Switzerland, the protecting power. Moreover, after the termination of enquiries, it was on its way to producing a final, conclusive, report. Meanwhile the British Foreign Secretary Eden shamelessly made the monstrous accusation in a statement to the House of Commons that the British prisoners had been murdered in Germany. This unqualified accusation of the British Foreign Secretary is sharply rejected in a message sent to England via Switzerland by the German government.

The note reads as follows: 'Without waiting for the results of the German enquiries, the British Foreign Secretary has produced a report on this affair, which the German government rejects in the sharpest possible way. We deny the right of a Foreign Secretary of a country which has initiated a bombing campaign against the civilian

population, which has wiped out tens of thousands of German
women and children through 'terror attacks' on private dwellings,
hospitals, and cultural monuments, which, moreover, in a 'Handbook
of Modern Irregular Warfare' has literally ordered all British soldiers
to employ gangster methods , i.e. to scratch out the eyes of enemies
lying defenceless on the ground, and to smash their skulls with rocks,
to make accusations against anyone.

The German government refuses to make any further statements
on this affair in view of the outrageous attitude of the British Foreign
Secretary.[412]

That the Germans allowed the senior British officer of Stalag Luft III –
plus several other prisoners who collectively had a large amount of knowledge about what had happened – to go home almost immediately after
the event seems remarkably short-sighted, if not downright incompetent,
on their part. They must surely have realised that the first thing the
repatriates would do when they returned would be to tell everything they
knew to the British authorities, and that there would inevitably be
repercussions. It could be that the Luftwaffe were prepared to let them go
and tell what they knew as part of their apparent desire to distance themselves from what had happened, on the assumption that the news would
get out somehow anyway. Also, the Luftwaffe could perhaps have been
concerned about possible retaliation against their own prisoners being
held in British POW camps, another reason to make it known that they were
not responsible for the murders. But even if these speculative explanations
were indeed the motives, then the Gestapo could have prevented Martin
and the others from leaving Sagan once they had arrived at the camp on
6 April, fully five days before the group was sent to Annaburg. Even after
reaching the repatriation camp, the Gestapo could have stopped them
going home, since 120 prisoners had had their names removed from the
repatriation list by the Germans on the grounds that the British government had failed to provide their quota of the agreed numbers, therefore
prisoners had to be withdrawn to adjust the figures accordingly.[413]
It would surely have been easy enough to have included Massey and the
others from Sagan in the group of those removed from the manifest and
to have kept them in Germany. Had Martin and the rest been held at
Stalag Luft III (or elsewhere in the Reich) and not allowed home, then the
full details of the shootings could probably only have reached the UK via
the Red Cross or the Protecting Power, and the Germans would have

surely done all that they could to subvert any investigation by those organ-isations through denial, delay and disinformation. Perhaps the Germans felt that their bluff of 'shot while resisting arrest' would be accepted by the British, along with their contention that the breakout was part of a wider campaign of planned sabotage across Germany. Whatever the reasons, the truth was now out.

A memorial service for the fifty dead escapees was held in London at St Martin-in-the-Fields church on 20 June 1944, attended by Massey ('in the first seat … with his lame leg stuck out into the aisle'[414]) and the other Sagan repatriates. But with the war still going on, there was little else that could be done for the time being other than to make representations and appeals through the international organisations. As Anthony Eden had said, those responsible could only be brought to justice when the conflict was won.

Once Germany had been defeated, though, the British government remained true to its word and a team from the RAF Police's Special Investigation Branch was despatched to occupied Germany to track down the culprits and bring them to justice. This was an immensely difficult task given that Germany was in such huge turmoil so soon after capitula-tion, with thousands of wanted former military, government and civil authority personnel doing their best to evade capture, perhaps by getting out of Germany altogether, and with a myriad of Allied and international investigative teams roaming the country looking for them. And of course, the Soviet authorities had their own agenda and were hardly likely to be forthcoming with either Nazi prisoners who were being held in their zone of occupation, or their information.

The RAF Police investigation team, led by Wing Commander Wilfred Bowes, nevertheless did an excellent job, and the first trial of suspects was held in Hamburg on 1 July 1947. One of the witnesses called for the defence was von Lindeiner, who testified that although he had been given no spe-cific direction from a higher authority regarding warning prisoners about the dangers of escaping, he had cautioned Massey anyway because he 'felt uneasy about the change in climate regarding escapes'.[415] When asked what he would have done if he had been ordered to shoot the escapers himself, von Lindeiner replied that 'I would have put a bullet through my head.' Of the eighteen defendants tried, fourteen were given the death sentence (one was later commuted to life imprisonment), and they were hanged on 27 February 1948 in Hameln prison by the British executioner Albert Pierrepoint.

But the pursuit of those responsible did not end there. A second trial was held in October 1947, and although capital punishment was handed down to two of the three defendants (the third was acquitted), both sentences were subsequently commuted. More trials took place on and off through to 1968 when the last Gestapo man to be tried was given a two-year prison sentence by a West German court. In all cases, the defendants pleaded not guilty to the charges, citing that they were simply 'carrying out orders' and therefore had no choice but to obey.

At last, Martin Massey had the satisfaction of knowing that the information he had brought with him from Sagan had been acted upon, and that 'exemplary justice' had accordingly been done. The murders of those fifty men – *his* men – whose welfare had been his responsibility, and whose attempted break for freedom he had personally authorised, had finally been avenged.

Massey's duty to the men under his command at Sagan did not solely rest with the dead. At the end of the war, when the Kriegies were released from captivity and repatriated to the UK, he insisted on being present at the reception centre at RAF Cosford that handled their arrival, to greet them personally and to supervise their processing. One of them, Alex Cassie, remarked that it was 'a nice touch ... the sort of thing that he would do'.[416]

The tributes to Martin's leadership at Stalag Luft III began to arrive as the war finished, first in the form of international recognition. On 22 June 1945 Colonel Delmar T. Spivey, who had latterly been a senior American officer at Sagan, wrote to the adjutant general of the US Army (there was no independent air arm in the US military organisation at the time – the Air Force was part of the Army):[417]

Subject: Letter of Commendation for Group Captain Massey, Royal Air Force. POW Stalag Luft III Germany

To: The Adjutant General

1. It is desired to commend Group Captain Massey, RAF, for his outstanding work as Senior Allied Officer at Stalag Luft III, Germany, for the approximate period July 1942 to January 1944.
2. When American prisoners of war first began to arrive at Stalag Luft III, Group Captain Massey immediately accepted them and treated them as he would RAF personnel. They were furnished with food,

clothing, toilet articles, and other comforts which the International Red Cross and YMCA had made available to the British prisoners of war, and not furnished by the Germans. Through his gracious and generous attitude much was done to make the American prisoners of war feel that his incarceration could be borne much more lightly than would have been possible had it not been for Group Captain Massey's fine attitude.

3. On many occasions it was through Group Captain Massey's untiring efforts that it was possible for the senior American officers to meet with the British senior officers in conference with the German commandant to protest against living conditions at Stalag Luft III. Group Captain Massey took into confidence the senior American officers at all times and even though there were very few American prisoners of war at Stalag Luft III at this time, they were always consulted before any decision was made on his part.

4. The American officer prisoners of war were housed and fed in the British compound and received the benefits derived from the experiences which the British had gained from being prisoners of war for a long time.

5. His attitude reflects great credit upon the Royal Air Force and it is desired that this communication be forwarded to Group Captain Massey through the RAF.

Delmar T. Spivey
Colonel, Air Corps
Senior American Officer
Center Compound, Stalag Luft III

A more personal acknowledgement, and arguably the finest, arrived in January 1948 in the form of a letter to Martin from one of the former British prisoners, Bob Herrick. Herrick was sending a copy of a photograph of Massey taken as he was leaving Sagan for Annaburg and repatriation, and wrote 'I do hope this photograph will remind you of what I (in common with very many others) consider to be one of your finest achievements as a commanding officer. I shall always remember the great joy, tinged with equally great sadness, as we saw the well-known figure, complete with stick and boot, disappear through the gate.'[418]

Chapter Ten

Later Life: 1945 – 1976

With the investigations into the murders of the fifty Great Escapers completed, the RAF next considered how best to employ Martin Massey.
Although he had been assessed as fit to fly 'light single-engined aircraft
only' by a medical board, it was probably obvious to him that, given the
extent of his injuries, his age (he was now almost forty-seven years old)
and his advanced rank, his military flying days were over. On 15 September
1944 he went to the Air Ministry at Adastral House in London's Kingsway
to work in the Directorate of Personnel Selection, where he spent one
year. Armed with the experience he had gained in the personnel policy
department at the ministry, he then moved to the Permanent
Commissions Selection Board, also within Adastral House, but he was
now in the rank of acting air commodore. He stayed in the recruiting and
selection sphere, moving in 1947 to Ramridge House in Andover where he
was president of the RAF Selection Board, a post he was to hold for the
rest of his service career.

Massey's old injuries were to dog him continually, though, prompting
further admissions to hospital in 1949 and early 1950, the latter at Princess
Mary's RAF Hospital at RAF Halton in Buckinghamshire for skin grafts
to his damaged, cavus-deformed, left foot. Following that operation, he
was evaluated by a medical board for the last time, on 24 May 1950, at
which he was assessed to be forty per cent disabled. The recommendation
of the board was that he be 'placed on the retired list on account of
medical unfitness for Air Force service', words that Martin probably knew
were coming, but nonetheless would have been hard for him to bear, having
spent all of his adult life in the military. Finally, after almost thirty-five
years of exemplary service to his country in both war and peace, Herbert

Martin Massey's extensive injuries, the first of which had almost killed him, had forced his retirement.

The Royal Air Force did, however, honour Massey's contribution to the service with two notable awards before he left. Firstly, in the New Year's Honours List of 1950, he was appointed as Commander of the Most Excellent Order of the British Empire, or CBE. The news of the award reached him in his hospital bed at RAF Halton. Secondly, on 21 June 1950 his acting rank of air commodore was made substantive, just under a fortnight prior to him becoming a civilian once more on 4 July. He had also been previously honoured when, in August 1949, the president of the Czechoslovak Republic had conferred upon him the Czechoslovak War Cross[419] in recognition of Martin's role in training Czechoslovak bomber aircrews during his time in command of No. 10 OTU at RAF Abingdon during the war.

Martin's injuries not only precluded him from further service in the Royal Air Force, but severely hampered his ability to follow a second career. He worked for a time with the family firm, Mrs Massey's Agency, but things in the world of that particular business were changing. There was a general decrease in the demand for domestic staff, with many of the great stately homes in the country going into decline for a variety of reasons. Firstly, crippling death duties levied on the upper classes meant that many houses were either being sold, left to the National Trust or similar organisations, or allowed to fall into ruin. Secondly, social changes, such as the demand for higher wages and better jobs, brought about by the two world wars, were having an effect. Thirdly, new domestic labour-saving devices were being introduced, thereby reducing the numbers of staff required in those households that had managed to survive.

There was probably not that much work for Martin to do, and his time with the agency appears to have been limited. In any case, he was to be in and out of hospital regularly for further treatment of his old wounds. But he did find something to occupy his time for ten years between 1955 and 1965, when he served as the president of the now-defunct Employment Agents' Federation of Great Britain, an association that existed as a professional membership body for recruitment agencies. Given his six years of service with, and latterly as the head of, the RAF's personnel selection directorate, and his brief association with the family business, itself a recruitment agency, he was an ideal choice for the post.

The Massey family moved at some point from Croyde to nearby Pilton on the northern side of Barnstaple. Here, they bought a property known as the Red House, where Peggy decided to resume her work as a teacher, opening a small private school within the house. She was apparently none too keen on Martin 'shuffling' around the place (as his daughter-in-law Eleanor put it to the author) when there were children there, and he was strongly encouraged to be out of the house as much as possible. He was a keen gardener and so spent much time tending his borders and vegetable patch, and he also travelled around visiting his sisters in various parts of the country to keep out of the way at home. His two brothers had by this time emigrated, one to New Zealand and one to Australia.

Massey retained at least some connection with Sagan and the Great Escape for a considerable time after the war. Alan Bryett, one of the Kriegies at the camp, kept in contact with Martin for several years, exchanging Christmas cards containing heart-warming messages. Massey's daughter-in-law feels that Bryett looked up to him somewhat, perhaps due to the polarity in their ages – Bryett was one of the youngest at Stalag Luft III (where he was known as 'Junior'), and Martin the eldest – a fact borne out by Bryett describing Massey as 'a father to all of us'.[420] Martin also joined the Royal Air Force Ex-POW Association in 1963, becoming member number 177.[421]

Although a 'father' to the Kriegies, Martin's relationship with his two sons was not so close. When he was repatriated, he must have seemed an unfamiliar figure to the boys as they had not seen him for two years; for the younger of them, John, this was almost half his life at that point. Massey was by all accounts a strict father to them, insisting on beds being made in regimental fashion, and carrying out room inspections with white gloves, looking for any stray specks of dust. Peggy had moved the three of them to Croyde after Martin had been shot down, where David and John had gone to the village school before being sent to a private governess for a year. Both the children were despatched to boarding school at Ampleforth in North Yorkshire at the age of nine, a long way from home in Devon.

In 1963, the Hollywood movie *The Great Escape*, based on Paul Brickhill's book of the same name, was released. While most of the characters in the film were amalgams of several real Kriegies, two were based directly on specific individuals, with only their names altered slightly. Richard Attenborough played the part of Roger Bartlett, in reality Bushell – he even had make-up to represent Bushell's eye injury sustained in a pre-war skiing accident. The part of the senior British officer was depicted by the actor James Donald, who had already appeared in a supporting role in another classic war film, *The Bridge on the River Kwai*, in 1957. Donald's SBO was renamed 'Group Captain Ramsey', but he walked with a limp, aided by a stick, and wore the ribbons of the DSO and MC, along with those of First World War campaign medals.

Martin attended the royal premiere of the film at London's Leicester Square Odeon on 20 June 1963. Apparently, he did not think a great deal of the picture because of the 'Hollywood-isation' of the events, although several other ex-Kriegies, including 'Wings' Day (who was also at the premiere), thought that it was quite good, invented scenes such as Steve McQueen's motorcycle jump notwithstanding. What Massey thought of James Donald's portrayal of him is unfortunately not known, but his family were certainly proud to see Martin depicted on the big screen, even if his grandchildren (watching years later on television) found it odd that his name had been changed. They watched Donald's every move and listened to every word of his dialogue, trying to work out what their grandfather had been like back then. The film was to become a family staple at Christmas, as it was in many households up and down the country, but with greater poignancy.

In 1988 Martin was portrayed on screen for a second time, in an American made-for-television film entitled *The Great Escape II: The Untold Story*. Billed as a sequel to the 1963 movie, the picture covered the escape and the post-war hunt for the executioners of the fifty. Unlike the previous film, though, this production used the real names of those involved, and Massey's part was now played by the versatile English actor Peter Dennis, still with the distinctive walking stick and limp, but with incorrect medal ribbons.

Martin's sons and their children came to visit in Devon regularly, and his granddaughter Camilla recalls weeks spent at the Red House during the summer holidays of her childhood, exploring the house and helping her grandfather in the garden, where there were always plenty of jobs to be done. But like many of his generation who had been through so much, Massey never spoke of his many wartime experiences to his family, which was hardly surprising given everything he had suffered.

For a number of his later years Martin suffered from angina, which was not in itself life-threatening but was certainly a warning sign of the risk of a heart attack or a stroke. And so it was to prove – a heart condition eventually claimed his life when, on Leap Year Day, 29 February 1976, Air Commodore Herbert Martin Massey, CBE, DSO, MC, died, just over a month after his seventy-eighth birthday. His death certificate records the cause as 'Ischaemic Heart Disease', now more commonly known as coronary heart disease. He was at home at the Red House at the time, and Peggy was there with him. A memorial service, attended by friends, colleagues and family, was held for him at the RAF church of St Clement Danes in London on 22 May. He is buried in the churchyard at Pilton, along with his wife who passed away a little over seven years later on 11 August 1983, also aged seventy-eight. After three wars, three serious wounds, two shootings-down, two years of imprisonment, one sinking, and six decorations, Martin Massey's life had without doubt been one of extremes of fortune, and one well lived.

Chapter Eleven

Epilogue

Martin Massey's childhood home in Derbyshire, Hilton House, is now a hotel. A blue plaque commemorating his residence there was unveiled in 2016. Of his schools, Derby School Preparatory and Spondon House School no longer exist, but Oundle School continues to flourish.

The outdated BE2s of No. 16 Squadron were finally replaced by the Royal Aircraft Factory RE8 (nicknamed 'Harry Tate' in rhyming slang after a popular music hall comedian of the time) in May 1917, although the BE2 carried on with the RFC, providing service in the communications and liaison roles. The RE8 was no better, and in some respects arguably worse, than the BE2, and enjoyed an equally dismal reputation. Some improvements were incorporated in the RE8's design, such as moving the observer to the rear seat, but like the BE2, it was built to be inherently stable so offered no real enhancement in terms of air combat agility. The RE8 was also more difficult to fly than its predecessor, particularly since it was much heavier and therefore needed a far higher landing speed than former BE2 pilots were used to. Because the aircraft gave almost no warning that it was about to stall, many unwary pilots realised too late that their airspeed was insufficient to remain airborne. The RE8's limitations were highlighted starkly on 13 April 1917 when six of them, all operated by No. 59 Squadron, were shot down within a matter of minutes by Jasta 11. However, Major Maltby said that, after his squadron's experiences with the BE2, the new aeroplane was 'more than welcome' and that 'everyone liked them very much'.[422] Whatever the truth, the RE8 was hastily withdrawn from service almost as soon as the war had finished, ironically before the BE2 was itself fully retired.

No. 16 Squadron, Royal Flying Corps saw active service for the rest of the First World War, becoming a squadron of the newly created Royal Air Force on 1 April 1918. The squadron disbanded in 1919 but re-formed in 1924, serving throughout the Second World War and then on into the jet age. During the first Gulf War of 1991, when Iraq invaded and occupied Kuwait, the squadron deployed its Panavia Tornado GR1 aircraft to Tabuk in Saudi Arabia, from where it carried out perilous bombing missions against Iraqi airfields and other military targets. Disbanded later the same year, the squadron numberplate was passed to 226 Operational Conversion Unit, which trained pilots to fly the SEPECAT Jaguar ground-attack/tactical reconnaissance aircraft, becoming No. 16 (Reserve) Squadron. With the imminent withdrawal from service of the Jaguar, the squadron was disbanded once more in 2005 and remained dormant for three years until, in 2008, another training unit, this time 1 Elementary Flying Training School, took on the squadron number and its reserve status. No. 16 Squadron continues to fly today, operating the Grob Tutor aircraft from RAF Wittering.

Major Paul Maltby, No. 16 Squadron's CO for much of Martin's time on the squadron, stayed on in the nascent Royal Air Force after the Armistice, rising steadily through the ranks. By 1942, he had been promoted to Air Vice-Marshal and was the air officer commanding Commonwealth air forces in Java (and subsequently commander of all British forces in the region) when Sumatra was overrun by the Japanese. He spent the rest of the Second World War as a prisoner of war, and throughout his incarceration he battled bravely with his Japanese captors over the appalling living conditions and treatment of his fellow prisoners. He was knighted after the war and was appointed serjeant-at-arms of the House of Lords in 1946, an office he held until 1962. Sir Paul Copeland Maltby died in 1971, aged seventy-eight.

Werner Voss, who shot down Martin Massey and Noel Vernham on 4 February 1917, was eventually himself shot down and killed on 23 September 1917, aged just twenty years old, during a furious dogfight with RFC fighters, one of which was piloted by the British ace James McCudden, VC. Voss fought seven British aircraft alone that day before being brought down. McCudden later said: 'As long as I live I shall never forget my admiration for that German pilot, who single-handed fought seven of us for ten minutes and also put some bullets through all our machines. His flying was wonderful, his courage magnificent, and in my opinion, he was the bravest German airman whom it has been my privilege to see fight. I saw him go into a fairly steep dive and so I continued to watch, and then saw the triplane hit the ground and disappear into a thousand fragments, for it seemed to me that it literally went into powder.' At the time of his death, Voss had been credited with forty-eight aerial victories, placing him fourth in the list of highest-scoring German aces of the First World War. His body lies within a mass grave among almost 25,000 of his fallen comrades at Langemark German Military Cemetery near Ypres in Belgium.

Hans Howaldt, captain of the German submarine *UB-40* that sank the hospital ship *Lanfranc*, became one of Germany's leading U-boat commanders of the First World War, sinking sixty-three Allied vessels (a total tonnage of 95,518 GRT) and damaging a further eleven, as well as taking another ship intact as a prize. Howaldt was awarded the Blue Max for 'outstanding leadership and distinguished naval planning and successful submarine operations'. He survived the war and went on to win a bronze medal in the International Eight Metre class sailing event at the 1936 summer Olympics held in Germany. The *UB-40* itself was scuttled in Ostend on 5 October 1918 as the Germans retreated from Belgium towards the end of the First World War. The wreck has been located in recent years and has been visited by divers. Hans Howaldt died in 1970, at the age of eighty-one. The wreck of His Majesty's Hospital Ship *Lanfranc* lies some forty miles off Brighton at a depth of fifty-two metres in the English Channel, where she sits upright and fairly intact, although there is of course a tear in her hull where the *UB-40*'s torpedo hit. She is a popular attraction for sports divers and is apparently an impressive yet ghostly sight, looking as if she is continuing her journey home to Southampton along the seabed. Access can be gained through a skylight inside to a dining area, where much of the ship's crockery lies strewn. Her name still shows from her starboard bow in eighteen-inch-high brass letters. Both of the *Lanfranc*'s sister ships, the *Antony* and the *Hilary*, were also sunk by enemy submarines during the First World War.

All three of the hospitals in England where Martin was treated after being shot down by Voss have since closed as medical facilities. The Royal Victoria Military Hospital at Netley was largely demolished in 1966, although part remained in use until 1978. The Queen Alexandra Military Hospital at Millbank closed in 1977 and most of the buildings are now occupied by Tate Britain. The Furness Hospital in Harrogate, formerly the Grand Hotel, is now an apartment complex named Windsor House.

No. 6 Squadron remained in the Middle East after Massey left in 1937, staying there (with a sojourn to Italy for some of the Second World War) into the jet age until 1957 when it re-equipped with the English Electric

Canberra aircraft at RAF Coningsby in Lincolnshire. During its service in the Western Desert in the Second World War, it successfully used Hawker Hurricane IID fighter-bombers against German armour, earning the squadron the nickname of 'The Flying Can-Openers'. No. 6 Squadron later became the last RAF unit to operate the SEPECAT Jaguar and disbanded in 2007 when the Jaguar retired from service. The squadron was re-formed at RAF Leuchars in Scotland in 2010, equipped with the Eurofighter Typhoon FGR4.

RAF Hinaidi was handed over to the Iraqi government in 1938 after the RAF moved to a replacement airfield at Habbaniya. Following the British withdrawal from Egypt in 1956, RAF Ismailia passed into the hands of the Egyptian Air Force. Today, it serves as a helicopter base. RAF Ramleh closed when Britain withdrew from Palestine in 1948 and the state of Israel came into existence.

Once the Second World War had finished, RAF Abingdon's flying training role ceased and the station became part of Transport Command. Aircraft from the station took part in the Berlin Airlift of 1948–49. The transport squadrons left in 1974, with Abingdon then becoming a maintenance unit for the major servicing of several types of RAF aircraft. Abingdon closed as an RAF airfield on 31 July 1992 and the site was transferred to the British Army, being renamed as Dalton Barracks, housing 3 Close Support, 4 General Support and 12 Close Support Regiments of the Royal Logistic Corps.

Horst Patuscka, the German night-fighter pilot who almost certainly shot down Massey and the crew of Short Stirling N3750 on their way back from Essen on 2 June 1942, went on to shoot down a total of twenty-three Allied aircraft, all of them at night. He was killed on 6 March 1943 when his Junkers Ju-88 crashed in Tunisia due to engine failure. In May 1943 he was posthumously awarded the Knight's Cross of the Iron Cross, one of Germany's highest military decorations.

Wing Commander Harry Day was held as a prisoner of war by the Germans right through until 28 April 1945, just over a week before VE Day, when he managed, aided by partisans, to cross the Dolomite mountains and reach the American lines in Italy. Post-war, he was awarded the DSO for his services while a prisoner, and was also made an officer of the Order of the British Empire. He was promoted to group captain in 1946, the rank at which he later retired from the RAF. 'Wings' Day died in March 1977, aged seventy-eight.

Oberst Friedrich von Lindeiner was arrested and court-martialled (along with ten other Sagan staff, including Pieber) by the German military authorities after the Great Escape. He afterwards blustered that his dismissal was 'without authority', and was an attempt by his higher command to 'save their own necks'. It seems that he could not accept that, as commandant, he was responsible for the prevention of escapes from his camp and so would naturally take the blame. He was charged on five counts:[423]

1. Intentional dereliction of duty, resulting in careless actions that furthered the enterprise of the enemy.
2. Constant disobedience of orders in matters of duty, resulting in detriment and danger to life or to a considerable degree to foreign property or danger to the security of the Reich.
3. Through constant irresponsible actions lessening the value of installations which served to defend the German land and thus endangering the preparedness of the German army.
4. Careless neglect of his duty of oversight over his subordinates.
5. Constant and deliberate offence against rules issued for the regulation of intercourse with prisoners of war, or else maintaining contact with prisoners of war in such a way that healthy national feeling was grossly violated.

The trial summary for his court martial states 'a failure in the field to apply discipline as commandant of the camp' and that 'because of slack application of his duty, von Lindeiner enabled the success of the massive escape of officers'.[424]

On 9 October 1944 he was sentenced to twelve months' imprisonment but shortly afterwards was diagnosed with 'an advanced stage of mental disturbance', a condition that he was probably faking to avoid custody (the psychiatrist who 'examined' him was a personal friend). He was admitted to a psychiatric hospital near Görlitz, where he stayed until January 1945 when he was released as the advancing Red Army closed in. He then apparently took command of an infantry unit defending Sagan and, although wounded, managed to evade capture by the Soviets. He made his way to the West where he was eventually made a prisoner, first of the Americans and then the British. He arrived in London in late August, where he was detained in a POW centre in London's Kensington Gardens known as the 'London Cage'. This facility (by that time) was used for the interrogation of those suspected of war crimes, and although von

Lindeiner was of course innocent of such criminalities, he was nevertheless a 'person of interest' to the British when it came to the investigation
of the Great Escape murders, given the amount of knowledge that he possessed. Indeed, when he was captured, von Lindeiner was carrying documents concerning a meeting regarding security at the Luftwaffe-run POW
camps (chaired by him just before the Great Escape) – perhaps he was
already preparing the ground for his defence.

There have been allegations that torture was used to extract intelligence
and confessions from German prisoners by the staff of the London Cage,
accusations rejected by its chief, Lieutenant Colonel Alexander Scotland,
who participated in the investigation into the executions of the fifty.
Scotland later said that 'it seemed to me that these manufactured tales of
cruelty toward our German prisoners were fast becoming the chief item
of news, while the brutal fate of those fifty RAF officers was in danger of
becoming old history'.[425] There was no suggestion by von Lindeiner that
he was tortured during his stay at the London Cage, but he did write in his
memoirs that 'the reception there and the accommodations were rather
shameful',[426] about which he says he complained strongly under the terms
of the Geneva Convention. But his words seem to be at odds with one
British report into his interrogation, which says that he 'is extremely
friendly to the British and his information is supplied willingly',[427] probably
a further example of his keenness to distance himself from the events
following the breakout from Stalag Luft III.

Von Lindeiner spent two years as a prisoner of war in Britain. After the
London Cage he was sent first to Shap Wells POW camp in Cumbria
(based in the town's small hotel) and then in September 1946 to Feather-
stone Park camp near Haltwhistle in Northumberland. He was repatriated
to Germany in June 1947, and in the 1950s he set about compiling his
memoirs, in which he claimed that he had been court-martialled by the
German High Command for: 'interceding on behalf of Allied POWs, 23
of whom were alive because of my intervention and were able to return to
their homeland. Among them were the Dutch Flight Lt, Bob van der Stock
[sic], as well as the British Group Captain Massey who otherwise would
have been court martialled for inciting mutiny. I have never heard from
them.'[428]

This statement is as bizarre and fanciful as anything quoted already in
this book from von Lindeiner, and is further evidence of his inability, or
refusal, to accept any responsibility for the Great Escape. He was arrested
by the Gestapo not because of any appeals for clemency, as he claims, but

for the fact that a mass escape had occurred from his camp, on his watch. Furthermore, the 23 to whom he refers are presumably those of the Great Escapers who were not shot by the Gestapo (who else would they be) in which case von Lindeiner did not have any influence over who was executed or who survived since he had been under arrest from the day after the breakout. The Gestapo are highly unlikely to have solicited his advice and opinion when deciding who to murder. Bram van der Stok was one of the three Great Escapers who made a successful 'home run' to Britain, and von Lindeiner claims that he had earlier resisted attempts by the Gestapo to have him sent to occupied Holland to face a court martial, which could have resulted in his execution. The apparent grounds for the trial were that since van der Stok was a member of the Dutch Air Force and had managed to escape to Britain after the German invasion of his homeland, he was therefore a deserter. Von Lindeiner said that, had he known then how the Dutchman 'would behave later on' (i.e. escape), he would not have 'compromised myself so much on [his] behalf'.[429]

The story seems as outlandish as the Massey mutiny tale, which has already been covered above. In his introduction to the former commandant's memoirs the editor, Arthur Durand, wrote that 'von Lindeiner … asserted that his memoirs were intended to be a "search for the truth" so that coming generations could have a factual description of the actions of German men',[430] but von Lindeiner's reminiscences are words written long after the event when bitterness, indignation and resentment over his treatment (and the resulting damage to his reputation) by his wartime German masters had set in. A 'search for the truth' and 'a factual description' seem to be somewhat loose statements and, in any case, if they were indeed the purpose of his text, he never had the memoirs published – the manuscript was discovered by Durand many years later in the German archives at Freiburg and only came into print in 2015. Why Martin never contacted his old gaoler after the war is not known; 'Wings' Day certainly kept in touch and visited von Lindeiner several times over the years, and Delmar Spivey corresponded with him regularly for fifteen years. Had they exchanged letters, Martin would without doubt have kept them in his extensive personal archive, given that he had retained such items as his old school reports. Perhaps Massey was aware of the preposterous claims that von Lindeiner had made about him. If a breach of trust did in fact occur as von Lindeiner believed, it very much appears to have been of his doing, rather than Martin's. Friedrich Wilhelm von Lindeiner genannt von Wildau died of a heart attack in Frankfurt am Main on 22 May 1963, aged eighty-two.

Stalag Luft III was evacuated by the Germans at the end of January 1945 with the remaining prisoners (along with tens of thousands more from other camps) force-marched away from the oncoming Soviets, in bitterly cold winter conditions. Hundreds of Kriegies died from exhaustion, disease and the effects of the weather, exacerbated by their poor diet and the lack of appropriate clothing, on what became known as 'The Long March'. Many others lost limbs, fingers or toes due to frostbite. The site of the camp at Sagan was left in disrepair post-war and eventually demolished, but in recent years it has been partially recreated and now houses the Museum of the Prisoner of War and a replica of one of the barrack huts, assembled from scratch in less than a fortnight by volunteers from the RAF in the mid-2000s. Also to be seen is the memorial to the murdered fifty Great Escapers, built at the time by the prisoners and which has been preserved.

In 1968 Mrs Massey's Agency passed to Carol Ellis (the founder's great, great granddaughter) and she and her husband took over the running of the agency. They were ably supported by Mrs Bates, the 'doyen of domestic staff recruiters', who retired in 1986 after serving the agency for over fifty years. The business was sold in that year to its present owners (thereby passing out of the hands of the Massey family after 141 years of ownership) 'who remain committed to maintaining the excellent reputation built up by the Massey family over the years'.[431]

Appendix I and II

Aircraft flown by Air Commodore Herbert Martin Massey
This list is taken from Massey's RAF Record of Service but is not definitive. Some of the aircraft that appear on it were not formally allocated to the units on which he served, so may have been squadron 'hacks' or were unofficial flights. Interestingly, the Maurice Farman Shorthorn, the Short Singapore, the Armstrong-Whitworth Whitley and the Short Stirling do not appear, even though he flew all of them.

Royal Aircraft Factory RE8
Avro (most probably the Avro 504N)
Royal Aircraft Factory BE2
Fairey IIID
Supermarine Southampton
Airco DH9

Armstrong-Whitworth Siskin
Fairey IIIF
Blackburn Iris
Fairey Gordon
Hawker Hart
Westland Wallace

Honours, Awards and Decorations of Air Commodore Herbert Martin Massey
Commander of the Most Excellent Order of the British Empire (CBE)
Distinguished Service Order (DSO)
Military Cross (MC)
British War Medal
Victory Medal
General Service Medal 1918 with bar 'Palestine' and Mentioned in Despatches oak leaf
Aircrew Europe Star
Defence Medal
War Medal 1939–45 and Mentioned in Despatches oak leaf (only one leaf worn despite two separate awards)
King George V Silver Jubilee Medal
Czechoslovak War Cross 1939–45

Massey was also a member of the Caterpillar Club, an informal association for people whose lives have been saved by parachute, and was thus entitled to wear the club's emblem, a gold caterpillar (representing the silkworm that produces silk for parachutes) with ruby eyes. The club's motto is 'Life depends on a silken thread'.

Appendix III

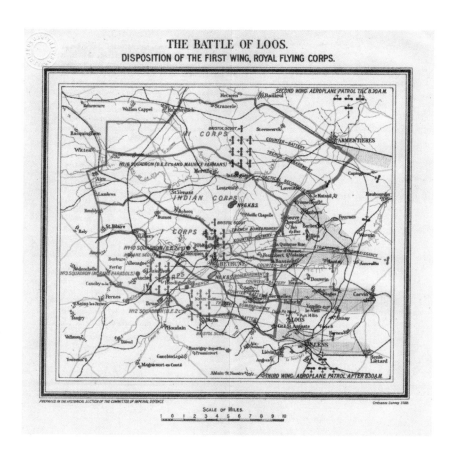

The disposition of 1st Wing RFC at the Battle of Loos 1915. Although this is before Massey had arrived, not much had changed by the time he came to France in July 1916. La Gorgue airfield is towards the top in the centre of the map, just inside the Indian Corps boundary.

(Alamy stock photo)

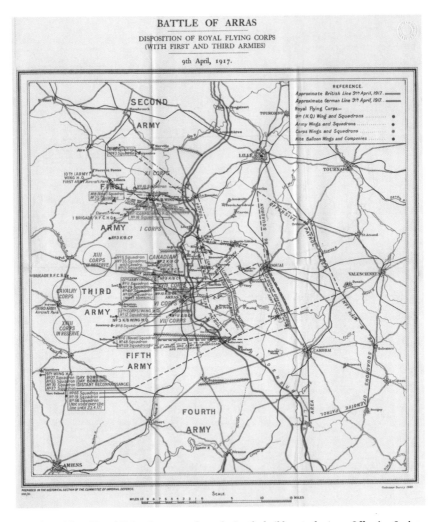

The disposition of Royal Flying Corps squadrons during the build-up to the Arras Offensive, Spring 1917. Bruay airfield lies between the words 'First' and 'Army', towards the top left . Givenchy, where Massey was shot down, is on the front line in the centre of the map, opposite the words 'Canadian Corps'. *(Alamy stock photo)*

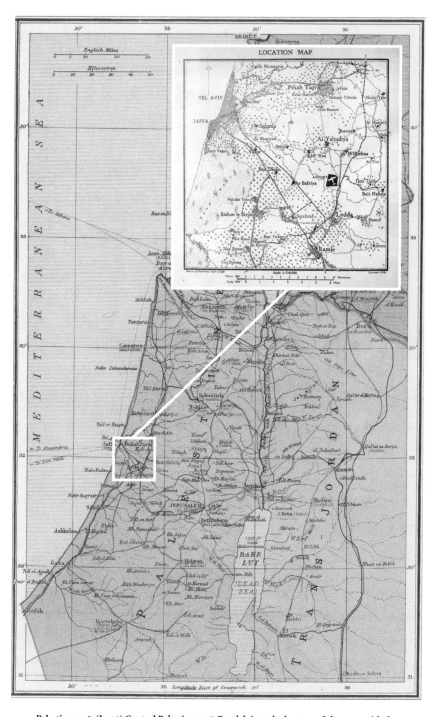

Palestine 1936. (Inset) Central Palestine 1936. Ramleh is at the bottom of the map, with the airfield marked.

Location of German Camps and Hospitals Where American Prisoners of War and Civilian Internees Are Held

(Based on information received to December 31, 1944).

PRISONER OF WAR CAMPS

CAMP	NEAREST TOWN	MAP SQUARE
Stalag II A	Neubrandenburg	B 2
Stalag II B	Hammerstein	C 1-2
Stalag III A	Luckenwalde	B 2
Stalag III B	Fürstenburg/Oder	C 2
Stalag III C	Altdrewitz	C 2
Stalag III D	Berlin-Steglitz	B 2
Stalag IV A	Hohnstein	B-C 3
Stalag IV B	Mühlberg	B 2
Stalag IV C	Wistritz	B 3
Stalag IV D	Torgau	B 2
Stalag IV D/Z	Annaburg	B 2
Stalag IV F	Hartmannsdorf	B 3
Stalag IV G	Oschatz	B 2
Stalag V A	Ludwigsburg	A-B 3
Stalag V B	Villingen	A 4
Stalag VI G	Bergisch-Neustadt	A 2
Stalag VI J	Krefeld	A 2
Stalag VII A	Moosburg	B 3
Stalag VII B	Memmingen	B 4
Stalag VIII B	Teschen	D 3
Stalag 344	Lamsdorf	C 3
Stalag VIII C	Sagan	C 2
Stalag IX B	Bad Orb	A-B 3
Stalag IX C	Bad Sulza	B 2
Stalag X B	Bremervörde	A-B 2
Stalag X C	Nienburg	A 2
Stalag XI A	Altengrabow	B 2
Stalag XI B	Fallingbostel	B 2
Stalag XII A	Limburg	A 3
Stalag XII D	Wahbreitbach	A 3
Stalag XII F	Freinsheim	A 3
Stalag XIII C	Hammelburg	B 3
Stalag XIII D	Nürnberg-Langwasser	B 3
Stalag 383	Hohenfels	B 3
Stalag XVII A	Kaisersteinbruch	C 4
Stalag 398	Pupping	B-C 4
Stalag XVIII A	Wolfsberg	C 4
Stalag XVIII C(317)	Markt-Pongau	B-C 4
Stalag 357	Oerbke	A 2
Stalag XX A	Torún	D 2
Stalag XX B	Marienburg	D 1
WK 8—BAB 21	Blechhammer	D 3

CAMPS FOR AIRMEN

Luft I	Barth	B 1
Luft III	Sagan	C 2
Luft IV	Grosstychow	C 1
Luft VII	Bankau	C-D 2
Stalag XVII B	Krems/Gneixendorf	C 3
Dulag Luft	Wetzlar	A 3

NAVAL AND MERCHANT MARINE CAMPS

Marlag-Milag	Tarmstedt	A-B 2

GROUND FORCE OFFICERS' CAMPS

Oflag IV C	Colditz	B 2
Oflag VII B	Eichstätt	B 3
Oflag IX A/H	Spangenburg	B 2
Oflag IX A/Z	Rotenburg	B 2-3

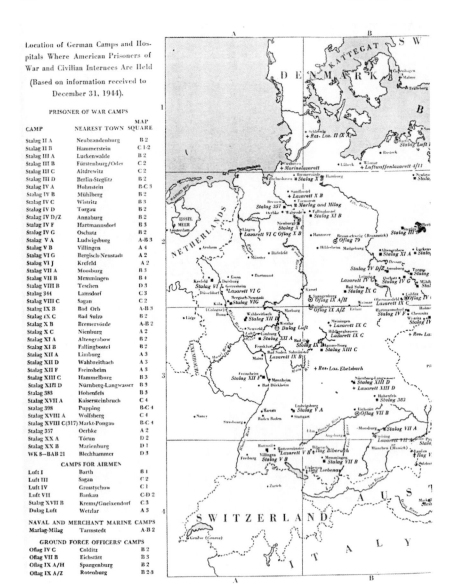

An American Red Cross map showing the location of prisoner of war camps and hospitals in Germany at the end of 1944. Dulag Luft is in square A3; Stalag Luft III in square C2; Obermassfeld in square B2-3; and Annaburg in square B2.

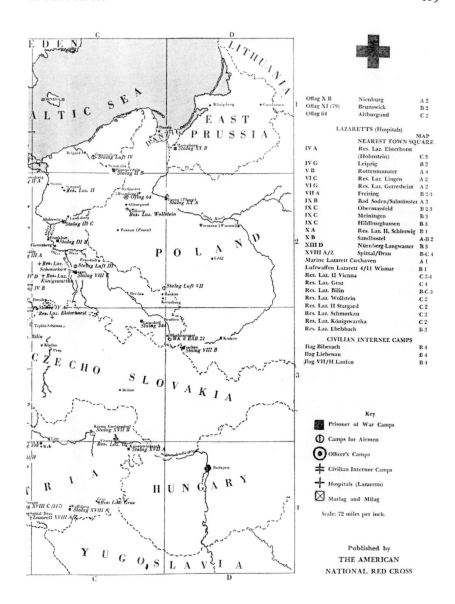

Oflag X B   Nienburg   A 2
Oflag XI (79)   Brunswick   B 2
Oflag 64   Altburgund   C 2

LAZARETTS (Hospitals)
                                                 MAP
                       NEAREST TOWN   SQUARE
IV A   Res. Laz. Elsterhorst
                       (Hohnstein)   C 3
IV G   Leipzig   B 2
V B   Rottenmunster   A 4
VI C   Res. Laz. Lingen   A 2
VI G   Res. Laz. Gerresheim   A 2
VII A   Freising   B 2-3
IX B   Bad Soden/Salmünster   A 3
IX C   Obermassfeld   B 2-3
IX C   Meiningen   B 3
IX C   Hildburghausen   B 3
X A   Res. Laz. II, Schleswig B 1
X B   Sandbostel   A-B 2
XIII D   Nürnberg-Langwasser   B 3
XVIII A/Z   Spittal/Drau   B-C 4
Marine Lazarett Cuxhaven   A 1
Luftwaffen Lazarett 4/11 Wismar   B 1
Res. Laz. II Vienna   C 3-4
Res. Laz. Graz   C 4
Res. Laz. Bilin   B-C 3
Res. Laz. Wollstein   C 2
Res. Laz. II Stargard   C 2
Res. Laz. Schmorkau   C 2
Res. Laz. Königswartha   C 2
Res. Laz. Ebelsbach   B 3

CIVILIAN INTERNEE CAMPS
Ilag Biberach   B 4
Ilag Liebenau   B 4
Ilag VII/H Laufen   B 4

Key
Prisoner of War Camps
Camps for Airmen
Officer's Camps
Civilian Internee Camps
Hospitals (Lazaretts)
Marlag and Milag

Scale: 72 miles per inch.

Published by
THE AMERICAN
NATIONAL RED CROSS

Endnotes

1   www.masseysagency.co.uk, accessed on 17 June 2019.

2   1901 Census.

3   1911 Census.

4   www.masseysagency.co.uk, accessed on 17 June 2019.

5   1901 Census.

6   Ernest had also lost another brother, Hugh, aged just two years old in 1866 and named his second son after him.

7   All school reports quoted are from the Massey family archive.

8   1911 Census.

9   www.countryimagesmagazine.co.uk/lost_houses/lost-houses-derbyshire-spondon-house/, accessed on 29 August 2019.

10 sites.google.com/site/denkporter2/theschools, accessed 29 August 2019.

11 www.oundleschool.org.uk/About-Oundle, accessed on 17 June 2019.

12 Oundle School Archive (OSA).

13 Massey family archive.

14 Lilford Hall in Northamptonshire.

15 Martin is presumably referring to the impending second innings of the house match he describes at the beginning of the letter.

16 OSA.

17 Ibid.

18 OSA: *Oundle School Commemoration July 3rd–4th 1915*, p. 9.

19 Holmes, Richard, *Soldiers; Army Lives and Loyalties From Redcoats to Dusty Warriors* (London: HarperPress, 2011), p. 184.

20 OSA: *Oundle School Commemoration July 3rd–4th 1915*, p. 36.

21 www.oundleschool.org.uk/Oundle-Remembers-Old-Oundelians-on-Somme-Trip?returnUrl=/Trips-News, accessed on 23 November 2019.

22 OSA: Oundle School Calendar and Lists; Lent Term, 1915, p. 39.

23 www.storringtonlhg.org.uk/the-college, accessed on 17 June 2019.

24 TNA: WO 339/59431; Lieutenant Herbert Martin Massey The Sherwood Foresters (Nottinghamshire and Derbyshire Regiment).

25 Ibid.

26 Ibid.

27 Morton, Dr Anthony, *Sandhurst and the First World War: The Royal Military College*

1902–1918 (Sandhurst Occasional Papers No. 17; Central Library, Royal Military Academy
Sandhurst 2014), p. 12.

28   Pugsley, Christopher and Holdsworth, Angela, *Sandhurst – A Tradition of Leadership*
(Third Millennium Publishing, 2005), p. 41.

29   TNA: WO 339/59431; Lieutenant Herbert Martin Massey The Sherwood Foresters
(Nottinghamshire and Derbyshire Regiment).

30   One of whom, Lawrence Dicksee, died just a month later when, while patrolling a quarry
in South Shields at night, accidentally fell into the pit in the dark. The other, Jack Brittan,
survived the war.

31   Supplement to the *London Gazette*, 6 April 1916.

32   Morton, *Sandhurst and the First World War*, p. 10.

33   The Sandhurst Collection Archive.

34   Interestingly, the form also asked for the gentleman cadet's educational background,
including the name of any 'crammer'; Massey chose not to mention Storrington at all.

35   http://www.shorehambysea.com/canvas-wood-wire/, accessed 16 October 2019.

36   No. 16 Squadron Royal Flying Corps, August 1916–June 1917; Notes by Air Vice-Marshal
Sir Paul Maltby (author's collection – source unknown).

37   Ibid.

38   TNA: Air 1/2391/228/11/146; An account by course students of service experiences:
F/Lt G. Martyn.

39   Lewis, Cecil, *Sagittarius Rising* (Penguin Books, 1983; first published by Peter David Ltd,
1936), p. 23.

40   Grinnell-Milne, Duncan, *Wind in the Wires* (London: Mayflower-Dell Paperbacks, 1966),
p. 19.

41   Ibid., p. 20.

42   Winter, Dennis, *The First of the Few – Fighter Pilots of the First World War*
(London: Allen Lane, 1982), p. 36.

43   Lewis, *Sagittarius Rising*, p. 51.

44   Ibid., p. 52.

45   No. 16 Squadron Royal Flying Corps, August 1916–June 1917; Notes by Air Vice-Marshal
Sir Paul Maltby (author's collection – source unknown).

46   Hansard; House of Commons Air Service Debate, 17 May 1916, vol. 82, cc1545–72.

47   Ibid.

48   No. 16 Squadron Royal Flying Corps, August 1916–June 1917; Notes by Air Vice-Marshal
Sir Paul Maltby (author's collection – source unknown).

49   Ibid.

50   Introduced in mid-1916 for aircraft; prior to that, the RFC used the standard infantry
forty-seven-round magazine.

51   No. 16 Squadron Royal Flying Corps, August 1916–June 1917; Notes by Air Vice-Marshal
Sir Paul Maltby (author's collection – source unknown).

52   Massey family archive.

53   No. 16 Squadron Royal Flying Corps, August 1916–June 1917; Notes by Air Vice-Marshal
Sir Paul Maltby (author's collection – source unknown).

54   Ibid.

55   TNA: AIR 1/2389/228/11/98: An Account by Students of War Experiences:
Wg Cdr P.C. Maltby.

56   Dowding's brother also served with No. 16 Squadron while Massey was there.

57   TNA: AIR 1/131/15/40/218; Pilots sent to Expeditionary Force with insufficient training.
General training of pilots.

58   TNA: AIR 1/2389/228/11/98: An Account by Students of War Experiences:

Wg Cdr P.C. Maltby.

59   IWM: Documents 20671: Private Papers of Wing Commander E.J.D. Routh.

60   Cole, Christopher (Ed.), *Royal Flying Corps Communiqués 1915–1916*
     (London: Tom Donovan Publishing Ltd, 1990), p. 189.

61   TNA: AIR 1/1342/204/19/1; 16 Squadron RFC Record Book – July 1916.

62   This involved watching for the muzzle flash of German artillery guns, and then directing
     British fire back against them.

63   TNA: AIR 1/1342/204/19/1; 16 Squadron RFC Record Book – July 1916.

64   Cole, *RFC Communiqués 1915–1916*, pp. 204–5.

65   Ibid., p. 205.

66   TNA: AIR 1/1342/204/19/8; 16 Squadron RFC Record Book – August 1916.

67   Ibid.

68   Cole, *RFC Communiqués 1915–1916*, p. 224.

69   No. 16 Squadron Royal Flying Corps, August 1916–June 1917; Notes by Air Vice-Marshal
     Sir Paul Maltby (author's collection – source unknown).

70   White, Andrew, *Fire-step to Fokker Fodder* (Fighting High Limited, 2019), p. 132.

71   Cole, *RFC Communiqués 1915–1916*, p. 245.

72   TNA: AIR 1/1342/204/19/12: 16 Squadron RFC Record Book – September 1916.

73   Ibid.

74   TNA: AIR 1/2389/228/11/98: An Account by Students of War Experiences:
     Wg Cdr P.C. Maltby.

75   TNA: AIR 1/1342/204/19/12: 16 Squadron RFC Record Book – September 1916.

76   Ibid.

77   Ibid.

78   TNA: AIR 1/1342/204/19/13: 16 Squadron RFC Record Book – October 1916.

79   Cole, *RFC Communiqués 1915–1916*, p. 276.

80   TNA: AIR 1/1354/204/19/67 A and B: 16 Squadron RFC Miscellaneous Correspondence.

81   TNA: AIR 1/1342/204/19/13: 16 Squadron RFC Record Book – October 1916.

82   Cole, *RFC Communiqués 1915–1916*, p. 276.

83   TNA: AIR 1/1354/204/19/67 A and B: 16 Squadron RFC Miscellaneous Correspondence.

84   TNA: AIR 1/1342/204/19/13: 16 Squadron RFC Record Book – October 1916.

85   Ibid.

86   Cole, *RFC Communiqués 1915–1916*, p. 285.

87   Ibid.

88   TNA: AIR 1/1219/204/5/2634/50; Combats in the Air: 16 Squadron Royal Flying Corps.
     October 1916– December 1916.

89   Ibid.

90   Cole; *RFC Communiqués 1915–1916*, p. 293.

91   Ibid.

92   Ibid., p. 319.

93   TNA: AIR 1/1343/204/19/14; 16 Squadron RFC Record Book – November 1916.

94   TNA: AIR 1/2389/228/11/98: An Account by Students of War Experiences:
     Wg Cdr P.C. Maltby.

95   TNA: AIR 1/1354/204/19/67 A and B: 16 Squadron RFC Miscellaneous Correspondence.

96   White, *Fire-step to Fokker Fodder*, p. 120.

97   TNA: AIR 1/1354/204/19/67 A and B: 16 Squadron RFC Miscellaneous Correspondence.

98   No. 16 Squadron Royal Flying Corps, August 1916–June 1917; Notes by Air Vice-Marshal
     Sir Paul Maltby (author's collection – source unknown).

99   TNA: AIR 1/1354/204/19/67 A and B: 16 Squadron RFC Miscellaneous Correspondence.

100 A contraction of Jagdstaffel, translated as 'fighter squadron'.

101 TNA: AIR 1/2389/228/11/98: An Account by Students of War Experiences:
     Wg Cdr P.C. Maltby.

102 No. 16 Squadron Royal Flying Corps, August 1916–June 1917; Notes by Air Vice-Marshal
     Sir Paul Maltby (author's collection – source unknown).

103 1911 Census.

104 IWM: Documents 20671: Private Papers of Wing Commander E.J.D. Routh.

105 Massey family archive.

106 No. 16 Squadron Royal Flying Corps, August 1916–June 1917; Notes by Air Vice-Marshal
     Sir Paul Maltby (author's collection – source unknown).

107 TNA: AIR/1/1354/204/19/57: 16 Squadron RFC Officer Casualties.

108 England and Wales, National Probate Calendar (Index of Wills and Administrations),
     1858–1995.

109 TNA: WO95/3989/3: Headquarters Branches and Services. Matron in Chief May–June 1916.

110 Massey family archive.

111 Ibid.

112 General Philip Game, later Air Vice-Marshal Sir Philip, governor of New South Wales.

113 Massey family archive.

114 Ibid.

115 Ibid.

116 Ibid.

117 Captain.

118 *The War on Hospital Ships, With Narratives of Eyewitnesses and British and German
     Diplomatic Correspondence* (New York and London: Harper and Brothers Publishers,
     1918, second, revised edition), p. 16.

119 Ibid. pp. 21–22; first published in the *Daily Telegraph*, 23 April 1917.

120 *Daily Mirror*, 23 April 1917.

121 Massey family archive.

122 No. 16 Squadron Royal Flying Corps, August 1916–June 1917; Notes by Air Vice-Marshal
     Sir Paul Maltby (source unknown).

123 A military overcoat.

124 *The War on Hospital Ships*, pp. 24–25.

125 Ibid., p. 16.

126 Ibid., p. 24.

127 Ibid., pp. 26–28.

128 TNA: WO 339/59431; Lieutenant Herbert Martin Massey The Sherwood Foresters
     (Nottinghamshire and Derbyshire Regiment).

129 Massey family archive.

130 Royal Army Medical Corps Training Manual (War Office, 1911), p. 351.

131 Ibid.

132 Supplement to the *London Gazette* dated 4 June 1917.

133 No. 16 Squadron Royal Flying Corps, August 1916–June 1917; Notes by Air Vice-Marshal
     Sir Paul Maltby (source unknown).

134 Giblin, Hal and Franks, Norman, *The Military Cross to Flying Personnel of Great Britain
     and the Empire 1914–1919* (Savannah Publications, 2008), p. 391.

135 TNA: WO 339/59431; Lieutenant Herbert Martin Massey The Sherwood Foresters
     (Nottinghamshire and Derbyshire Regiment).

136 Gunshot wound.

137 TNA: WO 339/59431; Lieutenant Herbert Martin Massey The Sherwood Foresters
     (Nottinghamshire and Derbyshire Regiment).

138 Ibid.

139 War fighting.

140 Instructional duties or staff work in the UK.

141 Massey family archive.

142 Ibid.

143 Ibid.

144 Ibid.

145 TNA: WO 339/59431; Lieutenant Herbert Martin Massey The Sherwood Foresters (Nottinghamshire and Derbyshire Regiment).

146 Ibid.

147 Ibid.

148 Ibid.

149 Massey family archive.

150 TNA: WO 339/59431; Lieutenant Herbert Martin Massey The Sherwood Foresters (Nottinghamshire and Derbyshire Regiment).

151 Ibid.

152 Ibid.

153 Ibid.

154 Massey family archive.

155 Ibid.

156 Ibid.

157 TNA: WO 339/59431; Lieutenant Herbert Martin Massey The Sherwood Foresters (Nottinghamshire and Derbyshire Regiment)

158 Massey family archive

159 Ibid

160 TNA: WO 339/59431; Lieutenant Herbert Martin Massey The Sherwood Foresters (Nottinghamshire and Derbyshire Regiment).

161 Ibid.

162 RAF Museum Hendon (RAFM): RFC/RAF Casualty Cards.

163 *Daily Telegraph*, 28 April 2010.

164 Massey family archive.

165 An amalgam of the words 'nine' and 'ack', the phonetic term for the letter A used at the time.

166 RAFM: RFC/RAF Casualty Cards.

167 Museum of Freemasonry.

168 RAFM: RFC/RAF Casualty Cards.

169 *Flight* Global Archive.

170 Ibid.

171 RAFM: A32; Minute to RTP from PA to CAS re film of R101.

172 Massey family archive.

173 Ibid.

174 TNA: AIR 5/170; Air Staff Memorandum No. 46 Notes of Air Control of Undeveloped Countries (Provisional).

175 All references to No. 6 Squadron flying operations in this chapter are taken from TNA: Air 27/73: Number 6 Squadron: Operations Record Book, unless otherwise stated.

176 Massey family archive.

177 *Flight* Global Archive.

178 Massey family archive.

179 Presumably meaning 'devoted' in this context.

180 Massey family archive.

181 Hansard; House of Commons debate 19 June 1936, vol. 313, cc1313–96.

182 The Nablus, Jerusalem, Saffouri and Haifa areas.

183 TNA: AIR 27/80 Squadron Number: 6 Appendices: Y; 1936 June 01–1936 Aug 31.

184 TNA: WO191/70 Military lessons of the Arab rebellion in Palestine, 1936.

185 TNA: AIR 27/80 Squadron Number: 6 Appendices: Y; 1936 June 01–1936 Aug 31.

186 Ibid.

187 Ibid.

188 Ibid.

189 Ibid.

190 Ibid.

191 The author recognises many parallels here with the rules of engagement for RAF aircraft during the invasion of Iraq in 2003.

192 TNA: AIR 27/80 Squadron Number: 6 Appendices: Y; 1936 June 01–1936 Aug 31.

193 RAF Air Historical Branch; *The RAF, Small Wars and Insurgencies in the Middle East 1919–1939*, p. 68.

194 TNA: WO 191/75; Preliminary notes on lessons of Palestine rebellion, 1936.

195 Massey family archive.

196 TNA: AIR 27/80 Squadron Number: 6 Appendices: Y; 1936 June 01–1936 Aug 31.

197 Ibid.

198 TNA: WO 191/70; Military lessons of the Arab rebellion in Palestine, 1936.

199 Ibid.

200 Massey family archive.

201 Massey family archive.

202 Forerunner of the Royal College of Defence Studies.

203 Massey family archive.

204 The Italian raid was against Turin and Genoa, within hours of Italy declaring war on Britain on 11 June 1940. To reach the targets, the Whitleys had to land and refuel in the Channel Islands, just two weeks before the islands were occupied by the Germans.

205 Bowyer, Michael J.F., *Action Stations: Military Airfields of Oxfordshire* (Wellingborough: Patrick Stephens Limited, 1988), p. 17.

206 Sawyer, Group Captain Tom, DFC, *Only Owls and Bloody Fools Fly at Night* (Goodall Publications, 1985 (first published by William Kimber & Co. Limited, 1982)), p. 19.

207 http://www.rafabingdon100tu.co.uk/id3.html, accessed on 20 November 2019.

208 Sawyer, *Only Owls and Bloody Fools*, p. 94.

209 *Oxford Mail*, 27 August 2012.

210 Sawyer, *Only Owls and Bloody Fools*, p. 97.

211 IWM Sound Archive 27064, reel 8.

212 Supplement to the *London Gazette*, 1 January 1941.

213 Ibid., 24 September 1941.

214 Bowyer, *Military Airfields of Oxfordshire*, p. 17.

215 IWM Sound Archive 26561, reel 4,

216 Bowyer, *Military Airfields of Oxfordshire*, p. 18.

217 Not all of which were for heavy bombers – some were for twin-engined medium bombers, specifically the North American B-25 Mitchell and the Martin B-26 Marauder.

218 Massey family archive.

219 TNA: AIR 14/2788: 7 Squadron Operations.

220 The target was supposed to be Hamburg, but was changed at the last moment due to poor weather over that city.

221 Hastings, Max, *Bomber Command* (London: Pan Books, 1999 (first published in 1979 by Michael Joseph Ltd)), p. 152.

222 Chorlton, Martyn, *The Thousand Bomber Raids* (Newbury: Countryside Books, 2017), p. 91.

223 Depending on the weight of bombs carried.

224 TNA: AIR 27/99/11; 7 Squadron Summary of Events 1–30 June 1942.

225 Hastings, *Bomber Command*, p. 153.

226 Chorlton, *The Thousand Bomber Raids*, p. 121.

227 Ibid.

228 TNA: AIR 27/99/11; 7 Squadron Summary of Events 1–30 June 1942.

229 Pino Lombardi email to this author, 1 February 2019.

230 Lieutenant.

231 Third Gruppe (Group), Night fighter Wing 2.

232 'Four-poster Bed', the code name for the system.

233 Boiten, Theo, *Nachtjagd Combat Archive – The Early Years Part Three (30 May–31 December 1942)* (Red Kite, 2018), p. 19.

234 Ibid.

235 Pino Lombardi email to the author, 1 February 2019.

236 Docherty, Tom, *No 7 Bomber Squadron RAF in World War II* (Barnsley: Pen & Sword Aviation, 2007), p. 58.

237 Only one of the eleven planned new Americas-based OTUs was created, No. 111 at Nassau in the Bahamas, that trained crews for Coastal Command.

238 A contraction of *Durchgangslager der Luftwaffe*, or air force transit camp.

239 Massey family archive.

240 A contraction of *Stammlager* or main camp.

241 A contraction of *Stammlager* Luft, or main camp, air.

242 *Stalag Luft III; An Official History of the 'Great Escape' POW Camp* (Frontline Books, 2016), p. 2.

243 Colonel.

244 Captain,

245 Walters, Guy, *The Real Great Escape* (London: Bantam Press, 2013), pp. 51–52.

246 Williams, Eric, *The Wooden Horse* (Glasgow: Fontana Paperbacks, 1980 (first published by William Collins, 1949)), p. 14.

247 Walton, Marylin and Eberhardt, Michael, *From Commandant to Captive: The Memoirs of Stalag Luft III Commandant Col. Friedrich Wilhelm Von Lindeiner genannt Von Wildau* (Lulu Publishing Services, 2015), pp. xviii–xix.

248 US National Archives (USNA): Record Group 389; American Prisoners of War in Germany, 1 November 1945.

249 Ibid.

250 Walton and Eberhardt, *From Commandant to Captive*, p. 82.

251 Day later exchanged his award for the George Cross when that honour superseded the Albert Medal.

252 IWM Sound Archive 26558, reel 15.

253 IWM Sound Archive 27064, reel 7.

254 Gill, Anton, *The Great Escape* (REVIEW/Granada Media Group Limited, 2002), p. 27.

255 Brickhill, Paul, *The Great Escape* (London: Arrow Books Limited, 1979 (first published by Faber & Faber Limited, 1951)), p. 11.

256 IWM Sound Archive 27271, reel 4.

257 IWM Sound Archive 27731 reel 4.

258 Smith, Sydney, *'Wings' Day* (London: Pan Books Ltd, 1970), p. 118.

259 Carroll, Tim, *The Great Escapers* (Mainstream Publishing Company (Edinburgh) Limited, 2004), p. 69.

260 IWM Sound Archive 27051, reel 12.

261 *Stalag Luft III; An Official History*, p. 3.

262 Massey family archive.

263 Martin was not from Yorkshire of course, but Derbyshire.

264 Massey family archive.

265 Walton and Eberhardt, *From Commandant to Captive*, p. 338.

266 IWM Sound Archive 27064, reel 8.

267 Gilbert, Adrian, POW – *Allied Prisoners in Europe 1939–1945* (John Murray (Publishers) Great Britain, 2006), p. 76.

268 Stalag Luft III; *An Official History*, p. 3.

269 Ibid., p. 98.

270 Walton and Eberhardt, *From Commandant to Captive*, p. 66.

271 British military clothing was provided through the Red Cross, and other clothes were sent by relatives from the UK.

272 Walton and Eberhardt, *From Commandant to Captive*, p. 65.

273 Stalag Luft III; *An Official History*, p. 3.

274 USNA: Record Group 389; American Prisoners of War in Germany, 1 November 1945.

275 *Stalag Luft III; An Official History*, p. 5.

276 Brickhill, *The Great Escape*, p. 28.

277 IWM Sound Archive 26558, reel 15.

278 van Drogenbroek, Ben and Martin, Steve; *The Camera Became My Passport Home: Stalag Luft 3, The Great Escape, The Forced March and the Liberation at Moosburg; The Memoirs of Charles Boyd Woehrle; A Time Document in Text and Pictures about an American Prisoner of War* (Stalag Luft 3 Archives of Holland, August 2016) p.198

279 IWM Sound Archive 26558, reels 14 and 15.

280 IWM Sound Archive 27731, reel 4.

281 IWM Sound Archive 27064, reel 8.

282 RAFM: X008-4793/001.

283 IWM Sound Archive 27271, reel 3.

284 Hartnell-Beavis, John, *Final Flight* (Braunton, Devon: Merlin Books Limited, 1985), p38.

285 IWM Sound Archive 11338, reel 4.

286 RAFM: X008-4793/004.

287 IWM Sound Archive 27051, reel 12.

288 IWM Sound Archive 26558, reels 14 and 15.

289 Walton and Eberhardt, *From Commandant to Captive*, p. 67.

290 Brickhill, *The Great Escape*, p. 68.

291 *Stalag Luft III; An Official History*, p. 5.

292 Gilbert, *POW*, p. 234.

293 *Stalag Luft III; An Official History*, p. 236.

294 Williams, *The Wooden Horse*, p. 13.

295 *Stalag Luft III; An Official History*, p. 14.

296 Ibid.

297 IWM Sound Archive 27051, reel 11.

298 *Stalag Luft III; An Official History*, p. 110.

299 IWM Sound Archive 26558, reel 17.

300 IWM Sound Archive 27064, reel 8.

301 IWM Sound Archive 27051, reel 12.

302 Gill, *The Great Escape*, p. 74.

303 *Stalag Luft III; An Official History*, p. 154.

304 Gill, *The Great Escape*, p. 73.

305 *Stalag Luft III; An Official History*, pp. 8 and 12.

306 Ibid., p. 11.

307 Vance, Jonathan F, *The True Story of the Great Escape* (Barnsley: Greenhill Books, 2019), p. 100.

308 Smith, *'Wings' Day*, p. 142.

309 *Stalag Luft III; An Official History*, p. 150.

310 Carroll, *The Great Escapers*, p. 168.

311 TNA: WO 361/1789/1 Part 1 of 2; Prisoners of war, Germany: Stalag IXC, Obermassfeld; hospital admission lists; reports of deaths; Meiningen cemetery burials.

312 The National Ex-Prisoner of War Association; Autumn 2006 Newsletter.

313 Walton and Eberhardt, *From Commandant to Captive*, p. 67.

314 Ibid.

315 TNA: WO 361/1789/1 Part 1 of 2; Prisoners of war, Germany: Stalag IXC, Obermassfeld; hospital admission lists; reports of deaths; Meiningen cemetery burials.

316 Ibid.

317 Ibid.

318 Ibid.

319 *Stalag Luft III; An Official History*, p. 150.

320 Brickhill, *The Great Escape*, p. 27.

321 Ibid., pp. 27–28.

322 Ibid., p. 29.

323 Ibid., p. 31.

324 IWM Sound Archive 27051, reel 13.

325 TNA: AIR 2/10121; Court of Inquiry: killing of 50 RAF officers from Stalag Luft III.

326 Walton and Eberhardt, *From Commandant to Captive*, pp. 189–90.

327 *Stalag Luft III; An Official History*, p. 10.

328 Ibid.

329 Ibid.

330 USNA: Record Group 389; American Prisoners of War in Germany, 1 November 1945.

331 TNA: AIR 2/10121; Court of Inquiry: killing of 50 RAF officers from Stalag Luft III.

332 USNA: Record Group 389; American Prisoners of War in Germany, 1 November 1945.

333 *Stalag Luft III; An Official History*, pp. 152–53.

334 TNA: AIR 2/10121; Court of Inquiry: killing of 50 RAF officers from Stalag Luft III.

335 Ibid.

336 Walton and Eberhardt, *From Commandant to Captive*, p. 133.

337 Ibid., pp. 131–32.

338 Ibid., p. 132.

339 Ramsey, Winston and Gail, *The Home Front in Britain Then and Now* (Old Harlow, Essex: Battle of Britain International Ltd, 2019), p. 155.

340 Walton and Eberhardt, *From Commandant to Captive*, p. 134.

341 Ibid., p. 66.

342 Ibid., p. 134.

343 Sergeant or staff sergeant.

344 TNA: AIR 40/2275; Statements by ex-POWs who took part in the mass escape from Stalag Luft III.

345 TNA: AIR 2/10121; Court of Inquiry: killing of 50 RAF officers from Stalag Luft III.

346 Ibid.

347 Ibid.

348 Ibid.

349 TNA: AIR 40/2275; Statements by ex-POWs who took part in the mass escape from Stalag Luft III.

350 James, B.A. 'Jimmy', *Moonless Night* (London: William Kimber & Co. Ltd, 1983), p. 94.

351 Ibid., p. 97.

352 *Stalag Luft III; An Official History*, p. 174.

353 Ibid., p. 175.

354 TNA: AIR 2/10121; Court of Inquiry: killing of 50 RAF officers from Stalag Luft III.

355 Brickhill, The Great Escape, p. 162.

356 Ibid., p. 156.

357 Walters, *The Real Great Escape*.

358 TNA: AIR 2/10121; Court of Inquiry: killing of 50 RAF officers from Stalag Luft III.

359 Ibid.

360 Lieutenant Colonel.

361 Cordes had himself been a prisoner of war during the First World War.

362 TNA: AIR 2/10121; Court of Inquiry: killing of 50 RAF officers from Stalag Luft III.

363 Ibid.

364 *Stalag Luft III; An Official History*, pp. 213–14.

365 TNA: AIR 2/10121; Court of Inquiry: killing of 50 RAF officers from Stalag Luft III.

366 Brickhill, *The Great Escape*, p. 219 and IWM Sound Archive 27271, reel 5.

367 TNA: AIR 2/10121; Court of Inquiry: killing of 50 RAF officers from Stalag Luft III.

368 Ibid.

369 IWM Sound Archive 27051, reel 15.

370 Brickhill, *The Great Escape*, p. 220.

371 Hartnell-Beavis, *Final Flight*, p. 52.

372 Ibid.

373 TNA: AIR 2/10121; Court of Inquiry: killing of 50 RAF officers from Stalag Luft III.

374 Some two weeks later, fifty cremation urns were bought to the compound,
     but by that time Massey had left Sagan.

375 TNA: AIR 2/10121; Court of Inquiry: killing of 50 RAF officers from Stalag Luft III.

376 Ibid.

377 Ibid.

378 Ibid.

379 Massey family archive.

380 TNA: AIR 2/10121; Court of Inquiry: killing of 50 RAF officers from Stalag Luft III.

381 Ibid.

382 A contraction of Heimkehrerlager, or repatriation camp.

383 TNA: WO 224/14B; International Red Cross and Protecting Powers (Geneva): Reports
     concerning Prisoner of War Camps in Europe and the Far East; Stalag IV/DZ Annaburg.

384 TNA: AIR 2/10121; Court of Inquiry: killing of 50 RAF officers from Stalag Luft III.

385 IWM Sound Archive 26558, reel 15.

386 Communicated to the author by Steve Martin, November 2019.

387 TNA: AIR 2/10121; Court of Inquiry: killing of 50 RAF officers from Stalag Luft III.

388 Ibid.

389 Clutton-Brock, Oliver, *Footprints on the Sands of Time: RAF Bomber Command Prisoners
     of War 1939 – 1945* (London: Grub Street, 2003), p. 176.

390 TNA: AIR 2/10121; Court of Inquiry: killing of 50 RAF officers from Stalag Luft III.

391 Clutton-Brock, *Footprints on the Sands of Time*, p. 177.

392 The other passengers stayed with the *Gripsholm*, eventually arriving in Liverpool
     (via Belfast) on 28 May.

393 MI9 was a department of the War Office, responsible for supporting European resistance
     networks and making use of them to assist Allied airmen shot down over Europe in
     returning to Britain. MI9 also manufactured escape aids, which were smuggled to POW camps
     in board games, playing cards and gramophone records, among other ingenious means.

394 Walters, *The Real Great Escape*, p. 26.
395 TNA: AIR 2/10121; Court of Inquiry: killing of 50 RAF officers from Stalag Luft III.
396 Ibid.
397 Ibid.
398 Philippe Goudreau was awarded an OBE for his services at Sagan by Great Britain after the war, and later became a missionary in South Africa. He lived until 1992, when he died aged 85
399 IWM Sound Archive 26558, reel 15.
400 Reproduced by kind permission of Steve Martin.
401 Pearson, Simon, *The Great Escaper – The Life and Death of Roger Bushell* (London: Hodder & Stoughton, 2014), p. 365.
402 TNA: AIR 2/10121; Court of Inquiry: killing of 50 RAF officers from Stalag Luft III.
403 Ibid.
404 Ibid.
405 Ibid.
406 Ibid.
407 Ibid.
408 Ibid.
409 Hansard: House of Commons Debate 23 June 1944, vol. 401, cc 477–82,
410 *Evening Standard*, Friday 23 June 1944.
411 RAFM: MF14/5; Press cuttings and public relations files.
412 van Drogenbroek, Ben and Martin, Steve, *The Camera Became My Passport Home: Stalag Luft 3, The Great Escape, The Forced March and the Liberation at Moosburg; The Memoirs of Charles Boyd Woehrle; A Time Document in Text and Pictures about an American Prisoner of War* (Stalag Luft 3 Archives of Holland, 2016), p. 232.
413 TNA: AIR 2/10121; Court of Inquiry: killing of 50 RAF officers from Stalag Luft III.
414 Vance, *The True Story of the Great Escape*, p. 341.
415 Ibid., p. 359.
416 IWM Sound Archive 26558, reel 26.
417 Massey family archive.
418 Ibid.
419 Second Supplement to the London Gazette of Friday 29 July 1949.
420 IWM Sound Archive 27051, reel 12.
421 The Kriegie; News-sheet of the Air Force Ex-POW Association, Number 3: December 1963 (sourced by kind permission of Ben van Drogenbroek).
422 TNA: AIR 1/2389/228/11/98: An Account by Students of War Experiences: Wg Cdr P.C. Maltby.
423 *Stalag Luft III; An Official History*, p. 215.
424 Walton and Eberhardt, *From Commandant to Captive*, p. 164.
425 Fry, Helen, *The London Cage – The Secret History of Britain's World War II Interrogation Centre* (Yale University Press, 2017), p. 145.
426 Walton and Eberhardt, *From Commandant to Captive*, p. 148.
427 Ibid., p. 202.
428 Ibid., p. 153.
429 Ibid., p. 81.
430 Ibid., p. 7.
431 www.masseysagency.co.uk, accessed on 27 September 2019.

Index